A FRACTURED PAST

A Fractured Past

Out, Black and Gay in 1970's Atlanta

TONY HOLLAND

Anthony L Holland

Contents

Foreward

Foreword

It is a rare pleasure to encounter a good man who is also a good writer. Rarer still is the pleasure of encountering a good writer with a great story to tell, one that includes a treasury of lessons for anyone with a beating heart. In *A Fractured Past*, Tony Holland provides his readers with rare pleasures indeed.

Like all great stories, his is an adventure in the classic sense of the word—a man's journey out into the world and into himself. It is not a tall tale, however, but a true story. It begins in adversity and is driven by insatiable curiosity and inexhaustible determination. The obstacles are daunting, the struggles severe, and the dangers all too real. It proceeds courageously in search of knowledge, and it arrives at wisdom. Specifically, it is the riveting story of a gay black man coming of age in the Civil Rights tumult of America in the 1960s and '70s and subsequently coming to the right to himself. It is also a love story. And it is a story of recovery. In one way or another, as protagonists, supporters, or antagonists, we are all participants in Tony Holland's heroic adventure, and we can all learn from recognizing ourselves in it.

In closing, I'll return to the "good man" part of Tony Holland. Without his heroic character, of course, we would have no real adventure to read or lessons to learn. The tragedy of innumerable lives is written in untold stories similar to his, but untold because of what has surrounded all of us, including ignorance, prejudice, and fear. Because of his courage, intelligent soul, and kindness of character, however, we now have Tony's invitation to his wisdom. In *A Fractured Past*, he has traced the way to becoming whole. Let us follow in his adventure and join him.

Ric Nardin

Prologue

PROLOGUE

Arguably, this could be considered the worst day of my life. As I sit here, I try desperately to make sense of all that's happened in the last few days. Why, with all the loss that I've experienced up to this point, is this so palpable? What is it that's setting this apart from the deaths that by all measurable standards should have been the worst? It takes a bit before the answer comes to me. *And to be truthful in this writing it is many weeks later before that answer arrives.* The secrets – so many secrets that are the staples of our lives as gay men - and the length of time that we've been friends has isolated me in this room from just about everyone else that has reason to hurt here today. Greg, we became each other's confidantes, each other's therapists, sounding boards, yardsticks of life. Most of the things that are painful and wonderful in our lives we would talk over and reason out before moving forward with them. And even then there were things I find today that you kept from me. Just as I know there are feelings and facts that I kept from you. But I also know that these were the things that I couldn't share with ANYONE; For if I could, dear friend, your name would have been the first on the list of consultation.

I look around here today and I see Ms. Dorothy. Such a strong black woman! In her, I see my own mother and every other strong African-American mother who possesses that un-yielding iron with a gentle and sweet center. The makeup that has carried her and her children through more hardships and strife than most can imagine. Today, her pain is obvious and I can only guess at what it's taken for her to make it through these last few weeks. Not only to bury a child, but you; her youngest at that. Next to her are your brothers and your sister and all of their children. The lost look that they are all wearing speaks volumes. None of us understand or can entirely comprehend just what has happened here. The sense of the surreal is astounding. On the seat just next to them is Peter, your partner. I think of the many discussions you and I had when you were contemplating becoming involved with him; all the fear of allowing yourself to drop your defenses. How wary you were of letting vulnerability creep in while allowing him entrance to your life. Also the wisdom that allowed you to see that he had fears as well. It was amazing how difficult it was to look at all sides of that particular situation. Sometimes your growth and insight were astounding to me. The things that it seems many of us have to work double time to get would come to you through the simplest of deductive reasoning.

And then on the other side of the church sits us three-Terry, Howard and me. It's funny how we all categorize our lives and our friendships. It wasn't until just recently, since your passing in fact, that I realized that we all filled a certain place in your life. It was a revelation to see that those places and purposes were quite distinct and totally independent of each other. Initially, that realization hurt and made me quite angry. But upon further examination I came to realize that it didn't diminish my part in your life. It was your right to go to whatever sources you chose to fill your needs. It's just that I loved you so much! You were MY little brother! My friend, my ally, and I couldn't imagine that you would ever not seek my counsel.

We've made it through the first portion of your service. Thank God Diane gave me the two anti-depressant tablets to take, or I doubt I could have walked in here, much less viewed your body and sat through these moments. And I sure as hell could not just sit here passively and watch the undertaker closing your casket, knowing that I will never see you again. I remember telling you of a dream that I had about this very day. Talk about grotesque Deja vu!

It's so very hard to explain the feelings that I have. I know what your blood family is going through because I've sat where they are sitting four times now.

Life has taught me there's very little that one will experience that's more painful. In fact, the only thing that I can imagine worse ,would be facing death in my own nuclear family for a fifth time. That would leave me the only original blossom left on my family tree.

I can only imagine that then I would feel TRULY all alone. Yet the isolating pain today is different inasmuch as this time I can't fully identify where I belong in the script. I'm not a blood relative and, as with most gay people of our generation, we've both kept our families at arm's length to a degree where our intimate lives and our close personal friendships are concerned. So though you are closer to me than many who carry my own blood, and I hurt for your loss so much that it's almost indescribable, I feel as though there's nowhere to really carry that pain.

All week, and indeed since you first started this last phase of your illness we (your family and I) have been in close; but somewhat uncomfortable proximity that only happens when something like this occurs. We know each other, but do we REALLY know each other well enough to cry on one another's shoulders? And I hope and pray that poor Peter, who's been a saint through all this, doesn't feel too strange. It must be hard being in his position - the only white face in the family entourage at a black funeral. Not to mention being the identified "spouse" in a same-sex relationship of the deceased! Talk about being outed!!! I note that he has some good friends here in the congregation supporting him, a few of whom I've met.

As we finish up now and head up the aisle, I see others in the crowd (quite an impressive one I might add) who dot our history together. Isabel and P.J., Greg from Decatur and Todd have all come to pay their respects. Not to mention the legion of people whose lives you touched professionally. After all these years of your speaking of them I've finally gotten a look at Richard and Susan. Richard spoke eloquently of your many years of service to the company and of the special relationship that you shared with them all. And even though they were not able to make it today, I talked with the two Jacks, and I'm sure you're in both their hearts as this day progresses. It's rather surreal to me as I wait in my pallbearer's position at the door of the church to help position you for your final ride. I see your cousin Moses looking at me and I know that somewhere around the corners of his mind, he's sure that he knows me. He may even remember from where, but either certainty is not totally there. Or maybe there've just been too many years from sixth grade to now for him to feel that he still knows me well enough to speak. I don't know and am in no mood today for extensive trips down memory lane with folks that may (or may not) be able to handle the reality of what's been going on in my life since they saw me last. Especially if that time was before I even reached puberty!

As your burled walnut casket is passed between the group of us - Terry and your nephew on the side with me, and Howard and two other guys on the opposite side, I'm surprised at how light my burden feels. The thoughts cross my mind that there's no way that I want you jostled. Greg, I can only hope you feel comfort knowing that Terry and I are right here at your side to see you through this. I'm here at your head and you can count on me.

As we start the drive to the cemetery, I'm surprised at the route that's being taken. It is once again down memory lane. We pass the area near Cascade where you and Dick bought your house, and once again I wonder if he's heard all the way in Chicago about your death. News like this has a way of growing legs and walking. I would have called him if I'd had a number for him. Even with Gloria's request that I call friends of yours, how could I explain to her the nature of our existence as gay men? Many of the friends you had, we did not share. And of the people that you and I had in common, most had preceded you from here long ago. Even more, I couldn't be certain of how Dick would have received a call like that after all you told me that had transpired between the two of you. Hell, of those that you'd been involved with, would you have even wanted them here?

Here we are passing the neighborhood where you grew up and just on the opposite side of the main street there's the community where my family lived when I was born and where I attended elementary school with your cousin Moses. As Terry, your niece and Howard are all chatting away here in the limousine, I sit here pensively exploring these thoughts. They cannot possibly know that our history extends back even this far. I can see you coming down the drive of what was then your parents' home over here. You're no more than a whippet at 16 years old, and as you rush down the drive to get into the car, your mom leans out the door to say hi to me. I'm sure she has no idea where we're off to, though I marvel at how you've always tried to be honest with them. It blows me away that you have told them that you're gay! I am totally undone at your courage and your strength. I should do the same, I know, but I'm scared.

As we pull into the cemetery, I think about all the times you would tell me that we didn't have time to feel bad about this, or "let's not talk about that. We'll deal with whatever when we're both old and sittin' in our rockers!" SO many situations could fill those blanks, and now our time has run out! Part of my pain is that I truly don't know how to be an adult with you not in the picture to bounce things off of. I don't know what the future will hold, or how the story will end, but I do know this was certainly NOT in the script when my story started....

Chapter 1

Chapter 1

CHAPTER 1

A big question that I think most of us stumble on at the outset is one that we never quite get answered. That question is simply; Who can determine what any of our outcomes will be? Certainly, I never anticipated the twists and turns that my own tale would take. I trust that many, many more chapters are to be written, but here's my attempt at making a start.

Out of a union bearing three prior offspring I sprang, in the year of 1958, on the twentieth day of July. Both my parents, being of a time when people worked to make their relationships stay together, enjoyed a place in all our lives. I was the last of the brood, and therefore my position was, and still is, quite questionable to me at times. Certainly my parents never gave me any intended indication that I was not expected or desired, but such are the feelings that sometimes accompany a youngest child. And surely those feelings are experienced by a sensitive child, and I really fit that category. Also, let's not forget the influence of my older siblings. Boy, Was I ever picked on! Mainly at the hands of my older brother, but my closest sister got her punches in as well.

Really, I looked upon her as a sort of mother figure. Since both my parents worked, she spent a lot of time babysitting my brother and me. There was such a vast difference in our ages, that to my young eyes, she appeared to be an adult.

There was a difference of eleven years between her and my brother, and fourteen years between her and me. To say that I seemed to be an afterthought certainly appears to fit the bill. I always considered myself a "change of life" child, since my mom was 39 when I was born and my dad was 41.

My eldest sister was sixteen years my senior and my earliest memories of her are as a young married woman. It is my understanding that she married right out of high school to get out of the house. Not unlike most mothers and daughters, a certain tension cropped up between her and my mother during those years. Nothing that they would not work out eventually, but right then it required that they get out of each other's orbit.

Basically, home life was good, though it did feature its tensions. For instance, there was the never - ending feud between my younger sister and my father. It was legendary. Never have I seen two people that totally disagreed on EVERY-THING. Years later, there would be speculation and irony concerning the why and how of this aspect of their relationship. Though never confirmed, my sister wondered if she may have been the illegitimate child of one of our aunt's, and given to my mother and father to raise as their own, since said aunt was without a husband. My sister thought that if this were true, it might certainly explain why she and dad never could get along, and always seemed to argue about mother most of all. She felt perhaps the basis was in his resentment at having the added burden of raising a child that was not his own, on what was an already extremely limited income. Though it seemed a wild theory, there were questions that were unanswered that could have certainly pointed in that direction. For instance, it was found that when my sister gave birth to her twin boys she had a different blood type that didn't show up anywhere else in our family. I suppose the test could have been flawed, but nevertheless it was a really peculiar finding.

During my early years, I think that the evidence of who I was to become should have been clear for all to see. I describe myself as a sensitive child. The fact that I often cried and was deeply touched by things seemed to escape my parents' notice. Or, perhaps it was constantly ignored because they assumed this heralded things that did not bear mentioning. I mean, I cried when looking at carnival clowns, for God's sake! Later, as an adult, I realize that the reason for that is that I was terrified by disfigured faces, a shortcoming that still affects me to this day. I am also happy to find that later in life many people have come out and admitted that clowns are just damned creepy! In my youth however, I did not possess the vocabulary to explain just what the issue was, but I can clearly remember being frightened at the Southeastern Fair when a clown came up and tried to pay attention to me. My dad got impatient and said that I cried over everything. I must have been three or four year's old, maybe five at the most. I could probably go so far as to say this was the first indication to me it was not okay for me to be sensitive or show feelings.

Another place that my sensitivity reared its head was around the lyrics of popular songs. I can remember certain songs making me very sad as a child, and not really knowing why. However, when I listen to them now, I do realize that the lyrics appealed to a deeper self, and that I would pick up on these lyrics and the sorrowful sounds of the music.

I'm not sure that it was the sole cause of my sensitivity, but a contributing factor was likely that I was never in head start or any other organized group of kids my age. I was very isolated from other children, and growing up in a family where feelings were not freely expressed or talked about at all. I spent those entire early pre-school days home with my mom. I remember them as being very bright and lots of fun mostly, as she had a very warm and loving spirit. She was a simple woman who found pleasure and beauty in nature. Her garden and the naturalness of that early neighborhood I believe were her mainstays. My mother loved plants and I can remember her tending to them there in the living room as the morning sun came streaming in. We spent wonderful times walking about the neighborhood during those early days. We would go around to the store that was on the next street over sometimes. It was run by a lady named Ms. Lily Rambo, and she ran it out of the front rooms of her house. It was on some of these walks that my mother started to introduce me to nature. I can remember her picking figs from a tree in the neighborhood and showing me how to wash them and prepare them to eat. She also showed me black walnuts growing right there on a tree up the street from our house. She was a wonderful cook. We had a great garden in the backyard at the very rear of our property. She would take these opportunities to teach me just how these foods that we found growing on the trees in the neighborhood, as well as the foods in our garden could go directly from the source to the table. It was a wonderful period in my early life.

Then came the culture shock of kindergarten. To set the scene here I must tell you that prior to going to kindergarten, I only remember one child in my life that was not older than me. All the others were either my brother's age, (three years my senior) or just between our ages, which still made me the youngest. Funny thing, that one kid that was my age, lived at the end of a street that was adjacent to our street. He would come to the top of his street to play wearing only a slip! My brother and I thought this was odd even then... The next time I saw him (we moved when I was five) we were both in a show at a club and he was a pre-operative transsexual. Yes! I think we can safely say our destinies were already on track! While I would never go out of the house "dressed", I certainly spent a lot of time playing dress up on the inside of the house in those early years... But I'm getting way ahead of my story. The point was that I got to play with practically no kids other than my brother and a couple of other older boys before kindergarten. Needless to say, when I went to school, they scared the hell out of me!

I know that some kids take a couple of days to get used to the idea of being without mom for a while, but for me, I spent the whole first school year in stark terror! I cried so much that I remember them trying to leave me and not being able to. My older sister almost got into a fight with the kindergarten teacher over wanting to take me back home when I cried. My sister did take me that day, but finally to persuade me to stay, the teacher had to take me with her everywhere that she went if she left the class. I would NOT stay in the classroom with all those kids. It seems odd to me now that no one noticed at that time the issue was not the school or the new building. I had just met this woman, just as I had just met the kids, but I clearly was able to consider developing a connection with her, but not them.

This set the tone for most of my relationships with peers for many years to come. I know that it was a good three years before I felt at home in the school environment. I know this now because the first and second grades are totally not in my memory at all. They all run together with kindergarten. However, the memories pick up again in the third grade teachers' class. By that time, I had enmeshed myself in the "cultural life" of school, so to speak, and had become more comfortable. Still, I remained a sensitive, wary and frightened kid. The next few years moved along pretty much without incident. As I became more and more adjusted to the environment it became easier and easier for me to excel in my studies. I look back at some of my old report cards from that period and I'm surprised at how well I did in school then. I even enjoyed some limited success with the band. Although, I must admit that the only reason I was even in the band was because my brother Ed wanted to be. I remember he came home talking about wanting that and wanting to play the trumpet. He was really excited and all pumped up about it. The actual interest that I had around music was in piano, but I was told that it would not be possible for us to get a piano, so I should play something that I could play in a band. I settled on an alto saxophone. The thing was awful! It was bigger than I was and made this God-awful sound when I blew into it that set my teeth on edge.

Here, I have a confession to make. The ONLY reason that I chose the saxophone was that while we were in the music store, I saw one lying in the display case with its case open. It was lying there gleaming goldenly on a navy blue velvet background, and it looked absolutely beautiful. Yes, that's right folks! I picked that damned sax because it sparkled and was pretty. It had mother-of- pearl keypads and the combination of all that brass and velvet and pearls was just too much for me! Yes, beauty and elegance were a requirement of mine even then...

Back then, we had a music director that was truly a joy. The guy was a lot of fun and seemed to really be a nice person. He made being in the band bearable for me. I also think that I had something of a crush on him. He was very nice looking. I remember that I heard some time later that the reason that he had left the school was that he had a nervous breakdown. Apparently, he and his wife separated because he was supposedly gay. I don't know that any of this was true, but I remember hearing it and I never forgot it. It was my younger sister that told me this, and since she worked in the medical field, I believed her. I think that even then, she suspected that I would turn out to be gay, and telling me anything negative was supposed to discourage that.

I once read that people born under the sign of Cancer in the zodiac are largely homebodies and love praise and flattery. That sums me up totally even back then as a kid. I did learn how to put myself in a position where once the kids got to know me, most seemed to like me, and in short order I had something of a social standing in grade school. That is, until the class bully came and called me on my shit!

Carey, with whom I later became friends, had mood swings even as a kid. One moment he was threatening to kick my ass after school, and a few days later he was complimenting me on my legs. Anyone who hasn't realized it, there are lots of folks out here that see slightly bowed legs as a definite asset. And even at my tender age I knew that his interest was intense. Carey was apparently batting on the same team as me, though it would be years before we knew that fact concerning one another. Even then, the compliment didn't throw me (I knew what to do with one of those!) but the threats left me in a cold sweat from sheer panic! Carey was a fat kid, even bigger than me (I always thought of myself as fat, even then) and known to be a bully. We got into an argument in class and he told me to "meet him out front after school". What in the world was I going to do? My dad used to pick me up after school and so I had to wait out front for him. We no longer lived in that neighborhood so it was too far for me to walk home alone. My brother no longer went to the school having gone on to the high school that year. Needless to say I spent the rest of the day sweatin' bullets! At 3 p.m. I wanted to be ANYWHERE but on that front stoop of the school. What would my constituency say when I got my ass kicked? Would I become a social pariah? Would no one look up to me anymore once my mask of "authority" as a grade school celebrity was stripped away? Well it turned out that Carey didn't come looking for me at the end of the day. To this day I don't know whether he forgot, decided that he didn't want the scene or what... All I know is that I was as happy as a clam that he was not there when I exited. What I've realized is that mostly, the bravado that he showed was a defense mechanism because even though he was a big kid, he was also somewhat effeminate, he still felt that he had to be pushy to keep the others from giving him hell. I also realized that his trying to give me hell one minute and complimenting me the next, was a way of making a connection with me.

During this time in school, things also began to take shape around my sexual desires. Now I know that most of our society takes for granted that kids don't have any sexual desires, however I have my own beliefs as to why this is so. I personally think that it's because we have so much internalized guilt about sex and sexuality, and so many hang - ups about it being "dirty" that we just can't get our minds around the concept that a child may have the same urges that we have as adults. I most certainly was aware of my attractions.

Those next few years found me pining away for a boy one year older than me. His name was James, and he was adorable. Even at that tender age I knew that to have it appear that I was even remotely interested in him would mean certain trouble. So the only way I knew to be close to him and not let him or anyone else, for that matter, know was to tell the world that I wanted to know more about his older sister. She was one year older than he was, and didn't know that I was alive, which was just fine with me! All I wanted was to gaze lovingly up at him! But my cover story was just the thing that would keep me with things to talk to him about. I think they stayed at the school for one more year, so that pretty much solved the problem of me getting caught up in fantasizing about him too closely. Nevertheless, he was my first real crush, and I did carry that torch for at least the whole next school term.

Seems that all the guys that I carried that torch for, from the very earliest, were light - skinned. This is very difficult to admit and certainly to acknowledge in print, but I don't think that it's all that uncommon. Lots of young, black kids were shaped by the attitudes of the day back then. The general overall feeling was that darker skin was not as desirable as lighter skin. And anybody that denies that we were all affected in one way or another is lying. James' complexion was that color of warm biscuits just from the oven; light with just a hint of honey gold. The mostly straight, but slightly curly hair that was also characteristic of the mulatto black was also apparent in him. And all that, combined with a ready smile and soft-spoken manner was all it took to slay me. It still surprises me the level of attractiveness that was there in that kid even then. I believe that we all are given the gift of the aesthetic spectrum. It's my belief that at some point in our lives we all get the opportunity to be the beauty and we also all get the opportunity to be the beast. It's just a matter of timing when we go through whatever stage. Have you ever noticed that some people are beautiful babies or even beautiful as children, but as they age, they lose their attractiveness? All too often the reverse is true as well. How many of us know or have seen people whose school day pictures were downright homely? Then, we see them as adults and they're absolute gods and goddesses. I rest my case...

The remainder of the school years at that particular school I was relatively comfortable, however I still was quite sensitive and a worrier most of the time. Fear was a constant companion. Never let anyone tell you that kids have no worries. Though their issues may seem small to you, to them, those issues seem gargantuan. For instance, by sixth grade, the problem of me getting home was becoming a big one. A lot of times it was a hardship for my parents to pick me up since both worked. As I've said, by that time we lived some distance from the school, and I'd never ridden the city bus alone. That particular school had no school buses serving the area since most of the pupils lived close by. One other kid lived close to where I did and his mom had made arrangements for him to stay with a lady in the neighborhood until she came to pick him up.

My sixth grade teacher also lived not too far from us, so my folks made arrangements for me to ride with her for a short period. During this period, I was late for school one day and had to stay in detention afterwards. It was a Friday and I guess she had things to do after school. She said that she wouldn't stay and so she'd give me money to take the bus. Not only did I not know how to do this (it involved me going downtown and transferring to get another bus connection), but she scolded me and made me feel really bad for not being able to do it. To some folks this might not seem like a big deal, but to a sixth grader in a city like Atlanta , who had never done the bus thing before , it seemed like solving all the problems of Congress. Here, yet again was another situation in my family and school life where it appeared I was creating problems. Since I was not responsible for getting myself to school in the first place, the detention felt really undeserved. I felt I was being penalized when all I was attempting to do was get home.

It's hard for me to remember now, but I think I called my sister at work and she came and got me. But prior to doing that, I remember being paralyzed with fear at not being able to get home that evening. The teacher had worked out this plan for me to take the bus home with no consideration whatsoever to what I felt, how I would cope or adapt. I remember feeling very betrayed because this was a woman that my family held in high esteem, so the shock was really doubled.

The year that followed set the precedent for a lot of the feelings and emotions that would be a part of me for many years to come. It was 1970, and forced busing in the Atlanta school system was definitely upon us. That year, I was to enter the seventh grade. It was determined by the government that all school students could no longer go to the school of their choice. All students had to either go to the school in their neighborhoods, or you had the option to go to a school in another district as long as that school was integrated by a certain percentage. Of course, this was not a problem for those in the white communities, since their schools were the best equipped and best funded. No one there was eager to change their kids' schools anyway. The only loophole for black families was if your parents worked for the school system. Then, it was determined that you could still go where you pleased.

Many parents were so eager to dodge the chaos that these moves were sure to cause in their children's lives they resorted to lying on forms. Some used the addresses of friends and former neighbors or relatives in the areas where they wanted their children to attend certain schools. It was widely known that this was going on within the communities, and openly discussed within my home. My parents talked about it. They knew full well that I'd had a difficult time adjusting to school as it was, and this might cause problems. And though it did cause significant problems for me, I'll always appreciate the fact that truth meant something to them. It was a value that I learned from them and that I hold dear today. It's not always easy to stick by, but it's very hard for me to turn away from. I believe that's because they instilled that in us.

Having moved to an upwardly mobile neighborhood in the black community in 1963, my parents were all too aware of the difficulty that my brother and I would encounter trying to fit in with the kids that we found there. As a result, they had decided to allow us to stay in the school that we had started, so as to try and keep us from losing ground and having re-adjustment problems on at least one front.

Many people may not be aware of the internal racism and discrimination that once occurred in the African-American community on a regular basis. Commonly called the "brown paper bag" test, this concept simply put, meant that if your skin color was found to be darker than the brown of a paper bag (i.e. the old grocery store variety), then you were considered too dark, or inferior. Needless to say, we were much too dark to pass this test. As a result, my brother and I spent a lot of time in those years fighting amongst the kids in the neighborhood to be accepted.

Eventually, we did okay as far as the battles in the 'hood' went, but up to then, we were spared the hardship of having to do this battle at school as well. I was all too aware of the fact that this would probably be a part of the whole "new kid at a new school" thing. And what's more, by this time my brother was in high school so I'd have to go it alone.

And believe me, in no way did they disappoint. The curious thing was that though a lot of "classism" and psychological abuse was directed from the kids, I found even more was directed from the teachers and the adults I encountered at the new school. They were all very class conscious. The unspoken truth was who your parents were mattered very much.

I remember that first day of seventh grade as though it were yesterday. One of the things that had helped me to cope with my old school was that we were eased back into the school routine at the end of the summer vacation. Usually, on the first day, we became acquainted with the new setup, the classroom and the new classmates (many of whom we'd just gone through the previous grade with). This was largely a planning day, so it was not necessary to bring anything to school with you when you came. Not so in the new class! I am fully aware now that time was of the essence, and that every moment counted. Perhaps that was why the sense of urgency.

I now know that this was certainly a more productive usage of the time in the classroom than what I was used to, but I'll never forget the burning shame that I felt when the teacher, Mr. McCullough, instructed the class to take out paper and pencil so that we could start lessons. Since I was seated near the front of the class , and he had just embarrassed me by noting to the entire body that I was new (as if they could not already see this), it did not go unnoticed by him that I was the only person that did not take out the paper and pencil as requested. He then asked me why I had not done as he asked. When I told him that I had not brought any because I did not think that they would be needed on the first day, he proceeded to berate me in front of the entire class because of this. So with a laugh at my expense, the school year was off to a rip-roaring start! To add to my shame and desolation, he then asked one of the classmates to give me some paper and a pencil so that I could keep up. It was then that I noticed that I was the only boy sitting in the front of the class! All my nearest neighbors were girls! This really did wonders for my image as "just one of the guys". Berated and besmirched immediately out of the starting blocks, I then did the unthinkable. I started to cry! Fighting with all my might to hold in the tears, I thought that I would die on the spot.

Basically, the rest of that day is a blur. The only good thing to come out of that entire encounter was that the three girls closest to me turned out to be some of the most popular and prettiest in the school. They took me under their wings and really felt sorry for me. They befriended me and became something of my "shelter".

Once again I was terrified but considerably older than kindergarten, and to cry was not only not cute, it was downright unacceptable! That taught me very early to bury those emotions along with any others that might appear as overt. I think from that moment on I realized that being a large person it was extremely difficult to disappear. The only option that was available to me was to show no emotion to anyone. To go as silent as possible, befriend as few people as I could get away with, carry on very few conversations and – above all – take any opportunity that I could get to be alone. I remember it as one of the darkest periods in all of my school history.

Many things made it a difficult experience. Not only the things that I've mentioned about being introverted and all, but also the fact that I'd never had a male teacher and certainly never encountered teachers that talked that way to students. I found any and every excuse I could to stay home from school.

In this school, something else that was different was that in order to get us ready for the rigors of high school, all sixth and seventh graders changed classes. I knew that I could do the work, that did not worry me, but the impatience and fast paced attitude took some getting used to. These kids were the mature and advanced variety compared to the crew that I had left at R. H. Wright, the previous school.

Collier Heights Elementary was located in the northwest section of Atlanta, an area well-known for its upper crust African -American families. There were many notable members of Black Atlanta society who had kids among the student body. Of the three girls that had befriended me that first day, one was the niece of a prominent Atlanta developer, one the daughter of a prominent restaurant owner and one the daughter of a gentleman who was rumored to have a rather dubious career that made him lots of money, but shall we say did not insure his health or that of his family...

I was still very much a sheltered child compared to these kids, and a lot of the things about me reflected this. I mean, these three girls for example; Their conversations were about catching the bus and going out to Lenox Square and Phipps Plaza and shopping at Neiman Marcus and Saks. Hell, of the adults that I knew, I doubt that very many of them were shopping in these places. The fact that I still wanted to carry a lunch box pretty much proved my immaturity. In my first school this would not have seemed odd at all, but in this school it was something that babies did. So when I showed up with a red, white and blue lunch box made like a mailbox and with U.S. Mail on it, they guffawed! I remember going home and spray painting the top of the thing gray so that it would be less conspicuous. No matter what I did I could not make a favorable impression with these kids.

I feel that at this point it is important to the story that I give you an adequate description of myself. I'm sure that will help you to understand and see me as they did. When I look back upon it now, as painful as it was, I can see how they might have thought it to be funny, but it was really very painful.

I am now and have always been a large person. Not necessarily always a fat person (though that's what I thought) but certainly always large and tall. My maternal ancestry is probably responsible for this. My Grandfather was nearly seven feet tall and my mother was five feet eleven inches, without heels. I probably was around five feet ten inches tall, and around 180 pounds in the seventh grade. No small character here. By today's standards this doesn't seem like so much, but back then kids were considerably smaller.

Now picture this kid about the size of a lot of the kid's parent's, but still very much an immature child, and carrying a damned post- office- box- shaped lunch pail. Needless to say, I needed an image adjustment and fast. Though this innocence was endearing to some, it definitely made me a walking target for insensitive folks. How lucky for the kids today that the schools are less tolerant of promoting differences in kids, and more aware of the teasing and other abuse that goes on. I have a niece who, at twelve years old, had already grown to five feet, ten inches tall and developed like a woman. I've witnessed her feeling the sting of unkind remarks that attempt to set her apart. Thank God my brother and his wife were able to find a school that did not allow the teasing. In her previous school her grades had begun to suffer because of it. So, in that respect, the school system has improved to some extent.

During that period at school, my feelings of isolation were at their peak. I was willing to do just about anything to blend in. And if that were not possible, I would just try and disappear into the surroundings.

About the closest I came to making this work was to volunteer to do the audio-visual responsibilities in the school. I truthfully cannot remember whether I volunteered for this, or if I was 'volunteered' for it. All I remember is that it allowed me time away from the classroom and time to be mostly left alone. I would take those large box shaped televisions that we had in school at the time around to all the classes that required their usage on any given day. This usually took about an hour to achieve.

Then came spring and the school presented a program called the "Around the World" tea. Several of the girls in the seventh grade class were choreographing a dance routine to perform at the tea, and I fell in love with the stage on the spot. I wanted so much to be up there working with them! I remember that I volunteered to spend hours stapling together programs in the auditorium just so that I could be there to watch them practice. And certainly, since I had to put out the record player for them to use , I got to be there even longer. I have since wondered what the teachers must have thought of me. Whether they thought that I was just enamored of the young ladies, or whether they understood that I wanted to participate. Either way, I remember when that Sunday came around (the program was held on a Sunday afternoon) I couldn't wait to go and boasted to my parents about all my help at putting this thing on. This one little bright spot in that school year was just about the only thing that made it bearable and got me through it. Even at this age, I was sure that I could not let people know that I had an interest in anything that would be considered feminine. You see, boys in my neighborhood played sports, and that was IT. Even at this age, I could see nothing wrong with being well-rounded and liking all sorts of activities that crossed all the usual pre-determined boundaries. I loved playing sports. But I also loved the arts. I loved to dance, cook and (soon to come) sewing. However, I also knew instinctively that to pursue those latter loves openly would bring about more ridicule than I thought that I could bear.

The beauty to come out of this artistic interest is a love for classical music and dance and all the more refined art forms that probably would not have been as pronounced without this open minded thinking back then. When all the other boys just looked at a school trip to the symphony as just a way to get out of class, I secretly could not wait to go. I felt so grown up and the music was so lovely.

As we moved toward spring at school , we moved toward the end of the school term and the prom. In those days, the seventh grade class in elementary had a prom just like the seniors in high school did. I did find that I wanted to go to this.

Don't ask me why. I still did not feel that I belonged with the overwhelming majority of these kids, but I wanted to participate. It was a dance after all...

I invited the only other kid in that class who appeared to feel as misplaced as I did. A young lady named Cassandra. At the time, she was probably the least popular girl at school. She was a really nice person and I felt somewhat comfortable with her. I will forever wonder what was going on with her though. I asked her to go weeks before the event was scheduled, yet when my father and I arrived to pick her up that evening; she was taking out the trash, and had not even mentioned the event or the invitation to her mother. So there I stood on the front porch with a corsage in one hand, my little gray suit on , my dad in the car in the driveway, and my date with blue jeans and a t-shirt on! Her mother made her rush and get ready, and off we went to the dance!

I don't remember too much about the evening, but I do remember the ride home. There I was in the back seat with Cassandra and my dad driving. It was my first date and I was trying to do things right. As we left the school, it had gotten dark. Should I attempt to kiss her? It was not too far to her house and if I was going to, I'd better move fast! I was really afraid that my dad would think that I was a jerk if I didn't, and yet embarrassed that he would see it if I did! None of this was about wanting to kiss her; just about what a guy 'should or ought' do. As we turned on her street, I remember thinking "oh well, it's now or never." And then I moved in for the kiss. Actually, I was surprised that she let me. And God knows it was just an experiment on my part. Not exactly unpleasant, but not really interesting to me either. Sort of like Jello for dessert...something a little sweet, but no slice of cake either! I think that I knew already that I was not interested in women, though I wasn't really going after guys at the time. However, it must be said that I've never doubted that I was gay.

That's knowledge that has been with me from the start.

During my very early years, there were many, many indicators that my sexuality was to be as it is. Even before I knew what sexual feelings were, I was aware that I had special feelings for males.

There were also the episodes of playing grab ass with one of the kids in the neighborhood when I was very, very small. My brother and I have talked about this incident since that time. When it was happening, he came rushing in to "defend me" ever the protective older brother. Recently, he asked if I remembered the particular night this happened. I told him that I did. He said, "All the time that I thought I was protecting you, when in fact, you were enjoying it!" We both laughed and really had a good talk about those days.

Those first years that we spent in the Collier Heights area of the city were some of the most enjoyable of my life. Even though we had to fight some to make our presence accepted by some of the other kids, it went okay. I don't think that it was really that unusual. Most kids have squabbles of some kind during those early years.

The thing that stands out the most for me however is the awareness of the other boys. As I've said, I've never NOT known that I am gay. But even then, the type of guys that would turn me on was evident.

It's funny--- even now I find myself reluctant to take the plunge and talk about it, but here goes...

I think that I've related to certain stories in our culture very well because they tell mine. The segment that Whoopi Goldberg used to perform in her standup routine of the little black girl with the shirt on her head that she pretended was hair. I think almost all black kids can relate to that child's feelings because we've all grown up in a society that tells us that entry to the "most exclusive club in the world" can only be achieved with lighter skin. So our development includes the perception that naturally lighter is better. (i.e., the interest in James at the earlier school)

Where relationships are concerned, I've always referred to this as one example of the "forbidden fruit" syndrome.

It showed up in me early on. Even as a child, most of the guys that I found attractive, like James, were much lighter than I am. This issue has caused me much pain and much turmoil in the past. It was only one of many things that I felt guilty about, but it was a major one. And through the years I've had many a conversation seeking answers as to why it manifested itself in me in just this way.

For me, I've gravitated to guys much lighter, much thinner, and much smaller than myself. In essence, guys that are just the opposite of what I saw myself as. Now, when I look at these qualities, I see that much of that is about self-hatred, low self-esteem, and low self-image. These are all the things that I felt were wrong with me as a child growing up. And though my goal is to talk about me and what my path has been, I have to acknowledge that over the years, I've seen these circumstances have differing effects on others. For instance, I've known black kids of differing hues ranging from extremely light skinned to coal black, that came up in the same era and circumstances that went the total opposite direction. They would stay as far away from a lighter skinned individual as possible. And almost always go for the black person that had the most ethnically perceived look possible, and it certainly did not hurt if the person was hefty and more introspective than most. One example that comes to mind happened during a period that I was attending a very popular black church in the Atlanta area. I happened to catch the eye of one of the 'newer members'. He's an extremely attractive brother, who just happens to be extremely light skinned. Though the church at the time had become popular with a younger, more contemporary crowd, and there were more 'men who have sex with other men' attending, it was still quite clear that all were "down low". This being the case, my new found friend and I had exchanged glances, but not much more than that. I mentioned the situation to another gay friend who was also attending at the time and he said to me, "wow! He is quite hot, but I'll tell you from experience, once you guys get to talking, DO NOT let him know you've dated white men. If you do, he'll drop you flat."

I'm sure his issues are that he's been teased and given so much grief in his life for being as light as he is, he doesn't want ANYONE trying to date him if he feels they're there because of his color. And sure enough, at a later date I did see him out on a date with a guy who was indeed darker than I am.

I also have one girlfriend that has a double master's degree and holds a doctorate, and in her relationships she seems to tack on that a guy MUST be unemployed and practically indigent. I think it's because she has always been considered "too smart"... Go figure... We as people are a strange lot.

In any case, I'm sure that this will explain why all the early boys, James, Jerry, Richard, William and Thomas, all little boys that I had crushes on, were all very light skinned.

And I think that my reluctance to speak on this even now has to do with the way that prejudice within and outside the black community is STILL a difficult topic.

As the days wore on, and we grew up, our differences with the other kids in the neighborhood were solved and we became friends having only minor infractions setting us apart from time to time. We went through all the rituals of becoming young teens within the community.

I remember the big thing back then was house parties. It was so much the rage that there was one every weekend; sometimes two and three in a night. Colored lights in the basement and slow records were the order of the day. It was the true proving ground and the place that you made your mark in the 'hood'.

Early on, I was the youngest of the group. So while the others were making out in the corners with the girls, I was relieved of that necessity because the older girls wanted to baby me. The only reason that I was there (this was my brother's age group) was because my mom wouldn't let him go if I didn't go too.

So to find my niche, I used my talents. I've always loved music and dancing. So I would wait until they played fast songs then I would ask someone to dance. My moves were wonderful and I knew I could dance rings around just about anybody. Before long, I could always draw a crowd. Usually the girl would just stop and watch with everyone else. In essence, I became the evening's entertainment. One night in particular I remember the kids started throwing money into the circle. Little did I know that there would be many nights in my future when people would throw money my way for dancing on a stage.

The end of the house party phase for me came one Saturday night when we had to cut through the woods to get to another neighborhood that was behind ours. I couldn't see why we just couldn't go through the streets. But all the other guys wanted to go through the woods because it would be faster. This also meant cutting through several neighbor's backyards as well. Now all this would have been fine, but it was dark, and I, being the youngest, the chubbiest, and the slowest, had a difficult time keeping up. We had all gone to the liquor store up on the main thoroughfare and bought a bottle of wine. There were maybe eight of us, so nobody got more than a sip of it, but we swore that we were drunk! So that's when the idea to cut through came about. We all started out on a run. The group was running and laughing and I was bringing up the rear. Well it all got out of hand when we jumped a fence and ended up in the backyard of someone with a really mean dog. I am now, and have always been very wary of aggressive dogs. To the rest of the guys, it was still great fun, but for me it had now turned to terror! They all ran straight across the yard and bounded over the fence. I, bringing up the rear like a man on crutches in a 10k run, got to the fence and missed the first attempt! The huge shepherd was gaining on my heels and I was screaming at the top of my lungs! All the others were cracking up, and my brother is really pissed off at me. He came back and grabbed a handful of my sweater to haul me over the fence, and my jeans got caught on the twisted top of the chain link. I hung there for just a minute, out of reach of the dog for the time being, but not quite on the other side either. For just the briefest instant all time stopped. Then we all heard this ripping sound. The fence had caught just on the inside of my right thigh. Fortunately, it was just in the seam. The tear started there and went all the way around to just about the same place on the left pants leg. *"KER-PLUNK"!* With a thud, I hit the ground. They all hooted and I was humiliated and miserable. And to add insult it was a brand new pair of jeans!

Well, what to do? I'm sure as hell not going back the way we came. And I don't want to sit in this party with my pants falling off! And my brother adamantly refused to miss the party just because I now wanted to go home. So I went on to the party and once there asked to use the phone. I called my mom, and sitting in this woman's kitchen that I did not know, humiliated with a sweater tied around my middle to keep my ripped pants from view, I waited for a taxi to come and take me home. I didn't know it then, but this would end my parents insisting that my brother and I go together when we went to parties. From that time on, the separation of my brother and I into our own distinct peer groups was the norm. The only problem was that I did not yet have a peer group. It was really strange. I fell right in the middle of the neighborhood age range. All the kids in it seemed to be either older than me or just younger than me. So where did I fit? And as yet, I had not started high school.

Chapter 2

Chapter 2

Chapter 2

Even though it was a blessing to leave Collier Elementary and all the discomfort there, I can't say that I was any more prepared for the coming of High School. I went in with lots of misgivings and feeling very tentative. Here once again was my old nemesis; the fear of mixing with new people. It mattered not one bit to me that I was one of an incoming body of about 409 other students. The fact that it was all new to me was more than enough to put me on edge. The first class turned out to be not so bad. Though I had really fresh memories of my first day at Collier, I was relieved to see that the initial class; homeroom, was nothing more than a check-in. Nothing was demanded of me, so I was free to sit there and do my best to go invisible.

The teacher was once again a man, but this one was very kind and open. He was really not demanding at all. He called the roll and got everybody situated and explained what home-room was all about. The whole affair lasted less than a half hour. Then we were off to our first class of the day.

Of course, my memory of those initial days is quite hazy, but I do remember that I understood immediately I was not the only one confused. There were several others that felt much the same. There was a calming effect brought on by that camaraderie.

With entry to the eighth grade, came an introduction to gym class. That woke up a whole new set of issues for me. Much of the gym experience was about playing sports with other kids. I was really good at most sports, so that was never the problem. What was at issue was that I had to wear special clothing in order to play, and that made me feel VERY un-comfortable. First of all, I was fat, or felt that I was. I was very ashamed of my body and the thought of disrobing in a roomful of guys was terrifying to me. Knowing how guys liked to tease, I was sure that I would end up the butt of most of their jokes. So as a result, even though I had gym clothes, I refused to 'dress out' for gym, as they called it. The coaches would not let you participate if you didn't wear the required shorts and

T-shirt, so I would not do it. The result was that for the first couple of years, I received failing grades in gym class. It was my understanding that lots of the guys thought that I could not play the sports. I have no idea what the coaches thought. But it was all about body image. Over the years, I had been made to feel so self - conscious about my size and the shape of my body that I was convinced that it was hideous.

Then came the demands that because of my size I should try out for football. Once again, I loved playing football with the guys in my neighborhood. There it was friends getting together and playing. Here, suddenly it was about who was the biggest and best man; an issue also not of interest to me at that time.

To this day, I'm not very impressed with exhibitions of testosterone. I mean, there is a certain type of "posturing" that guys do when they all get together. It's not particularly amusing to me. Perhaps that's just a part of my personality. Everything in the world is just not a competition to me. And I've found that ALL guys do it. Gay guys have adopted it as a part of their personalities as well. I think that's about not being thought of as a 'sissy'. To me, it's ludicrous and looks that way on just about anybody who participates in the behavior.

Because of the fact that I'm a naturally large person, all my life I've had to contend with people making erroneous assumptions about who I am and what I like. So of course, it was assumed that because I was probably one of the biggest and tallest guys in the class that I would just naturally try out for eighth grade sports.

The next point of contention for me was in the music department. I had not played in the band while at Collier. I can't remember why exactly, but with all the other disturbing feelings I don't think that I could have handled it at any rate. But now that I was in another setting I thought that I should maybe pick it back up again. Especially since my brother was once again here, and seemed to have found such a home in the band. WRONG DECISION! My brother LOVED playing trumpet and loved being in the band. He always excelled at it. As I said before, it was something that I did because my parents suggested it from the start. All I ever wanted to do as far as a musical instrument was concerned was maybe play piano. However, I went on and joined here at the high school.

I think that the main reason that I joined was in trying to structure my schedule. I needed some elective classes and this was one that I thought I could do well in and hide. I loved to sing and had a beautiful voice, but it was high pitched for my size, and I felt it would draw attention to me. Thus, drawing down ridicule, so naturally chorus was out of the question. Besides "guys didn't go out for chorus". The only way they took it was if it was forced on them. And everybody knew that if you didn't pick your electives then they would be picked for you. So I joined the band and became embroiled almost immediately in problems with the band director.

The first issue was the fact that the guy had produced one of the most celebrated High School marching bands in the city. Maybe even in the Southeast. But I'm sorry; he was a straight up classist asshole.

One of the worst characteristics about Frederick Douglass High School in Atlanta at the time was that once again many of the up and coming black families in town lived in the area and sent their kids there. As a result, the faculty and administration definitely were aware of that and played favorites to those families' kids. Pretty much, the only way that you got recognition otherwise was if you were truly a gifted kid in some area. Mediocrity or any personal issues were frowned upon and basically treated with insensitivity.

My brother truly loved playing trumpet and excelled at it. Therefore he was first seat, first chair, section leader, drum major candidate, the whole shooting match. When I got into the band room and this man saw that my abilities were not quite there, and that my interest in playing was not as focused as that of my brother, the very next thing he said to me was, "why can't you be more like your brother"? BIG MISTAKE! Hell, I got more than enough of that bullshit sentiment at home. I sure as hell didn't need it from this asshole! But being the shy, retiring type at the time, I suffered through his scorn and rough treatment that first year.

By the next term, I was having major issues with even being in the band. However, I was not the type of kid who stood up for himself at the time. This man so traumatized me, that all I wanted to do in his class was not be there. He would have periods of teaching music structure and music theory, and though I was listening

and could read the music, I never raised my hand to answer a question. By the second semester I was TOTALLY intimidated by him. So he took to calling me out with questions, singling me out to play movements that he thought I didn't understand in front of the entire class. In a band room with probably thirty or forty pupils it seemed I was the only one that he could see. This of course, provided great entertainment for the others. Often, I understood the lessons and could perform the tasks, but I was so nervous and cowering that I would make mistakes. That would blow the whole thing up and then I would proceed to mess up even further, never getting it right.

Finally one day I snapped. He asked a question and called on me. I answered, but in a very muted tone. I was to his far left in the room. He then asked a girl on his far right if she had heard what I said. Her name was Lulu. He said, "did you hear that Lulu"? And she answered that she had not. He asked me to repeat it.

Still he felt it was not loud enough. Once again, he asked, "did you hear him Lulu"? She replied that she still had not heard. He then asked me to repeat myself for the third time. I stood up and at the top of my lungs shouted the answer, and then added,"did you hear that LULU!!!! "?? There was a split second of shocked silence. Then some of the students started to twitter with laughter. I was totally mortified that I had done that! I was NEVER that type of kid. But this man had pushed me to the limit. Not too long after that I went into his office and informed him that I would be dropping band class in the next quarter. Nothing was worth the discomfort and misery that I felt taking this man's class. There are not many people that I can say that I've hated in my life, but he's definitely a candidate. As a kid, I felt that I had no recourse to his treatment of myself and any other kid that was not one of his 'golden chosen'. But what I did at the time was the best that I could muster. He had his phone number listed at the time, and I used to stay up all hours of the night. Knowing that he had to be up very early I would wait until about two a.m. and then call his house.

I'd wake him up, and then just hold the phone. There was no caller I.D. back then, and traces were expensive. Once I'd broken his sleep, I'd read a book or something for about another hour to an hour and a half.

I would wait just long enough for him to get to sleep again. Then I'd start the cycle over. I did this and then I'd quit and go away

for a while; for about two weeks. Then I'd do it again. I think I did this for about four cycles until he finally changed his number to private. Small reward, but as a kid it was the worst I could think of to do to him. As a side note, many years later I had a co – worker who had gone to the same high school. We talked about it once and she told me that her mom had to go to the school in defense of her brother over that same band director.

Fortunately, the remainder of the ninth grade year would bring some definite changes. I was not really finding my niche at school. And as a result my inner instinct was to begin thinking of what it would mean to start to become independent. I didn't really connect with the kids my age in school. In those days my mindset was always older than my years; further evidence of that adult child. I was a voracious reader and spent much of my time living vicariously through the characters in the books that I read. All too often the books would take me on journeys that I could only imagine. They also were a wonderful training ground for me in the ways of the world. Some might say that they carried me to places that I was not ready for in my young years, but I would have to disagree with that. They taught me about faraway places, and served as a training ground for my social, as well as, sexual education. Though I knew that I was interested in men sexually, I really didn't know anything other than what I felt inside. I didn't know where to find others like me, and am not sure that I even knew before finding references in books that there was a way to find those people. However, once I started to read more mature books; novels mostly, I found a wealth of information on the subject.

I'm pretty sure that the readings are what first gave me the idea of men finding one another in public washrooms. I don't know that the thought would have occurred otherwise. When I went to investigate however, I found that it was indeed so. My very first encounters were found in department stores in and around the city. I was really quite surprised at the system of communication and the network that had been formed by the guys that did this type of cruising. There was an entire science to it.

There were methods of communication with one another in the actual men's rooms that were astounding! Men had this rather simple code system of foot tapping that has since been discovered by the society at large, with politicians and rock stars being busted in restrooms. But back then I don't think that it was known by anyone but the guys that were using it and perhaps the cops.

There were also messages that were left for certain people or types of guys in the restrooms. These messages were woven into the graffiti that was written on the bathroom walls. Years later, I would find that this was a method that hoboes used to communicate in rail yards when traveling from city to city. For many guys I found that this was the only way that they "cruised"; which is a term used for going out to pick up men. For quite a while I was content to just watch the goings on. There was much to be observed if you just hung out, kept your eyes open and paid attention. It was as intricate a dance as I'd ever seen. But then one day I came across a guy that was purposely seeking me out. It was the first time that I actually did anything with anyone. I remember I was scared to death.

The entire thing seemed to take forever, since people kept coming and going from the restroom. He and I were each in a stall, and we were in a particular restroom that had an outer door and a long corridor leading to the inner men's room door. So you could hear when someone was approaching. But I remember this guy was the first person that I ever reached climax with.

It was explosive, and thank goodness no one came in during that period. I don't think I could have pulled myself together enough to make the situation look innocent! He had gone down and performed fellatio on me until I just about went bonkers.

I had never felt anything so great! Afterward, we both hurriedly cleaned up as best we could and I immediately left the place.

I don't know what happened with him, and I never saw him again.

I remember after that encounter walking along the street downtown. It was about 5:30 in the evening and there were many people about, getting off work and making their way home for the evening. I had to head that way myself since school had

been out for quite some time and my family would be expecting me there soon.

For the remainder of that year and into the first part of the next this was to become my pattern. I would leave school and go downtown to the stores and 'play' for a bit before going home. Often I would not arrive home until early evening. Sometimes I was as late as 6:30 or 7pm. It was those days that my parents would sometimes question where I had been and why it had taken so long for me to get home. I'd come up with some type of excuse and usually they would let it go. Pretty soon I started to widen my search.

I reasoned correctly that if this much action was happening downtown, that it was most likely happening in the mall shopping centers as well. And that there might be much more since the traffic was not quite as heavy. And I found that in fact I was right. I also found that certain stores had reputations for being the best for cruising. There were many reasons for this. Most often, it was because of the floorplans. Many were set up on the same type of floor plans in all their stores, no matter where the stores were located. I remember Woolworth's were usually prime. All their stores had outer doors to the restrooms with a long hallway to the inner door, and on top of that, there was a coin operated lock on the outer door. There were times that I've walked into Woolworth's men's rooms and found close to a dozen guys standing around in a room with two urinals and one toilet! Once it was determined that you were there for the festivities, a regular orgy would commence! With all that hardware to work through to get in, there was more than enough time for everyone to right themselves if anyone was entering. And often it seemed that the only people that were entering were there to play as well. Another well-known store for lots of action was a chain of discount stores called Zayre. Many of these retailers have since gone out of business and have been for many years. But back then I think the problem with them was that they almost never had floor security and the employees either didn't have a clue what was going on, or just didn't care. Those stores as well were usually quite busy. But by far, some of the very best were Sears stores. Reason being that their floor plans almost always had men's rooms in departments like appliances and furniture. These were areas in the store where there were not a lot of sales personnel and almost no customers. Therefore men could come and go (literally and figuratively!)with virtually no one noticing.

These places became my playgrounds. My 'afternoon delights' so to speak. And it wasn't long before I started to want to go earlier to see if I was missing out on any daytime traffic. The problem there was that I was in school until 3pm every day, and on the weekend it was just too difficult to get away. Pretty soon I started to cut class and leave school early to go downtown to play. I didn't do it very often but it was certainly enough. I was careful though. Each teacher would take roll calls in her or his class, and if you came up present in the homeroom, but absent in too many classes later in the day, the assistant principal would flag you for cutting. It amazes me sometimes but I was never caught cutting class.

The other big issue for me was that even though I knew in my heart that I had always liked boys, it did nothing to alleviate the guilt that besieged me. Just after I would climax with some guy, I would become wracked with guilt and shame. I would mentally chastise myself and berate myself for being such a horrible person. Back at that time being gay was really frowned upon. And in the African American community it was practically the worst thing a guy could be labeled. Our society at large was so against this. Yet I knew inherently that for me it was as normal as brushing my teeth in the morning. That's what set up the awful guilt and self-loathing. Because I knew that no matter how the world felt about it, I was never going to be able to change. It made me feel as though I was carrying the weight of the world on my shoulders. I had no idea how to stop, and was not even sure that I WANTED to stop. But I also knew that if anyone were to find out I would be disgraced forever.

Much was affected by those feelings. Suddenly I had a secret that I could tell NO ONE. I withdrew from the few friends that I did have at school, and spent almost all my time alone. Even when I attended classes I didn't really mix with the other kids. I was off to myself a large amount of the time. It was about that time that I really started to become very introverted and isolated. I didn't think there was anyone that I could talk to.

My family seemed to be clueless about just about anything that concerned me anyway, and I KNEW there would be nothing positive there. I loved my family with all my heart, but I don't think they understood me very much and I really didn't understand them. I also just didn't feel that there was

much concern about me. On some level, I believe that I thought they really didn't care much. Oh there was lip service given to what I was doing, but no great concern really on their part. I felt that my brother was doing well in school and that's all they were really concerned with. I don't think they expected much of me. Don't think they thought I was capable of doing more than average, so no one pushed it. However, the real truth was that most of what I would have liked to do was inhibited by the thoughts that if I showed those interests everyone would call me sissy and figure out my secret.

By that time I had found a true love for sewing but was ashamed of it because it was 'something the girls did'. I always loved to dance and sing but would never pursue those interests in school because I'd be laughed at. I remember there was a big joke in school about having to take Home Economics as a requirement no matter who you were. All the boys used to scoff and complain and say it was a total waste of time. They made a huge joke about it, so I knew that once in there, if I had to take it, that I couldn't let anyone know that I really could sew and was getting good at it. Nor could I let them know that I liked to cook, for that was shameful too.

That next year would bring lots of change. There would be opportunities and realizations that would challenge and delight me. In the tenth grade year it was a requirement that all male students must take a year of ROTC. Initially, I was indifferent to the classes. I had no real desire to take them, but there was a benefit in that they would take the place of the gym classes so I then didn't have to think about that anymore. However, once I was in the classes

I found that I really liked the orderliness of it all. There was a defined structure. Once I found that it was possible, it was not long before I decided that I would continue the classes throughout the remainder of my high school years. I found very quickly that I was good at it! I liked that there were rules and as long as you followed them you would be all right.

There were other changes that had come about as well. Midway that year, I was to start working at the Downtown Marriott Hotel. Even though I was still under age by just a few months when I started, I landed a job there as a Room Service busboy. It had become enormously important to me that I start to work. I knew that if

I was going to do the things that I wanted, I'd need money. I wanted clothes, a car, and the freedom to really check out the city. Like any other kid, I was beginning to pay attention to those things. However, in addition to that, I also wanted to start to purchase furniture for myself. I was already plotting my escape from home. All these would require that I get some cash flow going, and quickly.

I started working at the hotel at a really interesting time too. When I started, the Marriott and the Hyatt were the premier hotels in the downtown area. That meant that those two hotels were garnering the bulk of the convention business in the city. Most of the larger parties, most of the visiting entertainers and just about any other entity that was looking for a really nice place to house an event was finding its way to our doorstep. It was a wonderful opportunity for me. I was making good money right off the bat. I was tipped by all the waiters and made a good salary on top of it. Since I was too young to carry alcohol, they wouldn't let me serve any food yet. However, that would come soon enough. In the meantime,

I found loads of time to explore the hotel and all its nooks and crannies.

I found that in between my duties of going up onto the floors and retrieving all the dirty dishes I had time to check out the various departments in the place. That was how I really learned it. That also gave me the freedom to meet and talk to lots of guests. As much as I'd like to say that I was there doing the "it was SO educational" thing, the truth is that I was really no different from any other teenage boy. Inasmuch as I was full of raging hormones! The only difference was that my hormonal deluge was directed at other males. So I spent a great deal of time checking out the guys that were there in the place. And believe me, in the mid-70's there was lots of sexual tension in the air! It wasn't long before I realized that I could play the same games that I had played in the stores around town right there in the hotel. At that time, just about any place there were public restrooms, there were likely to be men there seeking sexual gratification with other men. The hotels were certainly no exception. And on top of the traffic in the men's rooms, there were guests that were staying in the hotel who took that opportunity to 'indulge' their pleasures. The sexual revolution was in full swing and most people were trying to get their fair share one way or another!

The waiters used to tell stories of people that were coming into the hotel and checking in solely for the purpose of having sex with its employees. All these stories sounded just too fantastic for words but soon I found that they were quite true. There was one woman ; an older lady of about mid-50's or so , who came in on a regular basis.

She had a very striking body. It became common knowledge to most of the hotel that when she checked in, she would be calling just about every department in the place that was staffed predominantly with men. For instance, she would call Room Service and order food, or she would call the engineering department with a complaint about the television or whatever, or she might call the bell stand and request that they bring something up to her. All this was to get the guys to come to her room where they would find her sitting in a chair wearing a negligee. The door would be ajar, and when you knocked, she would call for you to come in. Once you entered and got close enough to really see her, you could tell she was wearing nothing under the nightgown. She would then open her legs and flash you when she saw you had noticed her apparent nudity under the sheer robe and gown. There was also a couple that became pretty infamous. He was a really huge guy, maybe 400 lbs. or so. She was absolutely "fashion model " beautiful. They would invite guys up to their room and ask if the guy wanted to make love to her while the husband watched. The guys in the hotel were floored by all this. While these were two of the extreme cases, there were sexual situations popping up all over the place. I came to find that hotels are very much like little cities. There is just about every element in them that you find in the world at large. I never got tired of going to work. Every day was something new and unexpected. The world and the hospitality industry were different places then, so naturally it should have been no surprise to me that there was gay activity in the place as well. It also should have been no surprise that there were other employees that batted on the same team as me. The problem was that in those days I was nowhere near ready to admit to anyone that I was gay. In no way was I trying to be open about it. So I was frankly terrified when someone would even mention something to do with being gay to me. I remember that there was one waiter whom everyone would sort of whisper about. The story was that he had been in a relationship with another guy and it was known even though it was undercover. The other man had a wife and was one of the banquet managers. I used to hear how the people talked about them when they were not around. It was not at all flattering, and the waiter seemed to be a picture of masculinity to me. I seriously doubted the rumors were true, so you can imagine my shock and near panic when – standing at the elevator one day – he turned and asked me outright if I were gay.

I became totally flustered and declared indignantly that I most certainly was not! My God, how stupid I must have appeared! It was not rocket science to figure me out I'm sure. I've never been all that good at covering who I am. My problem was that I dreaded the outcome of the revelation. I totally expected to be ostracized and mentally beat down once people had the admission from me. Never mind that it was totally catastrophic thinking on my part. I just went straight to the negative. The interesting thing was however, that this particular waiter also was the first person to show me an example of being somewhat comfortable with who he was.

Much of that time was spent hoping that nobody knew about me. It was very painful and very stressful. I would go above and beyond the requirements of any tasks that my job presented. I think that I figured if I could be a better employee than anyone else, then they would want to keep me despite my flaws if they were to find out my awful secret. It still amazes me today that I thought no one knew! I was so sure that I was being "careful". I thought if I kept quiet and didn't really mix with any-

one then I would pass with flying colors. Of course now I know just how ridiculous that was. The people that I worked with I now know were very protective of me. They didn't tease me or put me down, or force the issue at all. I can just imagine the conversations when I wasn't around! But still, no matter what, I'm grateful that they took it easy on me for the most part.

Meanwhile, back at school I was becoming more and more distant from my classmates. It was not that I had anything against them; it was just that as I continued to find out more about myself and my sexuality, I didn't feel that I had much in common with them. And I was sure that they would be anything but accepting of me and my newfound self. It pretty much became that I was living to work. All I could think about was that the money that I was saving would buy me my freedom from school, family and everything. The work was fun as well. I had the opportunity to really learn a bit about fine dining and what was possible with different foods. Up to that time, I only knew the things that were common in my home. I was always willing to try something new and was totally dumbfounded by just what the chefs in the hotel were capable of; Desserts that I never knew existed. There were totally different cuts of meat from anything that I had ever seen. There were even different types of fowl. It was all a terrific new world for me. And I took full advantage of it.

Many times I've said that the food there was my downfall. I began to eat more than I ever had in my life. I was gaining weight by leaps and bounds.

Before long, I was really beginning to put together some money. I immediately started to think about getting a car. I wanted to save and get my own so that I wouldn't have to fight with my folks to borrow theirs. I think that was pretty much the beginning of my independent streak. I knew that things were really changing for me, and I wanted to be able to do my own thing without being beholden to anyone. It was not that my folks were really all that difficult; it was just that I didn't really know how to relate to anyone at that time. And I didn't want to have to answer a lot of questions about where I was going and what I was doing and when I would be returning. In my own car I felt that I wouldn't have to.

Almost immediately when I got the car I found the benefits of the freedom that it provided. I suddenly found that it was nothing to get to the places where I had played at the public sex game. And indeed, there were new venues to discover.

It wasn't very long before I discovered Piedmont Park. It's a very large park in the center of Midtown Atlanta, and to this day the park is a centrally located hangout for just about anyone that was into inner city culture. At that time Atlanta was just coming off of the early 70's; The hippy/flower child period. During that time the hippies had pretty much taken over midtown. Much of the flavor of that period was still lingering in midtown and as a result it was probably the most liberal area in the Southeast. All the hip kids, gay and straight alike, were partying in midtown. And on any given day or evening that summer the park was generally packed with hot guys. It is a fairly large park, and at that time you could still drive through in your car. On the south end of the park was a lake. It was well known by all the gay guys that all the boys that you found walking about on lakeside were hustling. Male prostitution was very prevalent on the streets here then. However, just about all the rest of the place was fair game! On the northwestern side of the park, sitting up on a hill and facing Piedmont Avenue is the Piedmont Driving Club. It is a prestigious private club and is still there to this day. The backside of the club looked out over the softball fields. Just on the northern side of the club lay the area that is now the Atlanta Botanical Garden. At the time, that space was set aside as the park for the visually impaired and the Piedmont Park nature trails. During the summer evenings there would be countless young men strolling about the grounds up there. Cigarettes glowing in the night like hundreds of little fireflies lighting up the otherwise dark nature trails.

Many of the paths had been trodden upon so well that they were worn smooth from all the foot traffic. There were little alcoves that created secluded rooms within the overgrown shrubbery and amidst the low lying branches of the evergreens. There were certain areas that had been cleared away behind bushes that were anywhere from six to seven feet tall. Those industrious gay boys had creatively found some interesting uses for those spaces!

The clearings were often large enough that you would have anywhere from a couple to up to fifteen or so guys behind those bushes at any given time. Sometimes there would be full-fledged orgies going on in the moonlight out there! Many summer nights I would go out there if I were off work and stay from dusk, around 8:30 or so, until the park closed around 1:00 a.m.

I remember one night in particular, it was in the middle of the week, so there were very few people around. It was maybe 9:00 or so when I climbed the stone steps to the hill heading back to the trails. There was a large clearing next to the park for the blind that you had to cross in order to get back to the more secluded area of the trails. Just at the back of that clearing there was a large old tree with branches that swept the ground like a giant umbrella. Unless someone wanted to be noticed, he could stand under those branches all night and not a soul would see him. That particular night, just as I was passing the tree I noticed the faint glow of a cigarette just barely discernible under the branches. I decided to check it out. Since it was a weeknight I knew the chances of there being lots of people up there were slim. When I parted the branches and entered that little clearing I could just make out a beautiful young man.

He had shoulder length dark hair and a full beard. As I got closer I could see he was wearing sandals and white jeans, but had taken his shirt off. It was quite warm that night. He was slender, but not unappealing. There was a liberal amount of dark hair sprinkled about his chest, with a definite line snaking a sexy trail into the waistband of the jeans. One of the rules of the game in the trails was there was virtually no talking. So as I walked closer to him, I put out my hand to touch his chest. His skin was warm and just slightly damp with perspiration. His nipples were very prominent amongst the dark curls of hair on his chest. He leaned into me and reached up and pulled my face down to his for a kiss. The smoky flavor of his mouth after the cigarette was exhilarating. As he looped his arms about my neck, I encircled his waist with my arms and we clung there in that embrace and shared the kiss for what seemed like a good long time, though in actuality it was probably only about two or three minutes. When we parted, he stepped back and unbuttoned the top button of the jeans and looked up at me and smiled. He quickly pushed them down to the ground and stepped out of them. He then stepped back into my arms and began to open my pants. He then sank to his knees and took me into his mouth to the base. His mouth was so warm! I thought I would explode on the spot. After a few minutes of his ministrations, he got to his feet and turned around presenting me with the most gorgeous ass I think I've ever seen! His butt cheeks were like finely sculpted marble with just the shadow of dark downy fur covering them. The crack between his cheeks was quite furry with long curly hair. He leaned back against me and moaned. He then said, very softly, "please fuck me". As he leaned back against me I caught the scent of coconut coming from his hair. It was full and lustrous and felt wonderful against my cheek. I told him that I didn't have any lube with me, and he said not to worry. He had a small tube in his pants pocket. As he retrieved it, I watched his body move. It was like a finely chiseled dancer's body. There was not a flaw on him that I could see. He once again came over to me and squeezed some of the lubricant from the tube onto my fingers. He then took my hand and guided it to his ass cheeks. As my finger slipped inside of him I could feel the heat of his body. He exhaled softly against me as my fingers explored his soft, smooth insides. He then turned around and without another word, took my member and guided it to his back door. He enveloped my manhood like a warm glove. There was just the slightest pressure and resistance. It was the tightest, most wonderful thing I'd ever felt! He suddenly pushed back hard against me and moaned loudly. He had impaled himself on me all the way to the base. As we began to find a rhythm and rock back and forth, I thought I'd come before I could stroke a dozen times. But it didn't matter. He was there right with me. In no time we were going like a well-oiled locomotive. Soon, I could sense his speeding up and holding his breath. I felt like my whole body was about to shake loose. When we both exploded he was trembling so badly that I had to hold his hips against me tight to keep him from falling over. I could feel his muscles milking my balls of all they had to offer. In a few minutes, when the tremors subsided, we disengaged. He reached down and pulled a wad of paper napkins out of his pants pocket, leaned over and whispered to me, "I always travel prepared", and chuckled. He stepped back into his jeans, gave me a kiss on the lips and said, "that was great!" "Maybe we'll see each other here again!" With that, he parted the branches of the tree and was gone. When I stepped from beneath the canopy, it was like walking back into another world. All around, nothing had changed.

The tennis courts down below were still brilliantly lit and people were still playing. There were people walking about just as though nothing had happened. And indeed, nothing had as far as they were concerned. I, however, had just experienced the most explosive orgasm of my young life! There were many such encounters at the park that summer, but none compared to the sheer perfection of that one.

As time went on that summer, I spent more and more time in the evenings at the park. Now that I had the car, it seemed that work was more of a hindrance than a help. I did realize however that income was still the key to my freedom. I had a taste of it now and I wasn't giving that up for anything! As much as I wanted to play in the city, I realized that it cost money to play. The good   thing about the hotel was that it really wasn't much like work at all. The money was excellent and I got to work strictly dinners, which suited me just fine. I was never much in those days for early rising. I would soon find that being able to stay on one shift in that business was highly irregular. Most hotels and restaurants wanted their staff to be as flexible as possible. You needed to be available when the business was there. The Room Service Captains were very good about that. The only time that I might have to cover early mornings/lunches was during the peak of convention season. During those times it was not unusual to be at the hotel for 12 hours running sometimes. I learned to just put my head down and work. When that was happening it was all about the money. I quickly became more than willing to do it. More often than not during those periods it was pretty common that we would each make anywhere from $125.00 up daily in tips. I think the most that I ever cleared in one evening was about $450.00 for a whole day's work. And we're talking 1977 here. The business was spectacular during convention season, and those type tips were there for the taking from about January through May.

In the summer things would generally die down a bit as the business travelers went away and the family style tourists invaded. Even then, if you were quick on your feet you could usually finish with $75-$80 nights. All in all, things were lucrative. I was still a bit naive, and didn't really grasp what I could have been doing with the funds at my disposal. As they say, youth is SO wasted on the young!

My parents tried hard to convince me to invest in property as well as some other things, but I was just too focused on the partying to see anything else. Absolutely EVERYTHING that was happening in my life was new! They had no way of knowing just how high I was flying and what all I was into. They were rather nervous that I was in the fast lane, and I wanted to be sure and keep the details from them.

Such was the mixed blessing there. While I was having the time of my life, I felt I couldn't share it with anyone. Least of all them....

As fate would have it, the park would be the place that would provide the setting where I would meet the people that would become my confidantes. The first of which would be Greg. The way that we met was actually a little funny. I was sitting on the hood of my car just across from the first set of stone steps going up the hill to the park for the blind area. It was a really sunny and beautiful afternoon and I was reading a book. Still, after all that was happening, books were just about my best friends. I heard a commotion and looked up in time to see a couple of guys come running down the steps laughing and kidding around. As they came close I said, "hi" to them. I truly don't even remember who the second guy was, but the first guy immediately caught my attention. He was very tall and rail thin. He had a little lighter complexion than mine, but had outrageous reddish hair. He was dressed mostly in black; Black shirt and pants, with a light brown/tannish belt and matching platform shoes. I realized immediately that he was gay, and that he couldn't be much older than I was. Yet, he was so open and out there! He spoke to me and they stopped to chat. I told him my name was Tony and he said he was Greg. Here was the first ever gay black person that I had met somewhat socially, and he was my age! There were many that I had suspected since I'd started to play around with guys, and certainly I had encountered black men in the public restroom scene, but none that had been my age, and none of ANY age that were so obviously out there and seemingly comfortable with themselves. I think that was the driving force behind my wanting to know this person. I was actually quite put off by his overt personality in a way; But fascinated at the same time. I was much more used to the reserved attitude of those trying to hide their sexuality. I vaguely remember that the guy that was with him was white, and I think it was his friend John, but to tell the truth I was so riveted by Greg that I don't remember. He elected to stay behind and chat with me, so his friend went on his way. In no time we'd discovered that we were both from Atlanta and that we were indeed about the same age. I was sixteen and he was fifteen; Due to turn sixteen the following February. We began talking and I soon found out his last name. I asked him if he knew someone else that I knew by that name, and it turned out that it was his cousin! I had known the cousin since kindergarten. That kinship seemed to draw us even closer. We talked well into the afternoon. We just hung out in the park and talked like kids do when they make a connection. It's truly on a totally different level than most adults I think. Although we were both out there playing a very adult game, we found a common thread in our similarities and that spoke to us deeper than anything else could have. Pretty soon Greg mentioned that he had to get going, but mentioned that he would be going out that evening. I asked him where he would be going, and he said, "I'll be at The Cove." It turned out I knew the place, having met this guy in the park a few days earlier and him having asked me to take him there. Greg asked me if I knew where it was and I recounted the tale about meeting Raven in the park and him having asked me to drive him there.

It was right then that Raven became the very first of a few men that Greg and I would have in common. He told me that he knew Raven and that they had had a brief fling. Well, we proceeded to compare notes! We both laughed and agreed that he was all right, but no great shakes! I told him that I had been to the bar a couple of times since then, and would be glad to meet him there that night. He said ok and we parted company that afternoon.

That evening I arrived at the Cove a little early. It was a Saturday night, and up to then I had only been in on week-nights. I'm sure my eyes were the size of saucers! There were SO many good looking young guys.

As near as I could tell, the crowd was all white. I don't remember seeing one other black guy there. Already I was noticing that on this side of town there were virtually no black people. It really didn't bother me however. For as long as I can remember there was a mystical quality about people of other races for me, but I've not been necessarily intimidated or worried when in groups that did not include members of my own race. Pretty soon I looked up and saw Greg coming into the room. He'd not seen me yet, and I was able to observe him speaking to lots of people there. Not long after he came in there was another black guy who came in, and Greg appeared to know him as well. I caught his eye and waved. They both came over to the side of the bar where I was sitting and Greg introduced us. His name was Conley, and he was maybe mid-twenties. He had a light complexion and was very tall. I remember he had on the shortest blue jean cut-offs that I had ever seen! True Daisy Dukes, before the term became popular! That style of shorts was all the rage back then. We talked for a few minutes and then Conley went off to dance with some guy. Greg asked me if I wanted to dance and I said yes. We got onto the tiny dance floor and just went wild! It was totally crazy!

To this day it surprises me the number of people that were crammed into that little hole in the wall bar on any given Sat-urday night. In later years, they added a whole second section in the rear that was a big dance club, but in those early days it was only one room in front, and it was really just a little shack, with a screened in patio out back. Most weeknights there was just the jukebox in the corner, but on the weekends they had a deejay that would come in.

Before long Greg asked me if I wanted to go over to another bar. I responded with, "You mean there's another one?" He looked at me and said, "Sure, there are lots of gay bars around town." He told me a little about this one. He said it was a drag bar and that he'd wanted to go for some time, but hadn't been able to. It was a bit far and he didn't have a way to get there. So I said "sure, let's go". Once there I found that he was also worried about getting in. They usually carded to go in if you looked too young, but I paid for us both and looked anything but young. Greg sailed right in just in front of me.

If I thought there were a lot of guys at the Cove that was NOTHING. This place was packed to the rafters. I remember the very first moment that we walked in. It was between shows, and the dancefloor/stage was filled. Gloria Gaynor's Honeybee was playing and the black lights and strobe were on. That summer many guys were into the look of what's now called the 'wife beater' muscle T- shirts with tight blue jeans. All those white T-shirts were positively glowing up there on that dance floor with the black lights shining down on them. I was in total awe. Hell, I didn't even know this many gay men existed on the planet, let alone here in Atlanta! All my reading had been primarily about New York and other faraway places. Never had I dreamed there were gay bars filled with beautiful men right here under my nose! Of course, the first thing I wanted to do was fly up onto that dance floor! There I was in my element. So we headed up and worked our way into a spot right up front. We danced like fools, and were quite good at it too. Naturally we garnered our share of attention, which was just what we wanted.

Greg of course was MUCH better at working a crowd and talking to people. I was extremely shy and didn't have a clue as to what to say. I felt very awkward and unattractive.

Because of my size, it was fixed in my mind that I was fat and ugly. And indeed in the gay community looks were EVERY-THING. At that time I had no way of knowing that my low self-esteem would be exacerbated in this environment. I was just totally entranced. Soon there was a pause in the dancing and there was an overture of sorts. Greg suggested that we find seats before everyone came off the dance floor. We found a table in the first tier of the balcony and soon the show started. There appeared to be mostly women in the show, though there was one man there. I watched and was fascinated. The clothes were so beautiful and all the ladies sang so well. Then I started to notice that many of the songs I knew from the radio. It was then that I realized that they were not singing at all. There were records playing in the background. What's more, when I really looked at some of the women I quickly realized that they were actually men. Hell that was even better! I thought they were fantastic! Most of them looked damned good. Even though I could tell a couple were most certainly guys, they still looked really beautiful and were quite good.

I found myself totally drawn in by the shows and the bar in general. Before long, I was going there practically every night that it was open. And that was every night but Sunday. I remember there was actually one time around tax time that when I had my taxes done and looked at my earnings I literally thought to myself, 'damn near every cent was spent at' The Sweet Gumhead.'

At the conclusion of the show on that first night there however, I took Greg back down to Amsterdam drive. He was staying with some guy down there. I asked him who the guy was and he said just some guy that he was staying with for a little while. He was not very forthcoming and it was obvious to me that he really didn't want to talk about it. So for the time being I just let it go. Even then Greg was the type to play his cards very close to his chest so to speak. We started to hang out just about every night. Eventually one night he told me that he had moved to an apartment out on Buford Highway. Back at that time that's just about all that was on that road; Apartments and a couple of fast food places. I asked him one night about his parents and he told me that he had run away from home. I was immediately concerned, but he told me that he talked to them from time to time and let them know that he was ok, but that he could not go back there just yet. It was all very strange to me. I knew that I couldn't have done it. And though he put up a brave front, I knew that it was very hard for him as well.

Meantime however he had taken up living with this guy on Buford Hwy. The guy's name was Richard, and I really don't think there had ever been anything between him and Greg, I just think that he took Greg in and gave him a place to stay. Greg was always talking about getting a job, but quite frankly he was really still too young. He had dropped out of school in ninth grade for God's sake! It was still a few months before his sixteenth birthday, so no one was going to hire him. I was working and would give him money from time to time, pay for him to go when we went out, and all. That was pretty much how he made it. There were myself and a few other guys in the community that knew him and knew that he was really under age, so we took care of him. Before long he was able to get little jobs as bussers or dishwashers in restaurants and that helped. I was actually quite amazed at the ingenuity with which he managed. (Little did anyone know, he would one day become one of the most celebrated chefs in the city, and indeed in the entire Southeastern United States.)

Personally, I was still attending school and living with my parents. It seemed like such a drag since my off hours life had become so wild, but I knew my parents would kick my ass if I even THOUGHT about dropping out of school. And besides, I was such a "good boy" that I could have never done that anyway. Even so, I was there only in name. I went to class on occasion but had really taken just about all my requirements by that time, so almost all my classes were electives. I still got into much trouble about not showing up to school though. Basically, what was going on was that I had reached a point where I knew that I could never go back to being the same person that I was before beginning to come out, so I just avoided it. My life pretty much consisted of going to school on occasion, then going to work at 4:00 pm, and after getting off at 11pm I would go pick up Greg and we would hit the streets.

My boss never made me stay late to work because he knew that I had to be in school the next morning. And my parents were working during the days, so if I decided to ditch, I was the only person at the house to get the phone calls if my homeroom teacher or someone else from the school decided to call. Soon I was in my senior year and there were only a few more weeks to go anyway. I had long ago decided that I couldn't go through college simply because I just could not take another situation where I would be the new kid, and now the new gay kid.

Many of the decisions that I made at that time were based solely on the fact that I was petrified of anyone finding out my secret. The one thing that I had enjoyed about those final years of high school was ROTC, but when I thought of doing anything like trying to go on to military school or going into the Army I was sure that they would find out my secret and I would be kicked out or worse. Any thoughts of college were met with the same feelings. I had no idea what it was like, but I was sure that it would almost certainly be the same experience with school that had always been true for me. So I figured it would be best for all involved if my schooling career ended right there. I told myself that I was only going to "take a few years off", and that I would go back before long. But deep inside I felt that once I got away I would never put myself in that type of predicament again. So on I went skipping school that first quarter of my senior year. I was so removed from it all that I don't even remember there being any discussion of a senior prom. Don't know if they took a senior trip, and quite frankly, could have cared less. I really didn't start to pay any attention at all that year until there began to be discussions about graduation rehearsal.

Many times that year I would only go to school after lunch and hit a half day. The reason for this was that I was really only interested in going to ROTC and it was fifth and sixth period. So while I did maintain some type of presence there, it had become increasingly obvious that I was cutting the whole early part of the day, not just a couple of classes. For the most part I could get away with it by now, because many of the senior class members were ditching classes as well. I'm sure they had their reasons, just as I had mine. The sticking point was that one of those early classes that I was cutting was Review of Grammar. It was the one requirement that I needed to graduate that I didn't already have. The only reason that I didn't have it was that they would not let you take it until you became a senior. For me, that was unfortunate but I just couldn't bring myself to go there much these days.

When the graduation rehearsals started in earnest the teacher that taught the review sent word down to the gym that I should come to her class to see her one afternoon after rehearsal. I was freaked out because I knew what she wanted.

When I walked in she made me wait while she was talking to some other students. She was known to be really rough. When she sat down with me she asked me what I was doing down in the gym every day. I told her that I was down there practicing for the graduation. She then asked me what made me think that I was graduating? I was silent. She then went on to ask me if I knew that I would not be able to graduate if I didn't pass her class. I said that I did. She said again that she couldn't see how I thought I could do that since I hadn't attended more than 2 weeks of the class that whole quarter. I told her that I had all my other requirements covered and that I only needed the one. I then asked her about my options.

She explained to me that most likely I would have to come to summer school and make it up, or come the first quarter of the following year to do so. She said I would be allowed to march in the graduation line, but would be presented with an empty folder. I said ok, and prepared to leave. She told me to hold on. She then sat me down and said, " I really don't know what's going on with you. I know that you can do this work, however there is something in your life that's causing you to do this." She then said, " I don't know what it is, and I'm not going to pry, but I have a feeling that if you don't graduate now, you probably won't do it at all." I readily told her that she was probably right. She said, "I did something that I don't usually do. I gave you a D and let you pass so that you could graduate.... Whatever it is that's causing you these problems I suggest you work it out." She then told me to get out of there and she wanted a big hug on graduation night. I broke into a huge grin and thanked her profusely. It was probably the single most important favor that anyone had ever done for me. I was so traumatized by the pain of coming out and the expected reaction of people in my community if they knew my truth that I was all about avoiding it at any cost. It is by far the one thing that if I could go back and change in my life, I would. Maybe then I would have not been so reluctant to continue my growth and development as a young person. Especially in the area of my education. Little did I know that in time I would find that no matter what direction my life took, I would still need to learn to stand up for my beliefs. To not do so is just not a free pass that life is willing to give any of us.

By this time, I was becoming totally immersed in the scene of the Sweetgum Head Bar. I had met and befriended some of the employees there and was virtually spending every night there after I got off work. Sometimes Greg would go with me, and sometimes not. He had begun to work himself at various little odd jobs, and was beginning to branch out on his own. As time went on, I found that while we were very close, we definitely had different tastes in some matters.

I was totally enchanted with the show bar, Greg was not so much. He liked it just fine, but also liked going to other places. I was cool right there. It pretty much had everything that I felt I needed. I could see a good show, there were plenty of men, and I could dance. What else was there? I was happy. At the time I didn't yet realize that gay men generally broke out into categories. I was still very naive as to the ways of the community. Once again, despite my size, I was slow in the maturity department. Greg, even though he was younger than I was, had already reached that place where picking up guys took priority. I was still in the fascination phase. It was much more fun for me to dance the night away and watch a great show than to get tied up with some guy for the whole evening. This was a whole new world and it pandered so much to my imagination. The sights and sounds and the fantasy that I had found here was so much of what I was largely about. While the intrigue of sex was great, it was not nearly the strongest pull for me at that time. On the night that my graduation was scheduled for, there was a drag pageant at the bar. I had never seen one, and most definitely wanted to be there. One of the city's favorite entertainers was competing and it was really the talk of the gay community. Lisa King was the odds on favorite to win the pageant, and was one of my favorite performers as well. I had never dreamed such events even existed. I knew that no matter what else was happening in my life that there is where I would be.

When the graduation ceremony ended, many of the people from my class were planning to go out together and have some fun. While I didn't have many friends in my class there were a couple of people that I considered friends. Stanley, the one person that I considered my best friend, told me that he was going to hang out with some people. My parents asked me what I was doing and I told them that I was going out with friends. I told Stanley that I was probably just going to go home.

I climbed into my car and headed for the drag club as fast as I could go! By the time I got there, the show had already started. I had not missed much, and indeed was there in plenty of time to see much of the remaining competition. I have no idea what I expected, but it was wonderful! It was like a fashion show and variety show all rolled into one. The entertainers competed in clothing categories; Presentation, Evening Gown and Sportswear. Then came the talent portion of the competition. Many performed elaborate productions, complete with backup dancers and really nice costuming. Needless to say, the odds on favorite won, and all the performances were really very good. Without a doubt, I didn't for one minute feel that I had missed anything by not going out with the people that I had graduated with. As far as I was concerned, that part of my life was over. One door was closing and another was most definitely opening.

Chapter 3

Chapter 3

Chapter 3

By this time, I was more than ready to move ahead and explore what was in store for me out in the world fulltime and away from school. Most of my time these days was spent either at the hotel or at the bar. I was meeting people at a lightning speed. Some were very nice indeed. It was all becoming such a thrilling experience for me.

Shortly before graduation I ran into a guy that I worked with at the hotel out at one of the bars and had become totally infatuated with him. His name was Michael and he had become my first real world crush. I mean, I had my crushes on teachers and the like just as everybody else did. But this was different. He saw me in the bar before I saw him, and when he greeted me and kissed me on the lips I just about died. In his defense, he had no idea what type of can of worms he was opening. I doubt it ever occurred to him that I could possibly be as young and impressionable as I was . I fell in love on the spot. I began to follow him about like a puppy whenever he was in the bars. I'm sure I became a real nuisance to him. I think he finally understood when I placed the graduation invitation on his car.

He then got just how young I was and that I was pretty much smitten.

I of course couldn't fathom why he was not as taken with me as I was with him. It never occurred to me that he just was not into me. I became convinced that if I were thinner, he would find me more attractive. It was the thing that sent me in search of my first serious attempt at dieting.

I went to the drug store and got these pills. I'd never taken anything like this before, but the women that I worked with were always talking about losing weight and using water pills or diet pills, so I thought that I would give them a try. I lost quite a bit of weight, but I didn't read or heed all the package warnings. And before long I was experiencing some serious side effects. I was having mood swings like a crazy person. I would pick Greg up when I got off work and I'd be so wired that I couldn't wait to get to the bar. Once there I would literally drag him to the dance floor and dance until I was just about hyperventilating.

If anyone said anything to me I would likely fly off the handle immediately. I would go into a rage at the drop of a hat, and then just as quickly lose it and start crying. Drinking booze on top of all this was only ramping up the behavior. After a little while I started to notice that things were off the wall.

The other thing that I missed before taking these things was that I hadn't paid any attention to the fact that the package clearly stated that I should increase my water intake when using the pills. Before long, I became severely dehydrated and developed a kidney infection. I luckily caught it before it got extreme, but my sides were hurting so badly that people had to help me out of my car like a senior citizen and I was only nineteen years old. I think that I was very fortunate that the diuretic effect of those things didn't do more damage. They changed the way that my bladder and kidneys worked from then on. I tended for quite a while afterward to only be able to pass urine very slowly. It took some time (some years in fact), but eventually things got back to moving a little more rapidly. The whole experience was very alarming. Though I was happy with the weight loss, it sufficiently scared me so that I didn't think I would be doing anything like that again.

That summer and the entire year following were very special . It was all I could do to work full days. I was so ready to get out and to Midtown with all my new found pleasures, that work seemed greatly a nuisance. However I knew that without it all this freedom would go up in smoke. While I found that I really loved the gay community and all its perceived freedoms, it also threw me into something of a panic. While many of my thoughts about issues with my weight were there in my head, they were also helped along by the strict standards imposed by that very same gay community. At the time, there was certainly an unspoken rule about what one's appearance should be just as there is now.

There's an old joke that says, "A thirty-four inch waist-line on a ballerina is unfortunate, but on a gay man it's a tragedy". Believe me that was adhered to rather strictly in those days. Things are not quite so crazy these days with the Bear movement and all, but trust me it still exists. Check out the personal ads and see how many guys are stressing 'muscular' and 'zero % body fat' in their ads. Even those magazine ads targeting men who like "bears" or larger men, always pick models that are thick muscular buff. There's no obvious unsightly body fat on the guys chosen to portray that look.

So while I was not willing to get into any type of artificial substance to lose weight again, it still was a great concern to me. Enter Ira; Another somewhat overweight guy. We were in the club one night and dancing when I made some remark about my weight. He told me that I really didn't have to diet. According to him I could eat all I wanted and still lose weight. All I had to do was take laxatives. Up to that point this option had never occurred to me. But the experience with the diet pills had more than frightened me off any really crazy behavior. By now I took reading packages very seriously. And the first thing I saw on the side of all laxative packages was that prolonged use could lead to laxative dependence. That brought me up short. So I devised a plan to eat and drink excessive amounts of food/beverages which produced a laxative effect.

For a time I got the desired effect, and I actually continued that practice for many years. After a while though, the foods themselves didn't quite do the trick, and - in search of greater results - I began to use some laxatives as well. I did not know at the time that this playing with the food intake was almost as bad for me as if I had just gone on and taken the laxatives in the first place. The true fact was that at that time, I had never even heard of bulimia, and certainly didn't know that laxative abuse was considered a form of the condition.

The main thing during that period however was that Greg and I were intent on getting to know people and having fun. We still would head out to the GumHead on Saturday nights and dance like fools. One night in particular, we were on the dancefloor and the place was jam packed. We were having a riot of a time, when I felt someone tap me on my shoulder. I looked around, but didn't see anyone that I knew, so I went right on laughing and having fun.

The next day was a beautiful Sunday afternoon. I didn't have to go to work so I headed out to the park. At that time you could still drive through. On Sundays this was difficult to do because it seemed EVERYBODY was trying to make his way into the park then. As a result, it would take what seemed like forever just to drive from one side of the park to the other. That day, as I was coming around on the side that backed up to the Piedmont Driving Club, I saw what was easily the most beautiful guy that I'd ever seen. He was sitting on the steps looking out at the softball fields. As luck would have it, there was a parking space about twenty-five feet past where he was perched and I swerved in quickly before anyone else could grab it.

I walked back to where he was sitting and spoke to him. He was so arrestingly beautiful that I was struck speechless for a bit. He had black hair, hazel eyes, and a thick, bushy moustache. His smile was so arrestingly gorgeous that I could barely tear my eyes away. It was quite disarming, but I quickly recovered as he was very friendly and sociable. We had a wonderful time out there that day. The park was always teaming with people in those days, so there was always a lot to see.

My newfound friend introduced himself as Ernie, and told me that he had recently moved up to Atlanta from Florida. He was originally from New York. He had not been in Atlanta very long but really liked living here so far. He asked me if I remembered someone touching me on my shoulder the previous evening while I was on the dancefloor at the GumHead. It took me by surprise that he knew this, since I didn't remember seeing him there at all. He told me that it was he who had tapped my shoulder. He said that Greg and I looked as if we were having such a good time, that he just wanted to get to know us. I told him that he should have introduced himself and made his presence known. He said that he'd wanted to, but was too shy.

It is this exchange which describes the way that he was when I first met Ernie perfectly. He was staggeringly beautiful, but really very unassuming. He was quite genuine and that was the most thrilling thing about his personality. There was a 'realness' about him that actually made him somewhat surreal. Unfortunately, the truth for most of us is that we just don't meet people who look like he did, and find them to be genuinely nice and not full of themselves.

As we talked there were many people that were milling about in the park. It turned out that he liked to study people as much as I. There was this one guy who was selling these strange wall hangings. They were made of two sticks nailed together in a cross like fashion. They then had been wrapped continuously in multi-colored yarn, forming a type of geometric image of sorts. They were very strange, as was the man who was trying to sell them. He came up to us and engaged us in conversation for a bit. He wasn't threatening in any way, just 'marching to the beat of his own drum', so to speak. We both talked to him for a bit until he moved on. We then looked at each other and cracked up. That became a private joke between us for years to come. It really was one of those moments when you had to be there.

Before long we realized that we had talked well into the afternoon. Ernie told me that he had to get home. I offered to give him a ride, but he said he didn't live far and would walk. We exchanged numbers and promised to stay in touch. It wasn't very long before we were hanging out and having a good time. Here was another link to what was to become the core group to my chain of friends.

In just a few weeks Ernie announced that he was starting to work at a new bar called RJ's. It turned out that the bar was something totally different from anything that most of us in the city had ever seen. It was a Cabaret style club, with live entertainment. The owners were a couple that were older guys. Their names were Rick and Juan. Atlanta was such a melting pot then. There were so many clubs opening , but there was always room for one more. The club was located on Spring Street in a very large old house that sat up on a hill. It had been a small dance club in a previous incarnation, and that particular endeavor had seen some success there; So the location was known to the gay community. However, I think that the cabaret idea was pretty much doomed from the start.

It was just so foreign from anything that most of us had ever seen. We were young club kids who wanted to dance the night away. Though many of us may have liked musical theater, it wasn't something that we were going to seek on our nightly forays out into the city.

That said, Greg and I would truck up there anyway to support Ernie. His lifelong dream was to sing live and this place gave him an opportunity to get close to that. Anyway, we were at that age where the announcement of ANY new bar was all it took to get us up and ready to go. The first night that I went, I ended up going alone. For whatever reason, Greg was not with me that night.

It was really a very nice place, with a comfortable atmosphere, and a cast with pretty good voices. I sat there on the bar and had a couple of drinks while the show was in progress. Ernie was waiting tables, so he couldn't really stand and chat with me, but he would come by and we'd exchange a word every once in a while. My intention was to wait for him to finish and then we'd go and get something to eat. Shortly before the end of the show, I noticed a blonde drag queen sitting at the bar to my right. Though she was not bad looking, up close I could tell she was a guy. There were only a few people sitting around the bar. I was aware of her there, but we didn't exchange greetings. I wasn't even sure that she had noticed me. However when Ernie came out of the back, after finishing and came over to me, she piped up with a cracked gin voice and said, "Come over here Ernie. Why do you want to stop and talk to that guy?" Such was my introduction to Vonda. She was outrageous from the very first time I met her. She was really a nasty piece of work in those early days, and I soon learned that I was not the only person with that opinion of her. In those days, I was somewhat thin-skinned, and was quite hurt by her remark. I couldn't imagine what she would have against me, since I'd never seen or spoken to her. We were all young at the time though, and she was as quick with a flippant remark as I was to get my feelings hurt. Quite frankly, I don't think I could have chosen anyone better to introduce me to the catty way that queens can be. Ernie however, spoke to her, gave her a couple of minutes and when we started talking didn't seem to make too much of it or her, so the incident was soon all but forgotten. This however, would not be my last time dealing with her. And indeed it was many years later, after she had left Atlanta for Texas and made a name for herself there that we would finally end up on cordial speaking terms. Even in those early days she had the makings of a true beauty, and that's what she became. Like all of us, as she grew, and found that she didn't really have anything to prove to anyone, she became a bit more personable. On a subsequent visit back to Atlanta, we found ourselves judging a pageant together. It was then that we mended fences and healed old wounds.

One of the things that I found to be the case in those days was that as many bars as there were to open in this town, quite often they were short lived. It really didn't take long to tell what would be around and what would not. The funny thing was that there seemed often to be no rhyme or reason as to why they wouldn't make it. Quite a few just didn't.

Soon, RJ's got the kiss of death. I think it was a few years before its time. The gay community then was largely young kids. There weren't many older, established out gay people. Of course, no one had a crystal ball and could tell that the community would come out as loud and as strong as it has; featuring generations of out, proud and professional gay people. That club's style would have been fine for a clientele which frequented on the weekends only; or a much older crowd. But for us kids we really wanted a dance bar or some drag queens! Piano music was just not the order of the day. Funny, not much has changed for the young set! If anything, today's youth are even LESS interested in the finer arts.

To my surprise, the closing of the bar was not the only big announcement that was on the horizon. As soon as that happened, Ernie made it known to me that he would be leaving soon, moving to Texas. It came as something of a shock, because he had not indicated that he was even thinking of leaving. I learned quickly that in those days this type of thing was really not all that strange. While I was still at home, most of these kids were already out on their own and doing their own thing. If the spirit moved them to pack up and hit the road, then all too often that's just what they did. So with very little fanfare I soon bid goodbye to one of my newfound friends.

Once Ernie was gone, for a while there it was just Greg and me running around again. Things had changed a bit, but not by much. Greg was still pretty much trying to get settled and working somewhere. It was very difficult because like most of us, he had no skills really, but an even bigger problem was that he was just so young. He didn't talk much about the job woes, but I knew that they were happening. Much of the time I would help him out here and there with money and whatever he needed. He was much like the little brother that I never had. There was also a good deal of sadness in him about the strained relationship with his parents. I knew that he spoke to them from time to time, and that his relationship with them meant very much to him, but it was very difficult for all our parents to understand what was going on inside us in those days.

I knew that he was hurting about it but he was always such a private person that I quickly learned not to bring it up. If and when he wanted to talk, he would. Even at that young age, Greg knew his own mind and what he wanted. It was one of the things that I admired about him the most.

The telltale sign that the emotions were beginning to get the best of him was when he would start drinking. Usually it would all come out then in a torrent of tears. As much as I may have wanted to fix things or to help, it was his business and his stuff to deal with. Frankly, I had a plate full of my own that I was doing one helluva bang-up job at denying. So we danced the nights away, drank sweet drinks that were just as much fruit punch as they were booze, and time moved on.

It's funny how things have a way of moving forward without any help from us. I was starting to change a good bit emotionally. I began to notice the amount of interest that the guys around me were paying to one another. I mean, there were many guys that I had found attractive since I had started going around in midtown, but I was having such a good time hanging out and dancing that the guys didn't hold the priority for me yet that they eventually would. Sometimes I think if I could have held onto that frame of mind I would have been a lot better off.

Most nights now I was in the bars with Greg and other friends that I was meeting. There were very few evenings spent sitting around in Piedmont Park as I once had done. Along with the change in mindset though was also the fact that I was now working a fulltime schedule at the hotel, so I couldn't spend as many evenings out there as I once had. The most interaction I had with the park on these nights was to drive through and change in the men's room on my way out to the clubs to party.

This one night however I was passing through and I saw this nice looking guy sitting in his car, so I decided to stop and chat for a bit. I parked and walked back to his car and we started to talk. He was in town from New York on business. After we had chatted for a while, he asked me if there was somewhere close by that we could go and be alone, since he was staying at a hotel that was a pretty good distance away. I of course was living at home with my parents so we certainly couldn't go there.

I took him around to this dead end street next to the park. At the end of the street was an obscure entrance into the tree trail area of the park. I had never been down into the deep part of the trails. There were some really rough stories about going down there at night, so I usually steered clear. However, up around that top portion it seemed ok. We went back a little ways off the road, but there were cars constantly coming and going up and down the street and that made both of us nervous. Soon I called it quits with that. I was not at all willing to put myself at risk of maybe going to jail out there. And it was well known that the cops sometimes came up and down that street in unmarked cars and in plainclothes.

My friend was in total agreement with me, and though we were having a great time necking and fooling around, we were both skittish and ready to leave that place.

He told me that his business was concluding early the next day and he would be free then to have some fun. I told him that I was working the next day until 11pm, but could meet him afterward. He said that would be great, and we agreed to meet in the park in the same place as before.

It surprises me sometimes how cavalier I was about the whole sex thing at that time. It really was just not that big a deal to me. Sure it was there and I liked having it like everybody else, but it wasn't all that important. I really could take it or leave it at that point.

I met him as promised, and we headed off to his hotel in Forest Park, just south of the city near the airport. I left my car in the park and got into the car with him. He promised that he would bring me back once we were done. Today I can't believe that I did that! Usually I don't leave my car and get into the car with a stranger to do anything! But away we went, and really had a nice time. However just to show where my priorities were, when we were done he wanted me to stay over all night. Well I knew that I couldn't do that. I had to go home before morning. And besides it was Saturday Night! I couldn't wait to get back to town and out to the clubs! I invited him to come with me, but he said that he'd rather not. He was quite a good looking man; probably mid – thirties, and I'm sure the clubs didn't hold the attraction to him that they did for me. Had I met this guy a few years later, I guarantee that the whole evening would have gone totally differently. I NEVER would have left him to head out to the bars. Ah yes! Youth is most definitely wasted on the young!

Soon, Greg found a job at the Harlequin Dinner Theater in Buckhead. Every night when I left the hotel I would head up to meet him as he was leaving work. There were a couple of other gay kids that worked with him, so often we would all go out together. During that period a great many kids our age were abandoning home and the whole idea of continuing education. It was not like things are today. Some left home to escape the decision of having to disclose their sexuality to their parents. Others left home because they had disclosed and then found that they had no choice but leave. For the most part things were good for us though. We would all hang out together and many of us formed friendships that would last for many years to come.

These friendships became substitute families and for that reason many people were extremely loyal to their friends. There was one guy in the group from the Harlequin that I seemed to get along with quite well from the very start. His name was Steve. He always seemed outrageously happy and carefree. He liked to hang out and dance just as much as Greg and I did. With Steve along I never had any problems with having a dance partner. Sometimes Greg would not be in the mood, or just simply wanted to cruise and didn't feel up to dancing. Steve on the other hand was getting over a breakup and was totally off the thought of dating any guys right then.

As it turned out, his roommate Larry had come between him and his lover and was now sleeping with the lover. Steve was pretty torn up about it, but I generally thought that he was handling it all pretty well. He would break into a whole long speech occasionally about how big an asshole Larry - the roommate - was, but usually that was as far as it went.

Then one night he asked me to take him somewhere. We got into my car and he asked me to drive him from his apartment over to Lindbergh Drive. It was really less than five minutes away so I said sure. Well, while I'd heard plenty about Larry the roommate and Mac the cheating lover I had never met either, so I didn't really know anything about them other than what Steve had said.

It was around midnight on a Sunday night so the apartment complex that we went to was largely quiet. There were some lights still on, so it was evident that there were residents still stirring about, but for the most part it was quiet. After I pulled up to the building Steve told me that I could just pull over and stop. That he would be right back. I had no idea what he intended and he didn't tell me this was where Mac lived until he was getting out of the car. All of a sudden he ran over to where a Gold colored Dodge was parked. He picked up a huge rock and started beating and kicking the shit out of this car! Lights started going and I'm freaking out! Back at that time, the city of Atlanta was still very much segregated as far as communities were concerned. Every once in a while you would see one or two minority people living in predominantly white areas, but not often. And here I am, black as night in an all-white apartment complex with this crazy-assed white boy beating up somebody's car! I just KNEW my ass was headed to jail! Lights started coming on and people started looking out windows. Steve came and jumped in the car and said, "Let's get the hell outta here!"

All the while he's cracking up, and I'm panicking like a cat whose tail is stretched out in a roomful of rocking chairs! Turns out that up until now he had only suspected that Larry was screwing Mac. They both had been lying and saying it wasn't so. Larry had suddenly moved out on Steve and Mac had broken up with him. Steve accused them of being together and they had both vehemently denied it. The car that Steve had just assaulted was Larry's and it being parked in front of Mac's apartment was all the proof he needed. And here I was like most black people thinking that white folks were rather calm about affairs of the heart. Boy, did I have a lot to learn!

Once Steve beat up the car he pretty much got them both out of his system. I think he just needed to get some justification. He then went back to being good old happy-go-lucky Steve just as if nothing had ever happened.

While hanging out with him I got the chance to meet many of the people who lived in the apartment complex that Steve lived in. It was my first real experience with a 'gay ghetto' of sorts. The apartments were off Cheshire Bridge Road at Woodland Dr., and they were called Four Seasons. It seemed that just about all the tenants were gay kids and before long I got to know a good many of them. There were Jan and Barry who lived just under Steve. Jan was a pre-operative transsexual and Barry was this cute kid from Bermuda. Then across the way there was Ben and his roommate whose name escapes me. Probably because he was so bashful that I don't think I ever heard him utter a sound. And then there was this wild red headed kid named Mike who lived on the other end of Ben's building.

That was just a few of the gay kids there. There were many more, but this group became our little clique. Steve introduced me and they readily accepted me into the bunch. It wasn't long before I was hanging out with them quite a bit.

Greg would come and hang out with us from time to time as well. It turned out that he already knew Jan. But largely he was off doing his own thing. He was dating someone at the time so we were seeing a lot less of him than we had been.

Even at that early period in our lives I noticed that Greg was much more into the disco crowd than I was. The shows were more exciting to me. As we got older it seemed that many of the guys in the dance bars were less interested in dancing and more interested in cruising and getting laid. I was getting there, but I wasn't quite there yet.

In the meantime I was spending most of my time with the Four Seasons kids. I would go over to the apartments or would meet Steve out somewhere and we would hang out and dance like Greg and I used to. If we were at the GumHead we would meet up with Jan and Barry and often Ben would come along as well. Out of the entire little group, I think that I was more impressed with Ben than any of the others. It was funny, but he was such a sweet guy! Very quiet and reserved, it would often surprise me that even though most of the kids our age were into smoking lots of pot, drinking a lot and getting wild, it seemed that Ben always had a bottom line that he would not cross. I never saw him overly drunk or stoned, and I didn't see him going after many guys either. For a long time I actually thought that his roommate was his lover because I NEVER saw him pick anyone up or even really talk to many guys. More and more as I got closer to him I found that it wasn't that the roommate was more than a roommate, it was just that Ben had some serious standards. In an age where just about everybody was having phenomenal amounts of sex he was somewhat determined to look for a certain type of guy.

When Ben found him, he came in the shape of a man that was in his mid-thirties and very much a business man. He was somewhat older than all of us, and for that reason I felt very ill-at-ease with him. They quickly became such a couple and an item that Ben seemed to pull away from most of the Four Seasons bunch. He and I had developed a sort of special closeness though and so we still talked a good bit. I think the reason for this was simply that like Ben, I wasn't yet having a lot of sex, I didn't do drugs and I also wasn't yet drinking heavily. Maybe our reasoning for how we conducted ourselves had been different; his being his standards, mine simply that I wasn't ready for those things yet. I think that may have been why we tended to develop the closeness we did.

The problem for me was that I was just too young to appreciate his new partner's conservatism, and because of their closeness I always felt as if I was intruding. It was not long before Ben moved in with him. I regretted that I was not more comfortable when in their presence, but the discomfort was palpable for me and our friendship started to drift. I often admired Ben for knowing what he wanted and going after it. It's been over thirty years now, and though I've not seen them in about ten years, last I heard they were still together. I did have the chance to apologize to Ben years later for drifting off. I felt as if I'd lost a truly good friendship when that happened. He accepted and said he understood. We chatted a bit, but were never really able to connect as we had before. Too much life had happened for the both of us.

Somewhere around the end of 1977 I began to notice that I was missing out on something. Many of the people that I knew out in the bars were drifting away from the whole 'lets all get together in a group and go party' mentality. Much more emphasis was beginning to be put on finding and getting to-gether with the cute guys.

Drag was very big here in Atlanta, but it was still very much about being a man when not on stage and the transfor-mation when on stage. The whole hormone and silicone craze had not yet happened. It was just really on the horizon. For me, I was getting caught up by both the boy craze and the drag craze at about the same time. I wanted the guys for sure. But I was also very curious about the whole drag thing. I think that I was heading toward it long before I actually headed toward it.

I always loved beautiful clothes and had been sewing quite a few years by then. I think that the seed was already planted though I didn't know that I would ever be bold enough to go onto a stage. I don't think that the idea of ever really doing it had gelled in my mind. And I certainly had no clue that an opportunity to do so would ever present itself.

Greg had made the decision to move to New Orleans, and though I didn't think he would do it, he surprised me and did just that. It was very sad for me to see him go, but I knew he felt that it was something that he needed to do. I also knew already that we would stay friends no matter where we were. So I bid him goodbye and really threw myself into work more. Though we had really sort of started to travel in different circles, our friendship was always very strong and was more like that of family than just the bar acquaintances that I had with most of the people that I had met in this new life. We both had a lot of growing up that we needed to do. I think that he was searching for something when he went there without really knowing what it was or how to get it. I know that the adjustment when he got there was somewhat unexpected by him. He was there a few weeks when he called me and told me that he needed my help with a problem getting settled.

As it turned out, he was still too young by a few months to get a job in any establishment that sold alcohol. Here in Atlanta you could get a job if you were sixteen years old, but you could not serve alcohol. Apparently there it was difficult to get a job at all if you were not eighteen. And since I had a few months on him and had already turned eighteen, he needed to use my birth certificate to get work. I know now how dicey that is, and how dangerous. When my parents found out what I had done they went through the roof! But already our friendship was close enough that I didn't feel any threat from him using my papers. So he came back to Atlanta for a couple of days and I got him a copy of my birth certificate to use for a few months. To this day I don't know if he used it. I doubt he did since there's never been any record of it showing up in my past.

Meantime there were lots of things going on in my world as well. For a few months there I was cut off from my new little band of friends because my car died and since I was still living with my parents it was just too hard to get across town to the clubs to party. That portion of time taught me a lot about bar acquaintances as well though. When I had the car and was there all the time, there were people all over midtown that were always yelling greetings and happy to see me. I was young, had an operational car, and a job that paid pretty good money. I was always there to set up a round of drinks and play taxicab for the group. The minute that car died, it seemed that not one person called to see how I was doing. I was at home going out of my mind and lonely as hell, but no word from the bar friends. I decided that I would work like a dog, save every penny and buy another car. It was very hard to come back from my perceived freedom and toe the line of going to work and just going home, but I did it. My father offered more than once to just fix the brake system on the car, which is what took it out of commission; but I declined. That had been the latest in a string of difficulties with it, and I was determined that it needed to go.

Soon, I did acquire new wheels and was back in stride with my partying. Though the crowd was still there, and I had been angry with them, I did still hang out with them. I had learned a valuable lesson however. So now I was much more in tune to doing what I wanted and not necessarily trying to buy my friendships by offering up myself and what I could do for people. The result was there were fewer people around, but those that stayed I thought were at least somewhat sincere in the bunch.

The beauty about those years in my life was that everything was new. As I moved through different changes and growth periods it was easy to accept a lot of things in that life because I really had nothing to compare it to. That was the positive aspect. The negative aspect was that by not really having any outside experience to compare with the situations that I came up against I was emotionally or psychologically hurt by situations before I could see the danger coming.

Soon what had been open innocence toward meeting people started to turn to the fear exhibited by many introverts when they start to shut down. In my naiveté, I had put myself out there for friendships and the hope of romance. While there's nothing wrong with that, I was not prepared for the incidences of calculation, manipulation, deceit and disappointment that can also go along with meeting people. My only reference for love and romance was what I had found in the pages of novels. So when I met guys that were a bit nice, I would sometimes go too far too fast. Or if someone were friendly I would sometimes let my guard down totally and call them friends before I really knew anything about them. Too many times allowing this to happen will make a person throw up walls really quickly.

In no time at all I could see myself shying away from people. Not everybody, but definitely it became more of an effort to meet people. There are lots of things in the world that were not defined as clearly as my adolescent black and white thinking would have had me believe. If I thought I had been slow to mature around the kids back in my grade school it was nothing compared to how slow I was in learning to deal with affairs of the heart out in the bars.

The truth of the matter was that – for all his being the younger – Greg was the social butterfly, and I was his wing man.

He could charm and get along in just about any social setting and with just about anyone. On top of this, he had an uncanny ability to read and size people up very quickly. This part of his personality was often the entrée to my social connections. Now, trying to do this on my own I often found myself feeling rudderless. I was ill prepared for the change of attitude from carefree party kid to young, gay man with romantic agenda.

With this change from running around like kids all lumped together getting drunk and dancing, to now being mostly about checking out the guys and trying to get with them I was clearly a fish out of water. I was then and am now a person that doesn't do deceit and calculation very well. I'm usually pretty up front about what I want. So the whole concept of playing the game in the bars just about drove me crazy. I was awful at bar cruising then and I'm still awful at it today! What I didn't know then however was how to calm myself and not let it all take me over.   As a result much of the whole *going out to pick up guys in bars period* of my life was pure agony. I would fret for hours over what clothes to wear, what look was right, whether I was cute with this shirt or whether this outfit made me look fat. It was years before one day it dawned on me that by the time the evening rolled around to the time for me to get ready to go out, I would sometimes have made myself so nervous, keyed up and miserable that the whole idea of having a good time was NOWHERE in the picture! I suppose I should have been able to see the next phase coming. Quite naturally I soon discovered that just like it had made the guilt go away to have a little drink if I were going to have sex, it would soon also be the balm that made the whole ordeal of whether I would measure up in the clubs bearable. And unfortunately, all of sudden whether I measured up in the clubs was of extreme importance. For somewhere in my mind the seed had sprouted that if I could just find a relationship; a man to love me then my life would be totally perfect.

I think that thought was borne of the fact that increasingly for all of us the interest was more on the guys. And I was suddenly seeing all these guys coupled up all around us. The influence of all these couples, along with my friend Ben's newfound relationship had a tremendous effect on me. Add to that the feeling that there was something 'dirty' about promiscuity; even within the gay community. We were all pretty much using the only template that we had for modeling our lives. That the template came from the very society that ostracized and ridiculed us was (and to some degree, still is) lost on most of us gay folk.

Soon, I found myself in such a frenzy over it all that I wasn't sure what was going on. Somehow in my mind, having sex with someone had become the entree to love and relationship. I tried returning to a happier, more suitable point for me but the world had moved on. One day during the week I remember going once again through Piedmont Park and meeting a very tall, young Hispanic guy. His name was Pepe, and he was quite friendly. Though we talked for some time, I could tell from the outset that there was an "arm's length" feel to the encounter. Before long he made it clear that he had a lover and was really committed to the relationship. We continued to talk and even though it had been established that was all there would be, I was still happy to chat with him. It was in this type of situation that I found I would open myself up to hurt. If I could only have been honest with myself about what I really wanted. Pepe would be the first of many. I could and would delude myself very easily into believing that if I was interested in someone and that interest was not returned, I could then 'satisfy' that interest by becoming their 'friend'. What I now know is that what I was really seeking was the consolation prize of being near them with the hope of changing their minds.

I found that I was not capable of really turning off the desire for the guy, and my decision to hang about as a 'friend' was often a bad one. This was my first sign of what I would later realize was my tendency to go after unavailable men. Whether physically, emotionally or geographically so, the fact that they were unavailable would seem to flip a switch in me that was overpowering. Upon that realization he would then become the man that I wanted, and no other would do.

With the ground rule in place that he was in a committed relationship, Pepe and I became 'friends'. We could chat for hours about all that was going on within the gay community as well as the world. I finally got the opportunity to meet his lover David one night at the Gumhead. He was a nice enough guy; Sort of quiet and bookish. He appeared to care more about the cocktail in front of him than anything else. By that time it really didn't matter much to me one way or the other. Or so I thought. Pepe was in love with David and that was the end of that. He (Pepe) and I continued to talk on the phone, and sometimes get together for lunch or whatever. This went on for about six months and the friendship had really blossomed. Then one evening I decided to go to one of the other bars in town. It was named Backstreet, and not a place that I usually frequented. It was a snooty dance bar, and more the type that Greg preferred than the kind that I really liked these days.

I went downstairs and immediately I ran into Pepe. He was sitting all tangled up with some guy and it DEFINITELY was not David! As I've said, David was somewhat bookish, about 5'10" tall, pale and sort of a mousy brunette white guy. This guy was about my height, with a great body, but darker than me! I think I must have startled Pepe as much as he did me. He immediately became belligerent and quite nasty to me. I had barely said hello to him. I was shocked and wounded. The script was moving way too fast here. I didn't even know what was going on; let alone what I had done to anger him. I turned and headed out of the bar. I was mad as hell, but also hurt that my friend would treat me that way.

It was a couple of days before Pepe and I talked. When we did he was totally dismissive of the way that he had acted toward me. And his only revelation about the guy he was with was that he and David had broken up. Well that was his business, and really had nothing to do with me. I was just flabbergasted that it had happened at all.About a week or two later I was in the Gumhead on a Saturday night. It was then that I saw David for the first time since he and Pepe had broken up. He was sitting on the side of the bar, and was getting drunk a little faster than usual. I told him that I was sorry about what had happened between him and Pepe. He thanked me and told me that he didn't know what had happened. They just seemed to fall apart. I told him that I thought that if he would talk to Pepe I was sure they could work things out. I then excused myself and went on my way. I can't remember now if Pepe had mentioned it or not in our talk, but apparently – broken up as they were supposed to be – they were still living together.

The shows that night were good as usual, and the girlz looked fabulous. It was turning out to be a really fun night, and I was getting high as a kite myself. As the night wore on, I looked down at the end of the bar. David was very obviously in a bad way. I went down to talk to him and try to maybe help him straighten up before they threw him out. He saw it was me and basically just fell apart. I collected him and took him out to my car. He was far too drunk, so I told him that I would take him home. He said that he didn't want to go there because Pepe was there. Well, I was living at home, and could not take him there. I thought of a friend that lived nearby. I took him there, and my friend said he could stay there long enough to sober up, but then would have to leave. David pleaded with me to stay with him because he didn't know the guy. I said ok, but I would have to get home before daylight. I think the next thing is pretty obvious. With both of us being somewhat intoxicated, and in the bed together, we ended up having sex. Afterward, I did feel bad, but convinced myself that he and Pepe were broken up, and if it had not been for that, it never would have happened. What a fool I was!

Before nightfall the next day Pepe was on the phone to me calling me a homewrecker! Telling me how David had come in crying and said I seduced him and then threw him out! Once again I was completely taken aback! It was then that I realized just how naive I'd been. David had played me totally to get back at Pepe. Pepe was embarrassed for being caught looking like a tramp after holding himself up as such a shining example of fidelity. David was a lying drunk, Pepe was a louse and I had been a total fool. There was no doubt that in this new and shady adult world I had a lot to learn....

Though I was sure that Greg would come back from New Orleans to visit from time to time since his parents were here, I didn't expect it at all when he called and said that he would be moving home. By this time he had been there for about a year, and I think he just was not as happy there as he thought he would be. It would be great to have him back home. I was beginning to move more and more out into the mainstream of gay life and meet more people, but I sure did miss my earlier friends. Once back in the city, Greg didn't talk in much depth about his time in New Orleans. Sure, there were stories of some fun he had, but I never really got the whole story about his decision to move back home.

I think it did him quite a bit of good to move away, but in the end he knew that he could do better here. When he got back he immediately got a job and was soon right back into the old routine. He met and moved in with a fellow named Ronnie who had an apartment over on Tenth St. I didn't know it at the time but that meeting would open up a whole new chapter in both our lives.

As it turned out Ronnie was working at another show bar in the downtown area called the Onyx Lounge. And before long we would have connections there even more so than we had at the Gumhead. One Saturday evening Greg called me at the hotel and asked if I'd like to go with him to the Onyx after I got off work. I said that I would, and arranged to meet up with him at his place right after 11p.m. It was really strange going all the way downtown to a gay bar. At the time most gay bars in town were either in Midtown right near Tenth St. or out around the Cheshire Bridge Rd. area.

When we first walked in I knew immediately that this was going to be very different from what I had seen so far. The place was considerably smaller than the Gumhead and had something of a shabby quality about it. But the charm was that many of the people there seemed somehow more approachable. The SweetGumHead, had a nickname of "the showplace of the south", and it enjoyed clientele that came in from all over; some that traveled from surrounding states on the weekend just to see the shows. The Gumhead was even known to host a few celebrities in the audience from time to time. The crowd here at the Onyx was good sized, but nothing like I was accustomed to at the other clubs. We got there just before the beginning of the show and I was eager to see how this show stacked up compared to the other. When the first acts came out onto the stage it was very different. These "girlz" were a little rougher around the edges, but still there was something intriguing and charming about them. NOBODY had me convinced they were a woman this time but that was ok. What I noticed was the bartender. He was your typical down home type white guy; Straight brown hair, thin moustache and lips. But he had a very nice body and an ass that wouldn't quit! Nice to look at, but I didn't think about much more than that.

I had long since learned that most of the guys that worked in the bars were pretty much off limits. They either had boyfriends or were lusted after by so many folks that it was near impossible to get noticed by them.

We stayed there for a bit and watched the show. It was really good and Greg's new roommate Ronnie was hot. He was working as the male dancer in the show. I remember that while it was good and we'd had a good time, I still wanted to go out to the Gumhead to see the last show there. At that time, there were so many choices in Atlanta that it was not unusual to make three, four or even more stops in a night. The city was loaded with bars to choose from.

It was a while before we started really going to the Onyx regularly, but it was definitely added to the mix now. And slowly but surely my circle of friends and acquaintances was beginning to grow again. Many of the kids at the Onyx took to Greg and I pretty quickly since Greg was Ronnie's roommate. In no time we began meeting all the employees there. The customers were another story yet again. Some were ok, but it seemed that many were older and drunken, so I didn't so much meet them, as just kind of 'sidestep' a lot of 'em. I think that was probably the reason that we were more hesitant to spend time there. I'm sure the clientele was as it was because the owners fit that mold themselves.

The Onyx was owned by a guy named Jim and his lover Keith. And while Keith was relatively quiet and easy going, Jim could be a mean and vile tempered drunk. I used to laughingly say that on Saturday nights at the Onyx you were guaranteed at least one fight. If the customers didn't provide it the management would! For all its rough edges however, this little bar was about to play a major role in shaping the next few years of my life.

A few days later I got another interesting piece of news. I got a call from a girl that I didn't know. Her name was

Nina(pronounced "nine-ah") and she said that she wanted to invite me to a party. Apparently Ernie had had his fill of Texas and was moving back to Atlanta. It was wonderful and welcomed news. Now both of my good friends would be back in my life. I was very excited that Ernie was coming back. Though the party wasn't for another week, he would be arriving in town in just a few days. It would be great to see him again.

Ernie called me when he got into town, and immediately we knew that we had to go out that night. I was in for quite a surprise when I saw him. He had definitely grown up in the time that he'd been gone. When he left Atlanta he had been a very beautiful, well-polished boy whose look was very clean and preppy. He always had very dark looks due to his Italian heritage, but the Ernie that I knew had kept his hair trimmed close. He usually waxed away the unwanted hair (and God, was there ever a lot of that!) and had been very model pretty. Now standing in front of me was the grown up man version. His look was very rough around the edges. I mean, the beauty was definitely still there, but it was a man's good looks not a boy's prettiness. He had let his facial hair grow out into a full beard, and the hair on his head was a mop; almost shoulder length. One of the issues that Ernie had always dealt with was the fact that he was naturally so hairy. The hair was everywhere. Even on the end of his nose! Before moving away he often spoke of how tedious it was. He would either have to wax or pluck all the areas where he didn't want it seen. In between his eyebrows was one place. Also, the brows themselves would turn into bushes if he didn't control them. It grew on the end of his nose, the tops of his ears, etc. It was EVERYWHERE. Clearly he had decided while in Texas to do minimal control. I can understand it. All that plucking and waxing would become tedious I'm sure.

The result however was a dark and somewhat brooding look. He had changed in other ways as well. I'd always loved

Ernie's upfront, but genuine manner. Upon his return it was obvious to me that I was not the only person whose innocence had been taken by this more mature and calculating world that we lived in. He was no longer as open as he had been. And I could see that there was a much more shrewd way about him now. He was still Ernie, but there was no doubt in my mind that Texas had changed him. Only time would tell if it had been in a good way.

One thing about him had not changed however, and that was his sense of being responsible. In no time at all he had come in, gotten an apartment and started working. He got on at the Magic Pan Restaurant in Lenox Square. That sent him to the barber shop right off, so soon there was at least the hint of the old Ernie. It seemed in no time he had gotten his new apartment set up and was back in business. I remember he didn't have much. But we got off work one night and I went with him to where he was staying and gathered his stuff. He'd gotten a little place on Charles Allen Dr. near Ponce de Leon Avenue. It took us until about 2 o'clock in the morning, but we got his stuff in and got him a place set up to sleep at least. He only had a mattress on the floor, but it was all his and he was not staying with anyone.

I think that sense of independence was the common thread between Greg, Ernie and me. I think that's what we each must have seen in one another. Anyway, we got him in and then starving, we headed off to find something to eat. Still, very much kids at heart, and both having this major sweet tooth, we headed for doughnuts. There was (and still is) a Krispy Kreme Doughnut Shoppe just up the street on Ponce from where his new apartment was. That time of night was the time when they would make fresh batches of doughnuts. If you've never had a fresh cooked doughnut right out of the kitchen then you don't know what you're missing. And if you've never had a Krispy Kreme, you've never really had a doughnut! OH MY GOD it's pastry heaven! We picked up about a dozen and a half and went back to the apartment to gorge ourselves. We were sitting there on Ernie's mattress and eating and laughing and somehow got to roughhousing like all boys do. I don't know what happened but I was so glad that he was home, and he was so glad to be back. There are those moments that you see in movies all the time where two people realize that they've reached a level of comfort and a place that they didn't expect to be. I'd never experienced it before, and I've not had it happen again. But suddenly we were looking in each other's eyes and we both felt it. NOTHING HAPPENED. And despite popular opinion by some people, that's the only time that Ernie and I even came close to intimacy. The weird thing was that I think we both knew that the friendship that we had was more, and if we'd gone beyond and moved into intimacy,it would have changed forever. Then again perhaps that's attributing more maturity to both of us than either of us possessed. All I know is that something would not let me proceed, and I saw in his eyes when he made the decision to pull back as well. I think for me I didn't really think that he would want me for me and it would have been just something for the moment. Surprisingly enough in those days I often thought like that about sexual encounters. Though I don't know whether it was a blessing or a curse, much of the time in that period I wanted it all with someone. And if I couldn't have that, I didn't want any... At any rate, the moment passed. We talked a bit more, and soon I got up and headed home for the evening.

In the upcoming days it was a real boost to my spirit that my friends had returned to Atlanta. We all had done some much needed growing and were beginning to find out just who we were as people. The three of us, Greg, Ernie and I were all pretty much still into partying and definitely were still friends, but we also had begun to develop personalities and those were taking us in different directions as far as the crowds that we preferred to associate with. Greg's crowd was more and more the preppy set, and Ernie's was definitely beginning to look more and more like the Levi/leather set. For me, I was still very much enchanted with the drag scene. It was the most colorful. And though it was not sexual to me at all, it was where I seemed to find the most pleasure for my entertainment buck.

I guess it would be fair to say that I was sort of straddling a couple of worlds. My sexual interest did then, and always has gone more toward men who are conservative in appearance. I enjoy doing many of the things socially that would attract a man like that. The theater, ballet, fine dining and art museums are all things that I enjoy and liberally participate in whenever I have the chance. And as a result of that, I found myself attracting more teachers and bankers than anything else. But the other side of the coin for me was the fact that I was very much into going to the drag bars. So I rarely met the types of men that I was attracted to out in the bars. Even though drag was much more popular then than it is now, the focus for most guys when they were looking for a date would be the dance bars, the cruise (Levi/leather) bars, or the hard core watering holes. However, in the latter, they were more interested in meeting Jack Daniels or Johnny Walker than any other guy.

But despite finding our different 'running crowds' Ernie, Greg and I still managed to find time to do things together. Ernie had settled back in well and the two of them worked closer to each other than to me so they saw more of each other I think.

For some strange reason, perhaps it was because I was so enchanted with the whole drag thing and all; Ernie had this strong desire to see me in drag. He would pester me about it from time to time. I took it as good natured kidding and though my own interest in drag was keen, I didn't really see it happening so I didn't give it too much thought. Then came the fall of the year, and Ernie informed me that they were having a Hallowe'en party at the restaurant where he worked. He asked me if I would help him to get his costume in order and of course I said yes. He also told me that he had one other favor to ask me. He said they were having a drag show during the party and he wanted me to get in drag and do the show for him! I told him I thought he was crazy as hell! No way was I going to show up at Lenox Square Mall in drag! He assured me that it would be after hours and most of the mall would be closed. Anyway I would be able to enter right off the parking lot directly into the restaurant so there would be no walking through the mall. Though I was curious about the whole drag thing, I wasn't at all sure about this! He and Greg both thought that it would be a real hoot, and Greg was saying that he would go with me so that I wouldn't have to do it alone.

Well, after some prodding, I agreed to do it. By that time, Greg and I both had become friends with Tina Devore, an entertainer in the cast of the Onyx Lounge. Tina's joining the Onyx cast had been something of a big deal because I'm pretty sure she was the very first black cast member that Jim and Keith had ever hired.

So I told Tina what I was doing and asked her if she would help me with my makeup. She said that she would, but I would have to get dressed at her house because she would have to work that night. That way she could do my makeup as she got dressed for work. That was certainly not a problem, since I was still living at home and had not given much thought as to where I would be getting dressed.

In the next few weeks, I began to calm down a bit about doing this, and decided that if I were going to do it, I may as well do it right. I knew that I would need clothes. Though I knew very many of the drag queens in town, I certainly didn't feel that I knew them well enough to ask to borrow clothing. And not many were as tall or as large as me, so that also would present a problem. So I immediately decided that I would need to make my clothes. And since I was doing this for Hallowe'en, and may never do it again, I decided to go to the bars from the restaurant as well. Might as well make a night of it!

I wasn't sure exactly how I wanted to look, so I made three outfits. One was a long gown with one sleeve in, and the other arm out. The second was a rag dress, which I would use for the 'performance' at the restaurant, and the third was just a tight fitting straight skirt and blouse with scarf that I could travel to and from in.

The next issue for me was shoes. As I've said before, I'm rather large, and have size 13 feet. I had no idea what I was to do about shoes. Tina said that if I wanted to buy a pair, there was a store downtown that sold larger sizes for women, but they only went up to a size 12 wide. Still that would have to be my destination. I remember the day that I went down to pick out a pair. I was freaking out. I really wanted to do this, but I hadn't counted on having to do things like try on women's shoes in public. The salesman in the store was very nice though. I guess because of all the drag queens shopping there he was used to it. He allowed me to look at, and try on shoes in the back storeroom. None really fit, but being artistic, I picked a pair that I was pretty sure I would be able to take home and 'alter' to make them work. I paid for them and got the hell out of there as soon as possible!

The big night came, and I headed over to Tina's house early. I had picked up Greg, and I think we got there before sundown even. I remember I was nervous as hell. I actually had stopped and picked up a bottle of Vodka to carry with me over there to get ready. I knew I'd need to get drunk to do this! Tina got me all painted up, and though I didn't look at all like I thought that I would, I wouldn't say that I looked bad. She had warned me that I should get accustomed to walking in heels, and that walking in them inside on carpeting had nothing to do with wearing them outside. While I had been practicing in my bedroom at home, I quickly found that she was 100% right. I imagine it's because the soles are so thin, and all your weight is concentrated on the balls of your feet. But the first time I stepped out on the pavement that night, I thought I would die from the pain! I didn't know my feet could hurt so badly so quickly! I immediately stepped back inside and pulled the things off! Fortunately I had brought some slides that I could wear. I immediately put them on! I decided right then that I'd be wearing them until I got to my destinations and had to put the heels on.

By the time Greg and I got out to Lenox Mall where the restaurant was located, I was already pretty well headed toward sloshed. I'd been drinking martinis since Tina had started making up my face, and had put a sizable dent in the liter of Vodka that I'd brought with me there. It was a good thing too. I didn't know very many of the people that Ernie worked with, but as long as I had my liquid courage that didn't much matter. The few that I did know were happy, and somewhat surprised to see me all done up like I was. But they were in costumes, and were already half smashed too, so what the hell! I changed into my performance dress and the show began. I can honestly say that I probably sucked at the performance, but it was my first time. God knows by the time the show started I was quite drunk. Oddly enough, one of the guys that worked there and was acting as the deejay would figure largely into my future. His name was Jules, and he would not only become one of the biggest show deejays in the city, but also became a close friend of mine and the Mixmaster of many of my future performance tapes.

We all had a great time that night, and when the show was over Greg and I decided to head downtown to the Onyx. The place was packed when we arrived. I can't even remember the drive I was so drunk. I do know that I went in and continued with one more martini. I decided that here I would enter their Hallowe'en contest for best drag. I didn't win, but apparently I made a good impression since several of the people in the cast and in the crowd told me that I should think about maybe performing. Tina agreed that I should think about it, and told me they had a newcomer's spotlight every Tuesday night. She thought that I should surely think about doing it.

While I wasn't in shape for much more that night, Greg wasn't ready to call it quits, so he told me that I could go to his place and change before going home. I knew where he hid the spare key, so off I went. It had been an eventful night! And while I was in no shape to continue it, I knew that it would provide several great memories and would be the topic of many conversations with friends for a long time to come.

What I had not realized that night was just how much it would change the next several years of my life. Indeed, after I went home and thought about Tina's and my conversation from that night more and more I began to give serious thought to maybe doing the newcomer's show and just seeing where it went. By now I'd come to know some of the entertainers around town and saw that they were really cool people who took what they did very seriously. In the course of talking to them I could see there was much dedication in them for their craft. After all, the rush that I'd experienced on Hallowe'en couldn't be denied. So I decided that I would give it my best shot.

Once again I knew that I'd have to prepare for this. My angle was always the clothes first. If I could sell nothing else in this I could always make my appearance something special. So I began to prepare my numbers to perform and the costumes for each spot. In those days the bars were doing three shows a night, at least five to six nights a week; Which meant that I would have to prepare about six numbers. That's two spots per show. That of course meant six outfits. I knew that I could use at least two of the pieces from Hallowe'en. However the others would have to be made. I started sewing and knocked them out pretty quickly. I remember I drew off outfits that I'd liked over the years, but never had cause to make until now. My love for garment construction and design had started way back when I was around 11 or 12 years old. The result was not bad I must say. I ended up with something like two or three Evening gowns, and a couple of pants outfits.

The night for the show came and since I'd told Ernie and Greg all about it, they both promised that they would be there. I remember that Ernie came in with a whole crew from the restaurant, and suddenly this little bar had what was like a Saturday night crowd on a Tuesday night. Of course the management was thrilled because all these guys were just getting off work and were ready to get good and drunk. They were drinking and carrying on and screaming for me and just generally having a ball. Naive as I was, though I thought I wasn't doing half bad. I also knew that they were screaming because I knew half of 'em, and Ernie had probably told the other half to cut up. Either way, the bar owner and manager made sure that the show director gave me six spots and two or three more for good measure. They came to me and asked me if I could do any more. I'd only really prepared the six songs, but I was doing some Diana Ross songs that night, and I really love her. So even though I'd not prepared more, there were some that I could improvise off her greatest hits album.

In the end, the management was happy, I was happy and the audience was happy so all was well. It was a great start to what was to become a pretty decent career in female impersonation for me.

From that little show, I started going down to the Onyx and performing on their Tuesday night lineup regularly. I was sewing weekly to keep up with the shows and as a result was acquiring quite the wardrobe. It was clear to a lot of the other entertainers; newcomers and seasoned professionals alike, that I knew my way around a sewing machine. Many of them were very complimentary of the clothes that I was producing.

As is the case in most shows, it wasn't long before people were wanting to 'trade' pieces, or some were just asking me to begin to sew for them outright. So suddenly what I attempted to work toward when I first started going to the show bars; the chance to sew for the entertainers, was happening for me right along with the opportunity to be an entertainer myself. It wasn't long before things were moving along smoothly. Right away I started trying to find a character that I could perform that would make me stand out amongst the crowd. Many of the popular artists' music was already being performed by other well-seasoned performers. I definitely wanted something that would make me stand out, and someone that I could deliver believably; where the illusion would not be lost because of my personal look. I settled on Millie Jackson. There were not many people doing Millie songs in town at the time. Dina Jacobs was doing one, but other than that, no one was really doing her.

Here, I'll give a little tutorial of sorts.

Back at that time, the idea was that the voice needed to fit somewhat with the illusion. For that reason, I felt that I needed a woman singer with enough of a "throaty" voice to not create a comic effect when matched with my size; And Millie's rough sound and brash nature would work perfectly.

I started with her early stuff. I liked the album "Caught up", but didn't really want to go there because Dina was doing the big tune from that album. I settled on the one right after it, "Still Caught Up". If you're not familiar with it, it's the album that has the song on it where Millie portrays a mental patient and cracks up. "I still love you, you still love me" is the name of the song, and it quickly became one of my favorites and a favorite of the audience that I was performing for. I affectionately started to call the number 'crazy lady'. It became my first big 'hit' with the show bar crowd.

I learned very quickly that doing drag isn't as easy as most people think. There's a lot more to it than just slapping a wig on and moving your mouth to a recording. I learned very quickly that there's work involved in making an act a good one. I was eagerly beginning to really get into it. And the kicker was that I was surprising myself and everyone else around too, I think. Often Ernie made the comment that when he'd asked me to do it that first time, he thought it would be a lark and quite funny. He said he never thought that I'd actually be good! But not only was I learning fast, I was beginning to gather a little 'following'. Pretty soon Tina, who was now the show director at The Onyx was telling me that there was going to be a pageant held at the bar specifically for newcomers, and that I should consider entering.

There's always been a lot of interest in pageantry in the drag community. There's something about a tiara that'll make drag queens go completely crazy! I think it's just the opportunity to compete in a fierce way at something that you know you're good at. I've seen people spend THOUSANDS of dollars to win a $500.00 prize and tiara. Of course, there's an upside to having that tiara. If the title is big enough you'll quickly make back your investment in bookings and appearances. It will pay for itself for years to come. But initially I think the primary drive is the chance to have one more conglomeration of rhinestones to wear....

My entry to the Miss Newcomer pageant that year was no different. I was drunk with the idea of winning in my very first pageant. I was totally gassed up about it. I had every intention to turn out some of the finest garments that I had ever made. I was selecting and purchasing fabrics for weeks in anticipation of the upcoming event.

I had decided to do Donna Summer's "McArthur Park" for talent and had enlisted the help of Ernie and another friend whose name was Reggie to be my 'backup' in the number. The contest was held in early fall, so I decided to do a cape suit for my sportswear selection and I had found some peach colored embroidered lace for my evening gown. That would cover the three categories that I would have to show in. And at the time, the presentation category was always a white gown, so I could quickly throw one of those together.

The night came and I was convinced that I had done all that I could and was ready. My clothes went over very well in the respective categories. And to tell the truth I was really never worried about those. I knew that I sewed well and that my clothing would always compete. What was at issue for me was the talent category. I also had no idea about bar politics back then either, so none of that was factored into my thought process. Anyway, I had drawn a number right at just about the middle of the pack of contestants, so they chose to have a break in the middle of talent, just before I was to go on. That break was sheer hell! I was nervous and about ready to pass out! I'd made this white bathing suit to do my talent number in, and it was tight as a glove!

The break ended, and the scene opened with Ernie and Reggie sitting in the 'park' as the music started. They were both in outer wear, and I came through the curtain in a floor length white fur coat. My hair was pulled back in a beautiful fall, with large, white cabbage roses framing it on either side of my head. When the music changed, and went into the fast break Ernie and Reggie came forth and took the coat off me as I started to dance. That was probably the longest 5 or 6 minutes of my life! I made it through the number and thought that I had done ok. Later on I was given some really good con-structive criticism, and when the mistakes were pointed out to me, I could certainly see why I didn't win. But hey, it was my first time out!

I like to think that's the night I really became an entertainer. It was tougher than any work that I'd ever done. It was also a great leveling of spirit for me in some ways. It taught me a tough lesson in humility. I was convinced going in that I had won, and when that wasn't the case, it was a bitter pill to swallow. It also represented the first time that I'd done ANYTHING that I considered work and ended up with NO compensation whatsoever.

I was to learn another lesson that night as well. It would be a hard one in humiliation. Earlier that day, Ernie and I had gone to the Piedmont Park administrative office to borrow a park bench for the talent scene. We had thought about just ripping one off, but there's a part of me that's been there since I was a child that usually causes me to think things through. And if I can do something the right way, it usually pays for me to do it that way. So I vetoed the theft idea and we went down and talked to the manager. He complied and told us he didn't have a problem with it as long as we brought it back. We promised that we would. That night after the competition and crowning were over, we were all exhausted. We'd gotten my things together, and as we were going out the front door to the club, someone opened the door to the backstage dressing room and I noticed the park bench. I mentioned to Ernie that we needed to get it, and he said, "Let's just come back and pick it up tomorrow". Well the last thing in the world that I wanted was for something to happen to these people's bench after I said that I would take care of it. So I insisted that we take it with us and we could drop it outside the door of the park office that night.

Reggie, Ernie, and Greg were all riding with me so we piled into the car and headed off. I was going to drop them off.

It had not even registered with me that I didn't have my male clothes. I'd left them over at Tina's where I'd changed and gotten ready for the pageant. At the time Greg lived on Peachtree St. just a block north of the Fox Theater. I was headed up Peachtree when I saw the blue light flashing in my rearview mirror. I was stunned and horrified! I had on the peach lace gown that I'd worn for evening wear, four inch heels, a face full of makeup and my hair was still slicked back with the fall and those damned huge cabbage roses! And to add insult to injury, it was then that I realized that not only did I not have my guy's clothes, I also had left my wallet in my pants' pocket, so I had NO driver's license or any other type of identification! I pulled over and the cop walked up to the driver's window. The very first thing he did was ask for my I.D. I explained to him that we were coming from a show at the Onyx Lounge, and that I'd forgotten my wallet earlier in the evening. I then gave him my name and suggested that if he would run my plate he would surely see that I was who I said I was. He told me to wait right there. I assume that's what he did when he went back to his car. He came back shortly and asked me about another name that was on my insurance. It was my father's name. I told him who it was and that my insurance was registered in his name.

By this time there were onlookers on the street and they were mighty curious. He told me to step out of the car, and my immediate response was, "do I have to"? Of course he said yes, and that I'd need to come back to the squad car. As I was stepping out of my car, it was hilarious to see I'm sure because this guy was not small. I'd say he was about 6 ft. tall. Well I'm 6ft. two and a half inches flat footed and I had on four inch heels! As I climbed out of the car, I just kept going, and going, and going.... Finally he was looking up at me incredulously! Back to the squad car we went. About that time another carload of cops drove up and I could hear them outside the squad car laughing and talking and discussing the situation. I immediately started popping off fake fingernails. I was prepared to strip buck naked in the back of that car if I had to. I was determined that if I had to go to jail, I would NOT go in drag!

After a time, he came and let me out of the backseat and gave me two citations. He explained to me that one was for illegally transporting city property. That even if I honestly borrowed the bench the man at the office never had the right to lend it to me. It belonged to the city. The other was for driving without a license. He explained that if I came to court with both my license and proof that I'd had permission to borrow the bench, the judge would probably throw both out. However, he was not finished with me yet. He told me that he would follow me over to the park to put the bench back right then. We were half a block from Greg's house and he was having a fit to get out of the car. I said, no way! It's just my luck the guy pops him for being drunk or something and we end up in jail anyway. Greg was mad enough to kill, but Ernie and I made him stay right there in the car.

We got to the park and this guy couldn't resist having his bit of fun. Here I am with three people dressed in regular clothes in my car, and he's there as well. He makes me and ONLY me get out and take this bench out of the trunk and carry it to the door. At that time, there were dormitories over the park office. I don't know if the people in them were workers or what, but it was late at night and all the commotion woke the people up. So here I am, in an evening gown with an all-male audience watching me manhandle this bench in gown and heels. It was a bitch, but it was a small price to pay if he wasn't going to take me to jail.

After that, I then carried Reggie and Greg home. Ernie was nice enough to stay with me and it was a good thing that he did. Because it was then that I realized that I still needed to get my clothes. When I got over to Tina's I discovered that she was obviously still out at the bars partying. Fortunately, there was a window slightly open. It was a sliding one so we forced it the rest of the way, Ernie crawled through, and unlocked the front door for me. I was never so glad to see the inside of a room in my life! I quickly changed out of my drag, washed my face, and then took him home. When I got home myself I fell into bed like someone who had been working on a chain gang.

I'd largely made it through the drama, but it still was not over. The next day I went to see the guy in the park about getting a note to carry to court. It was then that I realized that it must have been some of the park workers in those dorm rooms above the office. As I was driving up and they saw the car, I overheard whispers, "that must be the guy from last night"!!! Well, screw it! The guy wrote me the note so I guessed I could live with a little controversial scrutiny! But I tell you, for pretty much the remainder of my career doing drag I adamantly refused to drive ANYWHERE for years in makeup. I would paint at the bar that I was working in, but I would not go out into the city streets in paint unless there was just no other way.

That contest opened something of a flood gate. Prior to that night, while I still went to the Gumhead and was friendly with a lot of the entertainers there, I was spending more and more time around The Onyx. Not only had I also made lots of friends there, but I was getting more and more work opportunities there. It wasn't long before I got a weekend booking at the Onyx to appear with the regular cast. It was my first time working in a show with paid entertainers. While my first booking there was just for tips, I really didn't care. I was still making pretty good money on my regular job, and was much more concerned with getting the experience than I was with the pay. And besides I was doing ok with tips from the show too. I don't remember how many bookings I'd done at the Onyx, but before long the Gumhead started to open its weeknight shows to younger, less experienced entertainers as well. Suddenly there was a whole new fraternity of up and coming entertainers and the bars were taking notice. In this new found group were Ashley Nicole, Dawn Dupree, Lisa Alexander and myself. There were a few other people as well. Some were moving from other places and really weren't new to the trade, just trying to break into the shows here in town.

Either way, it was plain that there was going to be some competition if one was to find a place in this city to shine. That was the period of Glamour Drag in Atlanta. Damned near everybody that was doing drag at all wanted to work in Atlanta. It became the premiere showplace of the South; and some would say, the entire nation. Trying to be noticed could be challenging, but I was fortunate. I knew some folks and was quickly trying to meet others. I never really had difficulty working if I really wanted to. As soon as they started doing weeknight shows that showcased new talent in the Gumhead that gave me more opportunities to learn.

Then one day Tina approached me about a booking she was putting together on a weekend in Macon, Ga. As it turned out Jim, the owner of the Onyx, would from time to time pitch a fit and start firing people at the club.This was during one of those periods. I think Tina had quit during that period and Terry Douglas, another entertainer there, had left for a bit. So they were putting together a show to carry down to the We Three Lounge. It was a club in Macon at the time. Even though they had been ousted from The Onyx, the entertainers still had bills to pay. So the alternative was to go on the road and work smaller clubs.

Having never worked anywhere else other than the two bars in Atlanta, I jumped at the chance. This would be my first booking as an equally paid cast member in a show. The experience taught me how to read an audience that has no knowledge of you. I'd never been here and these people had never heard of me. I tried to open with Millie's "All the way Lover" which was popular at the time, but it only got lukewarm applause. I learned that weekend how to open with nothing but the top 40 hits to get them acquainted with me. I also learned that it was prudent to open with upbeat music rather than slow numbers. I immediately changed tactics after that first number and switched to some of the Ross numbers that I'd done on my first night out. Ross is practically always a crowd pleaser. My acceptance from the audience was better, but still conservative. No real matter to me though. I finished out the weekend. I can't really remember how the next night went. I know that I had a good time there. With each spot onstage that weekend I got more and more comfortable. I also watched what the more seasoned entertainers did in an out of town situation. That trip opened up a whole new image of doing shows that I'd not known about before. I quickly found out that some of the entertainers actually worked on the road quite a bit. They traveled to different cities and played clubs all throughout the Southeast. Some traveled and had follow-ings that stretched even further. The image of this just being playtime was fading more and more. Quickly I was becoming aware of the business side of female impersonation.

Along with that new influx of entertainers into the At-lanta area was a couple of new faces up from Florida. Tina had moved here from Tallahassee and had left some friends there. Before long, some of her friends came up and among them was a petite pixie of a queen who looked like a little girl. Her stage name was The Lady Chablis, and I doubt that she weighed 125 lbs. soaking wet. Not too long after Chablis' arrival there was another entertainer from Florida moved up. She came in from the Daytona Beach area.

Every so often there is an entertainer that comes along and EVERYONE is blown away by their act. Yeteeva Antoinette was in that category. When she blew in from Daytona, she danced in and took everybody's breath away. Beautiful, talented, a flawless dancer, she had it all. It was suddenly clear to all that there was to be something of a changing of the guard. With all this new talent around it was clear that the show scene in Atlanta was flourishing. There were so many quality entertainers that there were not really enough jobs to go around. Some of us began to look at booking out of town as the solution to that issue.

Since I was still not ready to give up my regular job, working out of town was often the answer for me. That way I could do both; Work some weekends at show clubs and weekdays at the hotel. I would book in clubs around town for sure, but the road work was both exciting and just a little scary to me. I never knew what to expect when I was outside Atlanta. And to be quite truthful, as nerve wracking as that could be, it was also one of the things that kept those shows good to me.

Macon was my first and quickly became one of my favorites. It was close by, and the patrons were beginning to get to know me. In many ways it was an extension of working in Atlanta. I suppose one downside to working on the road was that doing so directly resulted in being deceptive to my parents. Since I was still living at home, each time I would go out of town and would be gone overnight I would have to tell them something. I knew that I could never be honest with them and tell them that I was going out of town to work. That would raise all sorts of questions. As far as they were concerned every dime I made was coming from the hotel downtown.

I still had a boatload of discomfort around drag myself. I knew that talking about it to them or anyone straight was completely out of the question. So I lied and said I was going to parties with friends in nearby towns. The guilt and shame that I had for lying and worrying them was nearly unbearable. But to tell them what I was really doing would have likely killed them.

My guilt was a funny thing. It manifested itself by making me convinced that something terrible would happen. I was convinced that I would get hurt, arrested or something drastic. And of course the result would be that my deception would come to light in a bad way. I still to this day think that my paranoia was a result of the trauma of being stopped when I was very new in drag by the cops. Anyway, it made me feel horrible. I would pray incessantly when I was about to leave. All the time trying to hope that this time would not be the time that something would happen. I could never totally relax when I was out working. It was all making me a nervous wreck. I truly don't know how I was able to work with the level of irrational and catastrophic fear that I was dealing with. And I know my act suffered because of it. I would obsess about things happening to me onstage. Like someone would walk into the bar hating gay people and intentionally do something to hurt people. Of course, in my mind was the thought that entertainers being onstage in a spotlight would make us prime targets for some nut job to come in shooting or something. I would start down through a thought process like that and totally freak myself out.

It got so bad that I finally had to do something to calm myself. There is a very simple prayer that says, "The Lord watches between me and thee, while we are absent one from another". I wrote that out, tore it in half and hid part of it in my mom's curio cabinet and put the other half in my wallet. That little gesture helped some, but I was still quite a basket case.

In many ways all the emotions that surrounded doing the shows made it like an addiction. The back and forth love/hate tug was enormous. I would be out in the bars on nights that I wasn't working and someone would start to discuss me doing a booking in the club. Or I would have been drinking and actually approached someone about working. We would make all the arrangements and then the next couple of days would find me beating myself up for getting myself into it. It Didn't matter if it was booking or a pageant. I would have these terrible misgivings. They would then alternate between elation about the upcoming event and misery about why I'd agreed to do it. All the way up to the day of. Then I'd be in the mirror getting made up and nearly sick with worry. But inevitably once it was over I'd be glad that I'd gone through with it. And the next booking would start the same cycle all over again.

Thank goodness there were sometimes long stretches between the bookings. Before my popularity really got to growing I'd sometimes go two weeks to a month without a booking. And during those times I felt free to let my facial hair grow out and I'd often get serious about dating someone; Or at least having regular sex. For some reason when I was deeply involved in getting ready for a show, or going through a stretch when I had a lot of back to back appearances I seemed to never have sex during those times. In fact, the entire 8 years that I performed on a regular basis, I only picked up one person during a booking. And even then I made him come to the dressing room and sit with me when the show was over so he could watch me take off my makeup.

The two personalities- my show persona and my real persona, were so far apart for me that they just never intersected. One had absolutely NOTHING to do with the other. So as a result when I was in a period of doing a lot of drag I'd practically go celibate. And then when I'd have a drought of sorts from shows was when I'd play with the guys. It was during such a period that I first met George. He was like no guy I'd ever met before. My time with him turned out to be one of the most memorable experiences of my "dating" life.

It didn't occur to me at the time that my many casual sexual connections would affect my romantic life. Quite frankly, they scared the hell out of me. Just about any encounters that I had with men usually unnerved me so that I would come off sounding like a complete idiot. I didn't have the slightest notion how to talk to anyone. I certainly didn't know how to convey that I wanted to get to know them better. And the thought that they might want to get to know me? Well frankly, it never entered my mind. A guy would usually have to go straight to the sexual innuendos for me to think I had a "green light" so to speak. Otherwise, I came into the encounter with the thought that I would have to sell him on the idea of being with me. Even then I just automatically assumed that he would only want sex. Truth is, that seemed to be all it was ever about anyway. Some might say I had good reason for feeling this way. It was more the rule than the exception within the gay community no matter how much I might want it to be otherwise. I assumed that everyone thought the opening invitation to a committed, romantic relationship had to be sex. I had no idea there was any other way to become romantically linked with someone.

It seemed that the only time sexual situations were not baffling to me was if the game plan was established up front. That way I was not expecting anything more, so I didn't get disappointed as easily. That seemed to be the case with George.

He was a wonderful, but somewhat strange guy that I met late one afternoon in Midtown. He had an outgoing personality that was priceless. A quick wit and easy smile were the things that made him such a special guy. Very outspoken and never speechless, I knew almost immediately that he and I would be good friends at the very least. The thing that set him apart from almost every other man that I'd met in the gay community up to that point was that he always spoke his mind. I never had to wonder what was going on in his head, or how he felt about something because he would just put it right out there! That same direct approach carried over into our intimate correspondence. He let me know immediately after our first encounter that he enjoyed my company and wanted to see me again. However, he also let me know right away that he was not available for anything more than sex and friendship. He had a lover that he had been with for quite a while and had no intention of leaving. I asked him how he could be so blasé about it. He told me that they had an "understanding". I think the guy was married or something. George didn't quite go into the whole story. But what was really great to me was that whatever the issue, he was totally upfront with me. That freed me up to relax and enjoy his company. I could get to know him without all the mental clutter of, "will he want to take it further?" Not to mention all the other mind acrobatics that I was prone to go through.

The other thing that was so cool about George was that he was one of those guys that if you looked at him, you might just assume that he was something of a ne'er-do-well. I mean, he would wear very well-worn corduroy pants and a tee shirt that had seen better days. His boots looked as though they had been around for a couple of centuries. But if you looked closely you would see that he had a body that was as finely tuned as the engine in a '68 Mustang Shelby. And his mind was just as sharp. He was quite an adept classical pianist and was an avid student of fine art. Meantime he made his living waiting on tables, driving taxis, and all sorts of odd jobs because he simply didn't want to be tied down. Indeed, I remember one time he decided to just go off into the North Carolina woods and camp for about three months. This apparently worked out just fine with his lover. I could see that this behavior and the convenience of that relationship arrangement all fit together in a package that was this man's idea of a good life.

I've heard the ideology that one should 'wear life like a loose garment'. George was the epitome of that. As a result of these traits, the time that I spent in his company remains to this day one of the benchmarks in male/male relationships for me. George was the man that taught me the value of spending time with someone just for the pure enjoyment of it, but to not compromise yourself or the personal pleasures that you hold dear. He believed that it really did not have to be a big deal. George could have much fun watching the very first science fiction movie ever made (I'm not kidding, he actually took me to a silent film that was touted to be that.... Yawn...). Equally, a rare art exhibit could hold him transfixed for hours. And then, with just as much enthusiasm and interest, he could spend hours watching the latest silly sitcoms on television. And just watching him thoroughly get into his little joys in life was infectious. Pretty soon I would realize I was having a great time just hanging out there with him. I never saw him take himself too seriously. I think that's something that we all could stand to learn.

I soon started to notice how non-judgmental George was and it was something that I wanted to emulate. He pretty much measured the entire world with the same yardstick so to speak. That was certainly something that I was not used to seeing in dealing with people. It helped me see just how much contempt before investigation ran rampant in the gay community, and the world at large.

Chapter 4

Chapter 4

Chapter 4

By now, my life had many definite conflicts of interest. At the time, I was still very much in the closet as far as the African-American community was concerned. My life was split into three distinct parts. There was my work life at the hotel, my home life, and my social life. I was still convinced that no one in my home life knew that I was gay, and that's just the way I liked it. But just as in any situation where ideas conflict, my conscience started to get the better of me and the guilt started to creep in. I noticed it right off in my civic life. I had been an active member of the NAACP youth council during the latter part of my high school years and very much enjoyed the experience. However, I began to notice there were conflicts there that would tear me apart. I loved being a part of something that I felt could possibly change the world for the better, but at the same time the Organization had come out in force in opposition to the idea of a Gay Pride Day celebration in Atlanta, which, at the time was in its infancy. While I would dare not go and participate for fear of being seen and recognized (it was a hot topic then being covered widely in the press), I just could not bring myself to continue working with this group knowing what they must think of me and my "kind". Meanwhile, either members of the organization didn't know, or couldn't admit that I, and many others like me, were in their midst. In fact, the very first 'closed door/same sex' orgy I was invited to participate in was actually held at the hotel during an NAACP National Convention! It was hosted by some of the group members over that weekend.   So without hesitation I dropped my membership with the organization. Interestingly enough, I've said many times that if I'd known then of the hypocrisy and intense racism that soon showed vividly within the gay community, perhaps I would not have been so quick to make that change. For while gay people were anxiously march-ing up Peachtree St. during the day on Pride Weekend, by that evening, many gay establishments were practicing their own form of prejudice by either denying entry or exorbitantly char-ing people of color who attempted to enter their premises.

The myriad of feelings that were warring within me at the time was tremendous to say the least. There was so much random guilt about all that was going on in my life. My fear of straight black people was downright pathological and that was solely based on the way the community conducted itself around same-sex issues. Much of what has been said recently in the discussions of the "Down Low" phenomenon is certainly correct in that sense. And it is still slow to change. In the black community during the 60's,70's and even beyond, if you were a "sissy", that was just about the worst thing that you could be. You were a disgrace and everybody knew that you were. The only people willing to wear that label were the guys that were just so effeminate that they really didn't have much of a choice. As far as the remainder of the community was con-cerned, homosexuality simply didn't exist there.

I went through the angst of trying to determine just what I was supposed to do in my case. I knew that my life felt true to me, and that I didn't want to go the way of so many gay men. That is to say leave home and just disappear from all family and roots. I loved Atlanta and my family and really wanted to remain here. At the same time, because of my father's strong presence in the Methodist church community in Atlanta as well as nationally; I knew that I would be recognized by lots of people unless I put some distance between me and them. It wasn't difficult to come to the conclusion that seemed inevitable. After all, at that time there was really only one gay bar in Atlanta's black community. That was the Marquette Social Club on MLK Jr. Drive. EVERYBODY in the black community knew what that was. There was no way in hell I would have been caught DEAD at Marquette! At the time that street, along with Auburn Avenue, was the epicenter of business in the African-American community of Atlanta. My father knew just about every merchant along MLK Jr. Drive on a first name basis. No way was I going up there! Years later I learned of another gay bar in the downtown area named the Pear Garden. I think it was located somewhere near Poplar St. I know that a lot of black gay kids used to hang out around the Poplar St. area. But that too was just too close to home for me. So without much thought given it I chose to go to the northeastern side of town, which in those days was predominantly white.

I still wonder what my folks must have thought and the fears I must have awakened in them. They were raised at a time when they not only felt they could not trust most whites, but that the only thing that could come from spending time in mostly white areas was trouble. And while it was not as bad as it had been in their day, I can say there were still quite a few 'hair raising' moments. I can remember sitting in the living room at home with my parents one day and having my father try talking to me about race relations. He was walking that fine line of trying to be objective, but also trying to issue an extreme warning that he felt was of utmost importance. "I don't want to tell you that anyone is a bad person," he said, " however I do feel that I need to let you know my experience has been that most white people don't have your best interests at heart". He was quick to add that he agreed there were indeed white people in the world that had been kind to him and that he felt okay dealing with, but he stopped short of being able to say that he knew any he could call 'friend'. He just didn't feel that he could trust most to treat him fairly. And he certainly felt that should a situation arise where a white person who appeared friendly toward me was forced to choose between me and another white person, the chances were that the other white person would always be chosen over me whether the individual forced to make the decision knew that other white person or not. It was my father's belief that in such a situation, race would always be the deciding factor.

I argued vehemently that this was not the case with my friends. I intoned that things had changed greatly in the world and he must be mistaken. Of course, in time I learned that I was a little bit right AND somewhat wrong as well... Going through that period felt like what being a double agent must feel like. On the one hand, I was with my family who really didn't know my whole story, and I didn't feel I could ever be really honest with them. And at the same time, I was trying desperately to fit into a social community that didn't really know me or take me seriously. Often I felt that in the white gay community I had to keep what was deemed my 'unacceptable blackness' in check. That is to say that there were characteristics that people in the white gay community found acceptable; even quite novel. And then there were attitudes and attributes that were prohibited. For instance, in white gay bars as long as there weren't too many black patrons the management was accepting of our presence. As a black customer you were never expected to object to anything, and were generally expected to be agreeable and to have a pleasant disposition. A disagreement with a white customer would result in you automatically being ejected from the establishment. This however did not mean that the white customer would also be ejected. And a disagreement with a staff member could get you banned from the establishment altogether. Often, nowhere in this equation was any discussion of who was right or who was wrong. This was just how it was. In addition to these instances, there were many times that I spoke with other black kids in the bars who, just like me, had experienced the following:

You would be out socializing in a group of young people where all the members of the group besides you and maybe one other would be white. Someone would tell a joke that was basically a racial slur, and the other members of the group would watch the black people to see their response. If you responded negatively, there would be instant diminishing of the event as being 'just a joke', and you would be admonished to 'lighten up, and not take things so seriously'. If you "went along" and didn't complain, then it was deemed they could 'be themselves' more comfortably in your presence.

For years I had this intense dread of running into black straight people in situations where I would be identified as being gay. That is to say that if I were out at a restaurant with a group of gay men, no matter if the gay men were black, white or a mixed group (which usually was the case), I would see scorn in the eyes of straight black people and it would just about kill me. This was especially true with black women. I suppose it was due to the strong role that women play in our culture and the strong influence that the women in my family had on my life. As much as I loved my work at the Marriott downtown, that intense discomfort extended there as well.

Most of the people that worked around my area were black and all of the folks that were directly in my department were. Not to mention that the two women that helped me to get the job in the first place were friends with my mother and my sister respectively. So even at work I felt that there were eyes on everything that I did.

In fact, when I started to make friends in the gay community, I would often give them the number at work and have them to call me there. Anne, the woman that first told me of the job, was my oldest sister's roommate at the time. She was the evening operator in the department that I worked in. As such, she received all the incoming calls. She made no attempt to hide how she felt about all the men that were calling me. In fact she made more than a few harsh comments. I suppose she saw herself as looking out for me with such disapproving overtones. However, I wonder what she would have said had she known that many of the guys that worked there in the building and a couple that worked in our own department who appeared to be the very picture of heterosexuality, were soon making passes at me. My God, I was SO naive! With these guys I never dreamed this type thing would happen. My own experience was that I didn't know how to be anything but what I was. No matter how much I thought I was hiding my sexuality, some would say that I was pretty obvious. And while I thought I did a pretty good job of covering, I can look back now at certain scenarios and at some photos and laugh. Ha! Anyone could see I was 'batting for the other team' without me ever opening my mouth! Still I was trying to carry myself with a studied sense of dignity and that meant an attempted double life.

Meanwhile, on the other side of town I was beginning to get quite a different type of enlightenment. I have to admit that spending time away from my own culture and community offered me a chance to take an in depth look at the other side, so to speak. I think that anyone who says he or she has not at least thought about differences in the practices of people from a different background from theirs is just plain lying. How others live, think, act, work, conduct themselves, etc. is bound to be intriguing. Here I found myself spending time with people in very personal ways that previously were only as close to me as the television. Prior to coming out and becoming friends with some white people, as close as I was in passing these people on the street, my relation to their life experience was just as foreign as if they were inhabitants of the moon. I had never been into a white person's home environment. Had never known or seen any in a relaxed setting of any type. What it offered me was the similarity of the two worlds, yet an opportunity to glimpse the distinct differences. In many ways it simply boiled down to different points of view. At that time I had never heard the term 'white privilege'. It was pretty amazing to watch white kids do things and say things to people that I would have never dreamed of doing or saying.

One of the most apparent differences to me was the sense of entitlement that a lot of white kids had that a black kid did not; Simple things like being in a diner late night eating with friends. Someone's coffee cup might need a refill and the waitress would be busy with another table. This was a rather common occurrence. Often, we all went to the local Dunk n' Dine restaurant on Cheshire Bridge Rd. after the bars closed. I noticed that the white kids would think nothing of getting up, getting the coffee pot and pouring the refills. Though, even when there were black kids among the group, I never noticed one of us doing the same. One night, I was the one closest to the coffee station and one of the guys asked me to pass him the pot. I must have had this horrified look on my face because he said, "oh forget it, I'll get it myself." Well, after he'd poured the coffee and sat back down, I felt that I wanted to talk about what had just happened and started to discuss it with him. As we talked about it, it quickly became clear to me that he felt I thought I was "too good" to pour everyone's coffee. He thought I took it as an insult that he would ask me to pour his coffee. When I mentioned that, he readily admitted that had been his thought exactly. I explained to him that was not the case at all. I explained that being a black kid in the south, one of the first lessons that you learn is ,"boy, don't you go into nobody's house or business picking up anything that doesn't belong to you". I explained to him that the reason for that was that as a kid, our parents were eternally afraid that we would be accused of stealing or that we would damage something that they would have no way of paying for. He then exclaimed, "You know, I've seen this type of thing happen many times before and yet I'd never thought about the situation from that point of view". We went on to talk about other cultural differences that were just there in everyday life that people likely don't even notice. How comfortable most whites would be just simply browsing in stores while sometimes blacks would feel pressured because of the intense watchful eyes of store personnel as if we are about to steal something.

I know that the thought process often went the other way as well. I have known many white guys that have been quite frankly shocked when dating black men and finding that the black guys automatically assume that the white guys have loads of money. I remember one conversation in particular where I had gone out with this fellow a couple of times and we had become pretty comfortable with each other. I don't remember how we got on the topic, but he was telling me of a couple of other occasions when he'd dated men of color and the guys "just seemed to assume he was rich or something". I explained to him that most of the guys he was dating were products of a time and a socio-economic position where there were little or no positive black images on television or in the media at large. And nearly all these guys grew up in totally black communities. The only white people they saw were either always in business settings, on television or out at the mall. In the period these men grew up (this was in the 60's and 70's), they rarely or never saw white people with beat up cars, or ragged clothing, or teeth that weren't near perfect, etc. While the negative opposing images were very common sites in their own communities. So naturally in their minds the only reference most had to the experience of white people in America was one of success and affluence.

Sadly, in a lot of instances I think this image is still way too prevalent and the underlying message is, "to be successful in this country one needs to be a white male, 22-65 years of age, 5'8"- 6'0"tall; 165-180 lbs.; blond hair; blue eyes; size 9.5-11 shoe, etc..." The horrible thing is that to this day I still believe that most prejudice is simply the product of gross misunderstanding. If there were just a little more communication and openness between people and a lot LESS divisive drive by forces like the media and political personalities there would be fewer problems between folks. At any rate, the whole situation is still going strong here in Atlanta with racial problems. Maybe it's not as prevalent on the surface as it has been in the past, but it's definitely alive and well within our communities and it HAS to be stopped. Nowadays, I'm more prone to see guys in the white gay community make comments like, "I'm not prejudiced, I'm just not attracted to Asians, Blacks, or Latinos. I just prefer All-American looks. It's just my preference." Code wording like this is really the same monster, only wearing a different mask. All too often back then I would run into guys who would say things like, "I really want to talk with you. Why don't we go somewhere more intimate? You go ahead out. I need to run to the bathroom and I'll meet you outside". After about three or four encounters like this, I soon surmised that the truth was they didn't want their white friends to see them leaving the bar with a black man. Indeed, I later had a conversation with one friend, who when I told him of an affair I had with a mutual friend his jaw dropped. At first he accused me of lying, but once I described the guys' house and bedroom in detail, my friend looked at me and said, "Well I'll be damned! Tony, he's one of the most racist guys I know!"

I'm happy to say that I've been fortunate to have done quite a bit of traveling and as a result have found immeasurable pleasure in getting to know men of many different cultures and hues. Learning of their cultures and sharing different intimacies (including sexual ones) has been a priceless learning and growth experience.

After a time I rarely thought about the fact that I was often in social situations where I would be the only person of color there. In fact, unless it was mentioned by someone, I don't think I ever really thought about it. I guess I had 'adjusted or, more likely, compensated mentally for the foibles and faux pas that I encountered with people in the white gay community. As time went on and more black kids began to migrate into other sections of town, it became obvious what was going on. I began to see bars discriminate against the gay black kids more openly. It felt as though we had to go much further than the proverbial mile to get consideration in any type of a social situation. I started to notice that black kids were at best being totally ignored by the patrons in the white establishments, and at worst being treated anything but fairly by personnel of said establishments. It was nothing to see black kids come in and try to initiate conversation with the white kids and to have the white guys stare straight through them as if they weren't there. More times than I would care to recount I would see bartenders wait on every patron standing around the bar for the exception of the black patrons, and then STILL have to be literally chased down by those patrons (myself included) just to place an order. And even with all this, I still think that the most scandalous of infractions was the way many of the bar owners and managers managed to handle the issue of admittance for the black patrons. Outrageous cover charges and requests for multiple pieces of legal I.D. were the order of the day for minority patrons.

At the time Backstreet was one of the Nation's premiere discos. It ruled the Southeast Club scene like Buckingham Palace rules Great Britain. Absolutely everyone who was anyone who came to Atlanta wanted to be seen there. It had been written up in several of the Nations' major magazines and was known to be favored as a party spot for many of the top celebrities in the world when they came to visit. The door at Backstreet was manned for years by a guy named Todd. And he was known to be just about the rudest and unsavory doorman in the city. They had such a reputation for disallowing people into the club (especially black people), that outsmarting Todd to gain entry to the club became the stuff of lore around town. People were clamoring to be one of the "chosen". And never one to disappoint, Todd took that cue to sink to even lower lows. I had often heard that he would question guys coming to the door of the club extensively as to who they were, and if it were a mixed couple, he would even question the white member of the couple as to the identity of his date! This was due to the belief that black guys were stopping white guys outside asking them to help them gain entry.

With all that I had seen in Atlanta and throughout the south I still did not want to believe this to be true. Yet, one evening just as had been described to me, I had it happen! I went out with this fellow that I had been dating for a while and after an evening of dinner and the theater he suggested we wind it up with drinks at Backstreet. This was definitely his suggestion; NOT MINE. I had not attempted to patronize the place in years believing that there was no need for me to spend my money where I was not wanted. But since that was where he wanted to go, I relented and went along. We arrived at the door and Galen, who was my date and I walked up to Todd. He immediately asked for my I.D., which I produced. Todd then turned to Galen and asked, "What's his name? To which Galen replied, "His name is Tony." Todd then asked, "Where do you know him from?" I was flabbergasted! I looked at Galen and said, "You know what? Fuck this!! I don't have to take this shit off anyone!" But just like most of the guys in town at the time Galen was more than willing to try and smooth it over and asked me to please just let it go, have a drink and try and have a good time. To this day that still remains one of the most dehumanizing experiences that I ever went through. However, this scenario largely describes the conditions at many gay establishments in the south . It was certainly the worst encounter, but still I can't say it was the ONLY encounter I had of its kind. That situation happened in the 1980's right here in Atlanta, GA. So forgive me if it pisses me off when I hear gay boys say there's no prejudice in the gay community.

Things didn't change much here in the city for a while and I found myself in a rather unique situation. During that period there was definitely a sentiment of "the good blacks -vs- the bad blacks". What that meant was simply that depending on who in the gay scene knew you, you were deemed to be acceptable. I used to tell my friend Ernie that the rule seemed to be that each group HAD to have at least one... Needless to say that type of talk always made the white guys that I knew really uncomfortable. I think that was because while they saw what was going on, most were trying really hard to ignore it. All that said, it felt bad to be accepted in many places simply because I knew people and some subgroup of people deemed my presence there to be 'okay'. Once I began to gain some recognition as an entertainer, the gap between me and other black club kids widened even further.

Finally there was some relief where blatant discrimination from the clubs was concerned. There was legislation introduced that spoke directly to the problem of overcharging and denying entry to minorities, or any specific group in the city's entertainment establishments. Apparently it was not just going on in the gay clubs. There were challenges introduced around the whole concept of the entrance policies applied by nightclubs in general. Soon, the club owners stopped the madness around the requests for multiple pieces of identification and the exorbitant cover charges were curbed somewhat. Sadly Backstreet was one of the last holdouts on this front, and still went out of their way to discriminate where they deemed it necessary and possible. They were able to get away with this since they were a private membership only club. This became a work around that many clubs could employ. It gave birth to the $2 membership card. If a club instituted a membership to come in, it could then say it was a private club and deny membership to certain patrons. The whole thing was just a ridiculous mess.

By this time I was working in the bars a good bit doing shows and was beginning to become known to more and more of the gay community in my entertainment persona. Up until that time, my act had been fledgling and not as widely known as a lot of the people working in the craft of female impersonation. But as people began to know me through that work, they naturally began to set me, and other black entertainers apart from the black club kids in general. In Atlanta, drag was always a big draw. For years this was known as the 'drag capitol' of the United States. And indeed just about every top entertainer in this craft had come through here to work at one time or another. RuPaul, Crystal Wood (Diana Ross impersonator for "Boylesque" in Vegas) Lady Bunny, Lady Chablis, etc... All have lived and worked here at one time or another. So to be recognized as an Atlanta drag performer in those days was a position of elevated status within the Atlanta gay community.

Once again, I found myself feeling torn because of being set apart as a black gay person. Only this time it was a little different. While there were lots of black female impersonators in the clubs, you had to look far and wide to find a black employee in the gay clubs in any other role than that. The time that this whole thing hit home was one weekend quite by accident. I really had become somewhat removed from the struggles of the gay black kids. I was working in the bars so much then that less and less time was spent there as a patron. Now when I was there I was usually working so things were vastly different except for this one night. I had gone out to party at a club that I was scheduled to work in the next night. I really just wanted to check the place out. It was a new club, and I'd never gone there. I met the manager while booked somewhere else in town, and he approached me about guest spotting at his club. I wanted to see what the crowd was like and the setup of the room as it pertained to doing a show. The place was usually more of a dance club and didn't really have a stage setup per se. Rarely was I ever in any club these days without makeup so more and more people were not recognizing 'Tony' the guy. Only "Adrienne Lee" the performer. So when I walked in that night the people working there didn't recognize me. I was served attitude from the moment I hit the door from damned near everybody. Door man all the way through. At first I couldn't imagine what the hell was wrong with these fools! All of a sudden it hit me! I had not identified myself, so as far as they were concerned, I was just another black guy in the bar to be tolerated. So I decided to try a little experiment. It was early enough for me to stay there for a significant amount of time and then leave and return later. So I did. However, when I returned I was in full makeup. It was as different as night and day. The whole place was as cordial as if I were the First Lady. The entire episode just sickened me. Nevertheless, I was committed to doing the booking. I was afraid that not doing so would have ruined other work opportunities here in town. But afterward, I would never set foot in the place. I never took another booking from them and I sure as hell never went in for any other reason.

Chapter 5

Chapter 5

My whole life was changing rapidly. I was still heavily involved in my full time job at the hotel, however the money from the shows was increasing. It had caught up and, in some instances, passed what I was earning at the hotel. That meant giving priority to the shows. Yet the yearning to feel a part of at work was making me feel that I needed to continue to be the best there that I could be when I was there. Add to that the growing awareness of my fellow hotel employees about my outside activities and you'll get a pretty good picture of where I was mentally during that period.

I was not at all ready to deal with their newfound knowledge (or speculations). I still sported a good sized helping of guilt. I had the nagging feeling that I was doing something wrong as I got older. It seemed to be always with me, lurking in the background. Much of the conflict arose from not being capable of embracing what I knew my inner truth to be. Society made no bones about telling me I was wrong but I still knew that inside the entire gay scene felt natural to me. The categories didn't matter at all to me. I just liked what I liked.

There were activities and things that were distinctly masculine that I loved just as there were things out there that the world sees as distinctly feminine that I loved just as much.

I remember one day after much angst about all the mixed up feelings I came to a sudden realization. Even before I knew what sex was, I recognized that I was much more drawn to persons of the same gender as me. I started having memories of feelings that I had as a child. While they were not explicit, they certainly had homoerotic overtones. I remember one dream in particular involving a kid that lived down the street from us when I was five years old. He was a really cute kid and we played together a lot. I recalled a scene in that dream where we were playing and had a sleepover. In the dream I was in a position of authority. I suppose I was something of a parental figure, and he was there in my care. He did something that made me feel the need to spank him and I can remember how exciting the thought of delivering this bare bottom spanking was to me.

Of course I didn't know anything about going any further at five years old, but I doubt anyone could call that dream anything other than homoerotic.

With that memory and a few others I soon realized that there was no way anything could be wrong with who I was or my sexual identity. How could I have chosen to be this way? These were thoughts that I had even before I knew what sex was! Unfortunately by the time I began puberty and started to experience actually having sex, the social taboo had been made all too clear to me. That pressure was way too much for a fourteen year old kid to bear. I didn't really see any options though.

Shortly after starting to work in shows earnestly, I also began to discover the availability of sex venues in the gay community. That is to say venues that were there SOLELY for the purpose of sex. I was already going to bookstores in the city having been introduced to them by newfound friends. And of course the park was still a part of my life, though its attraction was waning fast. Not too much was happening there these days since it had been closed to motorized traffic. But I would soon discover a brand new venue. It would become my favorite by far and my main sexual outlet for many years to come.

I really don't remember how I first heard about the gay baths, but when I did it immediately sparked my curiosity. I was never one to enjoy the banal chatter and games that you have to be a part of the bar scene. I absolutely hate all the little immature posturing that goes on in gay bars. I believed that if two people were interested in one another they should just honestly admit it and go from there. Public opinion has no place in the decision of who one should date, sleep with, talk to, marry, etc. That's what makes the games in the bars so ridiculous to me. Enter the baths.

I started to notice ads for them in the gay magazines and decided to check them out. Now for someone like me who chose to accept a failing grade in high school gym class rather than show my body getting dressed in front of a lot of guys, the whole idea of walking around in a building of naked guys was intensely erotic, but also scary as hell. Of course all the ads you saw showed the most flawless beauties with the most stunning bodies imaginable. So I just knew that I would be ostracized.

Because of this I worried if I would be able to go at all. It was so mysterious, yet exciting at the same time.

I quickly found the sentiments surrounding the baths in the gay community were divided. Some thought that the baths were cool while others thought that the place was probably full of old trolls and still others felt it was simply degenerate. What I actually found when I finally visited was that in my opinion, there was a little truth in each claim.

Strangely enough almost all the people that I talked to who felt the places were horrible were usually the people who'd never even gone to the baths. This is not very different from most situations in life. People fear what they don't understand.

At any rate, in my first experience there, I seemed to get a little taste of each sentiment. It was slightly scary, exciting as hell, and even a little repulsive, but not much! I remember when I got to the door and the guy asked for the I.D. I didn't quite know what to expect and wasn't at all sure that I wanted to give him my credentials so readily. But I quickly realized that it was just for the purposes of making out my membership card. Most of the bath houses in this country are private clubs after all.

I paid my entry fee and went in. He asked if I wanted to rent a room, which consisted of a small changing cubicle with a cot inside, or a standard locker for my clothes. With all my body image issues this was a no brainer for me. I took the room and went on my merry way.

Once inside I found that while there were lots of men, some quite attractive, most were flawed mortals just like the rest of us. Not all were gym produced bodies. Most were just average guys, some indeed were a little older, and some sported paunches. Once in a great while however I did encounter the actual living god which would take my breath away.

Very quickly I got the hang of how this was done. It was not very different from the way of park cruising. The one difference was there was a somewhat more relaxed atmosphere since there was no worry of unexpected police presence there.

It's a funny thing but after a while being in the company of many men in various stages of undress, it was strange that a new guy coming in off the street still clothed could generate more interest than all that exposed flesh. Once he disrobed however he would become just like the rest of us.

I got settled in my room and began to tour the halls just like the rest of the patrons. I was surprised at the decor of the place. It was quite tastefully done. Well lighted and clean; Not at all what I'd expected. Upstairs were two hallways on which there were about thirty rooms each. And the front of the building was a well-furnished television lounge and snack area. Off to the right just as one entered was a separate room housing lockers for those who chose to check their clothes without the benefit the private room provided. Downstairs was the wet area. This included the indoor/outdoor pool, the steam room, the dry sauna and the whirlpool. The latter seated up to fifteen people. There was also a maypole style shower with multiple showerheads. The place was well laid out and well appointed.

At this point I would be remiss if I did not address some of the things that I hear out in the community about the baths and their patrons. I've been a patron of these establishments for approximately thirty odd years and in that period I've traveled North America and Europe a good bit. I personally take offense at all the negative connotation that's placed on the baths and the patrons therein. People, especially gay people, seem ready to instantly label them as the harbor of disease and filth. Not so. In the establishments that I've patronized throughout the United States, Canada, the United Kingdom and Europe-and there have been many- I have found quite often that the opposite is true. Not only are a great many of the establishments clean and well-maintained, but the patrons of most bath houses are as responsible as any guys that you see patronizing many a gay bar. Sometimes even more so.

Most people that go to the baths regularly for sex usually get the bulk of their sexual needs met in just that way. So there develops this body of regular patrons there. That means that by and large the members recognize each other and just about know one another's patterns. It's true that occasionally there will be a newcomer or an out of town guest, but mostly all are familiar. When the variations do occur they are easily identified and their pattern usually easily recognized.

I have found that patterns of behavior rarely change from location to location. Men that are conscious of cleanliness and safer sex are going to be that way no matter what bath house they patronize. Most regulars will go in and have one, maybe two encounters while there; with intervals of shower and toilette in between. There are of course those that will just go with anyone without any thought given to cleanliness. They are easily spotted however and equally easily avoided. Most regulars know them on sight.

In all fairness I have to add here that recently at the conclusion of a long term relationship I once again returned to patronize some of my favorite clubs. I was appalled at finding the number of men in some establishments that were apparently participating in more risky behavior that I had encountered in earlier years. But there again it's not the fault of the establishment. Most bath houses provide free condoms to all patrons; All that you want. Also many provide free HIV and STD screening and have time set aside for patrons to come in and have anonymous free tests done right on sight should they choose. The services are there for people should they choose to take advantage of them. So it's always been surprising to me that people are ready to cast the baths and their patrons as the main cause of the STD problems when all the time I've known many gay men that were going to the bars on the weekend, meeting men and picking them up for sex; Sometimes not even bothering to take the men home. Many are having sex in the parking lot or whatever and then often returning multiple times in an evening picking up additional partners; all the time with no thought given to safety or protection. Many are doing this while certainly not cleaning up very well in between. And a lot of these very guys will be the first to label the baths as trouble.

All this being said, I find what's difficult here is to talk about 'then' and keep it separate from 'now'. So much has changed since the period of which I'm speaking. So recognizing that, I'll just return to describing the events of the first night that I attended...

I was just about blown away by the casual atmosphere that I found there. Not the least bit stuffy or judgmental on the surface, the place was an instant hit with me. Pretty soon I was talking to a young man that turned out to be a very nice guy and we spent a pleasant time just chatting and getting to know each other. I guess he must have figured out this was all new to me, as I'm sure I must have looked wide eyed at it all to any experienced observer.

Before long we turned our attention to more intimate things and it was, and still is one of the most memorable encounters that I've ever had with a man. I remember his name was Rob and I was totally flabbergasted to find out he was married and had two kids at home! I was still somewhat naive at the time.

His gentleness and easy manner struck me as unusual. Even then I was beginning to form the opinion that a lot of gay men have not had the luxury of dating and learning to be considerate while lovemaking that is found with guys that started out with women.

We talked a bit more but soon he had to leave. I then decided that I would go exploring to see the remainder of the club - much of which I had not seen yet. I found myself in a dark room area of the club. I'm sure that when most guys give a club a bad rap this is one of the areas being referred to. But for the purpose of this writing, I will once again ask the reader to remember the time period. I'm speaking right now of the pre-AIDS period.

When I entered I was totally swallowed up by the darkness of the place. I could see only shapes and even those were not very clear. I could not see my hand in front of my face. It was so dark in there!

As I shuffled through, my leg bumped against the edge of a raised platform. I could just make out several bodies lying there. It was a rather large area covered with mattresses. There were many guys on it. Some were just lying there while others were engaged in various sexual activities. I was simultaneously freaked out and excited at the same time. Wow! Other than the quick, furtive encounters at the park, I had never been this close to absolute strangers totally stark naked and engaged in sexual activity. There was no sense of fear, or hurry. It was fascinating. Here I was watching a live sex show and I could have reached out and touched the players!

Soon after just sitting on the corner of the mattress for a while I looked behind me and noticed a space between this hefty guy sleeping there and the wall. That was perfect. He would be between me and the action and that was just fine with me! I'd had my fun, so I wasn't interested in joining in the play, but dammit, I wanted to watch!

For a minute the whole thing struck me as hilarious! How the hell could this guy sleep with all this going on around him? Nevertheless the big man was knocked out.

Confident that he would not bother me, and secure in the fact that he was so far gone that an air raid probably wouldn't have roused him, I settled in for a little voyeurism. My eyes were just beginning to get really adjusted to the darkness. I was beginning to see clearly some of the action going on around me when - OH NO! The hefty guy rolled over and trapped my arm underneath him! I was such a timid kid at the time. I just lay there trying to work my arm free without disturbing him. It took a bit of effort but I was finally able to free myself before my arm was completely numb. I got up and got the hell out of there while I still could!

I left the club that night with a sense of opening a new chapter. I had found a new adventure. It would not be long before I would expand my exploration to new cities and new clubs. I just always thought that being upfront about what I wanted was the best way. Better to go on to the baths and meet someone there than standing around in a bar getting drunk, wasting money and telling lies. Perhaps making choices that if I hadn't gotten drunk I would not have made. So it made perfect sense to me to do it this way.

I have to admit though that not every city and situation has given itself over to this theory. To be fair, I have been in some cities where the bath houses were simply atrocious. But it's just like anything else. I wouldn't check into a hotel that's an obvious flophouse, and by the same standard I've been known to turn around and walk right out of a bath house if the place was a dump and its patrons were sleazy. There are too many well-run upscale establishments in the world to put up with that.

Back around the time when I first started to patronize the baths, Club Miami was one of the nicest clubs in the country. It was well run and boasted a clientele from all around the globe. Featuring ' in and out' privileges for its members (meaning you could leave and come back within your allotted rental time), onsite masseurs, and a small restaurant and snack bar, it actually functioned as something of a precursor to the luxury spas available today for gay men. Sadly, Club Miami went through a really rough period and was quite a dump for a while. Though at the time of this writing I've heard that it's slated for remodeling and a much needed facelift.

Today there are many more clubs that fill the bill of glamorous multi-complexes. Many of them function as total entertainment complexes for gay men and feature far more amenities for their clientele than just sex. So you see they are not all just sex clubs. One that comes to mind is The

Deutsche-Eiche in Munich, Germany. It is one of the finest that I've ever come across. It's a very large establishment and houses a sauna, a hotel and a very nice little restaurant all under the same roof. It's quite professionally run and very comfortable. With a very personable and gorgeous staff . I cannot recommend it highly enough.

As I think back on the earlier times; the 1970's and 80's, I notice that as I would move into newer discoveries, I would often leave older practices behind. By now I was firmly a fixture at my new haunt; the bath houses. I had largely left bars behind except for working the shows. These years were quite a bit of fun for me but I now know that my life was largely a mess. I was in such denial about all that was going on that I didn't even know who I was. The food, the booze and the sex were flowing freely. And it seemed everyone around me both in the hotel and in the gay community at large was partaking of it. I was running wild, but there were many that made my exploits seem conservative by comparison. But my own conscience was winning out in lots of ways. I was never totally comfortable with either total conservative ideals or with being liberal to the point of having no boundaries at all.

The result being that I spent many years deriding myself and humbling myself in my own mind about what life should be for us all. Looking back on it I can see the tremendous toll it took on me, and just how ridiculous it was that I should have felt the need to hide who I was or what I thought just to please others.

I should have known that there would never be peace of mind as long as I was reacting to the shame of what I assumed people would think about me and my life. I think I gave into fear and obsessive thinking because I was still in such close proximity to those in my family and my native community.

Amidst all that fear, it never occurred to me to stop and look at the profession I was in. The hospitality industry is probably one of the most accepting of alternative lifestyles of any work environment out there. There are so many younger and unskilled people in that type of work that partying is the norm anyway. But no way was I thinking about that. I was just caught up and spinning in my own head about it.

Hiding from myself and using things to numb the pain and fear was a way of life. Then one night I was coming out of the baths and it dawned on me just what I was doing. It was one of those times when I've had the briefest glimmer of what was going on in my own subconscious. I suddenly could see the merry-go-round in my mind clearly. If things went well with meeting men I would go and eat something as a reward for a job well done. If I went to the clubs or to the baths and no one talked to me I ate to console myself because I was so horrible. I would usually make a pact with myself right then and there to get my eating under control the next day. However just as soon as the next set of circumstances presented themselves - positive or negative- I would find a reason to eat over them.

During all this I was still entertaining and liked working on the road from time to time. I was guesting at several clubs around town. But it was becoming more and more difficult to acquire out of town bookings without some type of title or pageant placement. Of course my weight was at issue here as well. One of my friends, Bill, who had been the bartender at The Onyx Lounge in the earlier years when I first started performing, said as much to me one night. We were chatting and I asked him what he thought I should do to finally break through and become headliner in the drag shows. He looked at me and said, "It's simple. Lose weight!" That brought on new concerns. I knew that to place in pageants I had to look good. And that was hard to do when I was getting fatter and fatter all the time.

I remembered reading a book that was written by someone in a personal relationship with a famous actor. He talked of how the entertainer in question would only eat salad greens and drink champagne when preparing for on screen appearances. It didn't sound like a half bad plan to me, so I decided to give it a try.   It was imperative that I do some pageants if I wanted to get my name known to club owners. I'd have to do something about the weight. The only other option was to try and go full time with a show here in town. And to do that would mean giving up the hotel job. I just wasn't willing to do that. It still felt more secure than just doing shows. I don't know how the salad and champagne thing did for the star, but for me it was a bust. I don't think I made it a week on that crazy routine.

I even started to make my clothes for pageants tighter as an incentive for me to lose weight in time for the upcoming event. Needless to say, this practice didn't last too long. It was much too uncomfortable and way too much trouble. I never lost that much doing it anyway. It was just one more way of trying to control a situation that at the time I couldn't see had nothing to do with the food.

It would be many more years before I would see the connectivity between my food consumption, my alcohol use, sexual behavior and my self-image. From time to time little things would come to light; like the time I went on vacation from the hotel and lost ten pounds just from not being around readily available food every day. I also noticed that when I was not at work at the hotel, or not doing drag somewhere I could and would spend endless hours on the hunt for anonymous sexual partners. I now see that all these behaviors exhibited similar qualities; Extreme highs and then falling to extreme lows. They also had an 'all or nothing' quality about them. I can now clearly see there was classic 'black and white' thinking.

Also, the food, sex and booze were all ways to try and fill a void that seemed to constantly be there.

As my presence in the gay community grew my worlds showed signs of collision. Frankly, I had no intention of letting that happen. I made some really stupid mistakes and allowed a couple of things to be delivered in the mail to my parents' home that had to do with my gay life and my sister caught on with no problem. Also, my nephews were growing up and becoming more inquisitive every day.

They started to make forages into my room and went through my personal belongings. That's when the problems started to make real headlines in the family.

I came home from work one evening to find an array of gay porno magazines spread across my bed. Apparently my nephews had been snooping in my room, found the things and one was headed to school with one of the magazines in his book bag to show his little friends!

Another time I came home to find pictures of myself in drag out in plain view on my bed in my room. It was clear that it was time for me to move on from the current living situation. It didn't help that one of my nephews was showing what I suspected to be clear signs of being gay. With things like they were I could see that I would probably be blamed for that if I stayed around. Not to mention the fact that all these different personalities were hell to keep separate. I had more facades going than that girl 'Sybil', in the 1970's story about multiple personalities, it seemed.

By now it was approaching the end of 1979. Many things in my life were taking on a new shape. But through all the changes my primary friendships with Ernie and Greg remained constant. The funny thing about true friendship is that no matter what goes on in your life these are the people with whom we seem to maintain contact. Despite distance, long hiatus, love affairs, or whatever, they are the 'go to' in our lives. For me, these were the folks that never changed. That's the real 'until death do us part'.

Greg and Ernie had both become more a part of the Backstreet pretty boy crowd, while I was more a part of the show crowd at the time. However, we still talked on the phone on a regular basis and still saw each other from time to time. Over the preceding years Ernie had been in a relationship with a guy named David. He was the manager of Stephen's Saloon, one of the local bars. Their relationship had been a rocky one, but it had lasted for a while. It was one of the strangest relationships that I ever saw Ernie enter. He and David didn't seem to have anything in common. Nor did David seem to like any of Ernie's friends. In fact, he didn't seem to have any friends of his own or to socialize within the community at all. He seemed to be something of a nerd so when they finally parted company it was with more of a whimper than a bang. Perhaps at the outset that was the very thing that Ernie saw in him - the fact that David was somewhat removed from the rest of his bar buddies.

It wasn't until the relationship hit the rocks that David began to thaw and try socializing with some of Ernie's friends. Much later on Ernie even said that he (David) made no secret of the fact that he didn't get why Ernie insisted on 'hanging out with fag hags, black guys and the like'. He said that David would question him endlessly about us when they were home alone. Maybe he just was insecure and didn't really know how to mix with the masses. At least that's what later events led me to believe.

Whatever the issue had been, after they split David started to call me trying to make friends. Hearing from him was a total shock, and I had no clue what the hell was going on. I immediately called Ernie and told him what was up. Suddenly David was calling me asking me to hang out and do things! This was when Ernie told me he didn't get it either since David had never made a secret of not liking black people. So we decided that I should go with it and see what developed.

Pretty soon it became clear to us that David was on a mission to re-make himself. I agreed to hang with him and when he would call I would go over and run around with him. Apparently he felt that his being such a stick in the mud was why the split had occurred.

First thing I noticed was that he'd done away with the glasses and was now wearing contacts. Pretty soon his hair had grown out some from its usual short conservative style and he was buying more stylish and better fitting clothes. I laughingly told Ernie before long that David was indeed on the road to becoming a budding hottie! Ernie laughed and said he didn't give a damn what David became. He wouldn't be going back to him.

David did make great strides that year toward becoming a different guy; At least on the outside. I soon learned what my role in the whole thing was. As I've said I was beginning to become known in the gay community, so my 'celebrity'; how-ever acquired, was necessary for the opening of certain doors and getting noticed by people. If he ran with me he could get in just about anywhere with no charge, often drink for free, etc.

I assume it was working because by that New Year's Eve we were hanging out regularly. We decided to go to Numbers, a bar on Cheshire Bridge Rd. to ring in the New Year. Lisa King, one of the local drag stars who was also a good friend of mine was to perform right after the countdown. We went early to get there before the crowd was rolling well. Since I'd worked Numbers on occasion we breezed right in with no cover charge and no need to stand in a line.

David had learned his lessons well. I remember looking at him as we danced before midnight and being a bit shocked. I had noticed before that his look was hot, but that night he'd outdone himself. He had on a black turtleneck sweater that clung to his chest just right. His hair (natural yellow blond) was cut to just graze his shoulders and shone like luscious corn silk. He had on a pair of black jeans that were fitting his ass just snugly enough to make your eyes go right to the prize, but not so tight as to look uncomfortable. In short, the guy had it going on that night! I too had gone out of my way to look the part of the hot big black stud man and was playing my role well. In those days it was perfectly acceptable and actually a plus to be a hot man when out of drag, and yet be able to look lovely when made up. Drag was still an art back then.

As we danced to the Village People's song 'Ready for the 80's' I looked around and saw that much of the attention and approving glances on the dance floor were centered on us. I was thinking; does it get any better than this? Well I didn't know about better but it certainly got livelier.

Soon it was time for the countdown and the ringing in of the New Year. I looked at David and wished him a Happy New Year. We kissed each other briefly at that instant. In my mind, the kiss was no more than a 'friendly peck'. Then he said the damnedest thing. He made it very clear just what my role had been. He actually made the comment, "Tony what are you doing? I'm sure Ernie told you that I don't really like black guys". I guess he wanted to make sure that I didn't mistake that kiss for anything more than just a friendly gesture. Well, fuck him. I really didn't think he was worth getting upset about. I decided to just watch the show rather than let him get my head in a bad place.

I don't remember much about the show, but that's no wonder. We were all pretty plastered in there that night. I do remember that while Lisa was attempting to do her first number she was being upstaged terribly. For all of us that had managed to secure a spot down front of the stage were being treated to a live sex show by these two guys who were obviously determined to have a REALLY Happy New Year. They had laid out on the floor right in front of the stage and were commencing a pretty hot 69 session right there on the floor! After her number concluded Lisa grabbed the microphone and attempted to talk to the crowd. Noticing that she was not being paid the least bit of attention she nudged the two guys with the toe of her shoe and said, "excuse me honey, but you guys can't just lay here and do this! You've got to go! Get a room or something." They both got up and adjusted what was left of their clothing. They stumbled off drunkenly to the roaring laughter and applause of the crowd.

The whole little scene lightened my mood considerably. I finished out the evening not the slightest bit bummed over David or his clear attempted usage of me. Did I really want to even know David as a person? Even though he had a new look, under the clothes and the haircut, wasn't he still just the same uptight asshole he'd always been ? Weren't those two guys doing it on the floor taking things just a little too far? Weren't we all in the community taking things just a little too far? Drugs were everywhere. We were all sexing it up all over the place like never before. Were any of us really "Ready for the 80's" as the song implied?

Had I known then what was to come perhaps I would have looked at the whole evening differently. Little did we know that all of this craziness was the calm before the storm.

1980 ; the start of a new decade. There was so much that had happened in the seventies. I doubted much could top all that had happened to me since I finished high school. It was all constantly changing and so far it really had been wonderful. But then, seemingly overnight it all just seemed to go wrong.

I doubt there is anyone who was around and out in the gay community in the early 80's that will tell you the period was anything other than horror filled. This is why many of us now have a hard time with the cavalier attitude that the generation of today seem to have toward HIV.

To say that what was going on was akin to a living nightmare doesn't really do it justice. It's so easy to say those words. But to live through that situation was a million times more devastating than just mere words can express.

For most of us it started as a series of little articles in the local gay community newspapers, and then small mentions in the local major newspapers about this strange new illness that people in New York and San Francisco were getting. There were reports of purple colored bruising that people were showing up in hospitals with. These physical markings along with flu-like symptoms were the earliest indicators that something was amiss. Many of the reports were quite conflicting. It was hard to know what was real and what was conjecture and paranoia.

After the initial symptoms appeared, it was said that they would often go away for a bit, only to return in a short time. It was also said that several people coming into the hospitals were coming up with strange lesions. The media said that the doctors were saying they had some type of cancer. By far the biggest news was that this appeared to only be happening to gay men.

The illness was first dubbed the Gay Man's Cancer. My friends and I began to breathe a little easier because everyone knew that cancer wasn't contagious! Surely this was just some blip on the news. Not unlike the reports that had come out a couple of years earlier about some type of issue that was found within gay men concerning amoebas. They had called it Amoebiasis. Before long the talk about that had died down. Surely this would do the same...

But little by little we began to notice that people were not letting this new thing go. They were actually talking about it, and it appeared to be spreading. It seemed that throughout the community someone would know someone else in another city that knew someone that supposedly had it. And then it hit.

Almost like the plagues that you read about in history books that came about in times of old. People started getting sick at an absolutely staggering rate. It seemed that you would see someone this week and he'd be a young, vibrant and healthy looking young man. Then in a matter of days you would see him again and he would be skeletal. It would look as though he'd aged forty years in a weeks' time. People were becoming gaunt with sunken eyes and their hair falling out in a matter of weeks. And then within a few months you wouldn't see them anymore. The horror stories were taking on a whole new dimension and there was plenty of evidence to make them believable. We started to hear stories of people who "had it" all over town and in every bar. As you went about in midtown it was the conversation that was on everyone's lips.

There's a realization that I've adopted. It has come to me as a result of the things that have happened in my life. Many of which threw me into complete panic and near hysteria even though I knew there was literally nothing I could do to change them. That realization is that no matter how horrible and shocking something is, I can only stay in a state of hysteria for a certain amount of time. Then I have to move on through other emotions.

That sentiment describes the mood of the gay community here in Atlanta at that time. This new illness which soon had been dubbed AIDS was very much on everybody's mind. However, since there was no cure, and it seemed nothing could be done, we had no choice but to go on with our daily lives. Oh - you can bet it was always there just under the surface, but we still had to try and function the best we could despite the updates of illness and terror that we all were constantly hearing. We went about our jobs, we did benefits, we whispered amongst ourselves and we tried to ignore and forget. And many of us did this quite effectively. But inevitably there seemed to be always a reminder coming up somewhere very near. For the first time I saw obituary sections popping up in the gay community newspapers and magazines.

Even with the worry about AIDS, it seemed that maybe drag might be a workable profession for me. Things were really off to a good start with this New Year. I was more established than ever in the community of female impersonation. And in the Southeast my bookings were really taking off. My reach was expanding. Bar managers and Show Directors were beginning to request me. I no longer had to solicit bookings as much. In just about every contest I entered I was placing in the top three. The bar owners and managers were seeking me out.

In addition to the work onstage I was also beginning to gather more costuming clients from outside the drag community. More legitimate theater clients.

While I had long realized that my living situation needed to change, now it was really imperative. All that was beginning to happen was making home life harder and harder to deal with. And besides that, I was older and it was just time to move on.

It's hard to describe just how difficult the thought of leaving my parents' home was to me. I've always been careful no matter how it looked on the outside. The main reason it had taken so long for me to make the move to go - even though I'd wanted out since before leaving high school - was that I didn't want to live in the manner that so many of my friends did. They were all mostly moving from apartment to apartment, not able to make rent; with roommates that were making their lives hell. It just didn't seem like the direction I wanted to go in.

I've always been pretty self-sufficient and wanted to be sure I could make it on my own before I went stumbling out there. Trying it out as a tipped employee just didn't seem do-able to me. I'd had plenty of experience with how erratic tips could be. But whatever I had thought in the past, I knew the move must come now.

As I've said my nephews were becoming more and more inquisitive every day and since they spent a good deal of time at my parents' home, I didn't want the friction this could potentially cause.

Looking for somewhere to live when you've never done so and being a bit of a perfectionist with limited funds makes for an interesting mix. I first started by asking friends what they thought I should do. Many were more than helpful. All the suggestions they gave were taken into account. Many were things that I had never considered and it gave me a new outlook on the whole situation.

My biggest obstacle was the fear of the unknown. Much of the fear of failure stuff that lurked in the shadows concerning my entire life really showed up here. I have no idea what I thought would happen. After all, by this time I was in my twenties and certainly able to think for myself. So I guess it was just that little extra push that I needed at the start to get out there.

One suggestion that I took was that since it was my first time out on my own to try and get a place near someone that I already knew. That was received with open arms at the time, but now I can see it was really a mixed blessing.

I ended up moving into a small complex with two apartment buildings. It was off Cheshire Bridge Rd. and my friend William already lived there. He was doing shows as well and I thought it a good idea that he lived in the same building just a few doors down.

Most folks who knew William knew that he was just a little eccentric, to say the least, but I had no idea just how much until I lived next to him. He would often have these wild imaginings that people were watching him and trying to figure out what he was up to. For instance - there was this

Hispanic woman and her husband that lived in the apartment next to mine. William lived upstairs over them. Because the woman would be outside often when he left to go to work at night, he became really paranoid that they were out to get him. Mind you, it was not surprising that she would stare. William worked one night a week at The Sports Page. It was a lesbian bar down the street from the complex. On Wednesday nights rather than getting ready for work there at the club he would leave home in full drag in front of the neighbors and walk to work. Of course they became curious. After all, he was as tall as I. Six feet and two inches flat footed. Put on a pair of heels, and that's a spectacle!

This was another reason that I opted to dress at the club where I worked. Just to avoid just these types of scenes. I really think that in his mind William was convinced that they didn't know it was him that came out of his apartment on Wednesdays! He basically said as much.

The other sticky point that I ran into living that close to him was his invasion of my privacy. I'm a rather private person and I enjoy my solitude. He took to coming over all the time when I got off work in the evenings. It was usually around eleven or so. And the bad part was that he would not leave. One time I was there with a date and I literally had to take William out into the hall and ask him to leave. He simply would not take the subtle hint. It was very difficult to get him to understand that I didn't want him or anybody invading my space on a constant basis. I didn't mind the occasional visit, but when it was all the time it became a problem. He even took to inviting his guests to come down and use my phone since he didn't have one. On one occasion he sent some guy down to meet up with me to ask for a ride. William knew that I would be leaving shortly for work. I went out and the guy was waiting by my car. He introduced himself and told me that William had said that I'd probably give him a ride. He then asked if I minded him using my phone before we left. Since I still had a couple of things to do before leaving I said ok. Later I found out the guy had placed a long distance call on the phone, which, at the time, was rather costly.

In other ways the complex was a little strange all on its own. There was the man living in the building across the way whose Doberman lived in his station wagon. And then there was the couple who lived across the hallway from me. They had a young son, a Doberman, a cocker spaniel mix, and a poodle all living in the apartment. Their apartment was the same floor plan as mine - a one bedroom with living room, dining/kitchen combo, and bathroom. Where the hell they put themselves, the kid, and all that livestock is anybody's guess!

But despite all this, it was my first apartment and I loved it. I quickly became something of a hermit there. My friends were beginning to ask after me. They no longer saw me in the bars as much. I was just glad to have somewhere to go to find some solitude. In the last few years at my parent's home I mostly just slept there and went in to change my clothing. I couldn't really have any privacy there so often I would go out to the clubs even if I didn't want to. Once I had my own place, I began spending more time at home rather than haunting the bars so much.

I'll never forget the advice Ernie gave me about making rent. He told me that he totally understood the fear of not being able to handle it when you worked for tips. He told me that in his first place he figured out how much it would take per day to make his month's rent. And he would isolate that amount every day in a jar in his cupboard in order to insure the rent would be there when needed. I thought that was really sweet. And while I never actually put that system to test I did have to learn that some sacrifices had to be made at times to keep things on the even keel.

All was going along swimmingly until Donnie came to town. It was then that I learned just how unskilled I was at setting boundaries.

Donnie was a friend of Ernie's that I had met a few years earlier. When we met, he was in the process of leaving a relationship to move to southern California. Well one early spring evening I was working in the show at a Midtown bar called Illusions, when in between numbers I went to the bar to get a drink. It was a weeknight, and the first show, so the bar was still pretty empty. There he stood; not looking a day older or any different than he'd looked when he left Atlanta.

We quickly greeted each other and struck up a conversation. I told him that it was really great to see him. I had liked him before he left and remembered him to be a very nice guy. He seemed to always have a smile on his face. He told me that he'd just returned; had just gotten in that evening in fact. I welcomed him and offered to buy him a drink. We soon started talking about old times and he said that he'd missed Atlanta and all the fun he'd had here.

Donnie was originally from Rome, Ga. Not too far from Atlanta, but pretty rural at the time. He asked if I'd seen Ernie lately. I told him that Ernie had gone to Texas for a couple of weeks' vacation. This disturbed him. He said that he'd been counting on finding Ernie so that he could ask if he could stay with him while he got on his feet. He said that more than anything, he didn't want to have to go home to his folks in Rome.

With my own home situation such as it was, I could certainly understand that. So when he asked if he could stay with me for a few days until Ernie returned I said sure. I explained that my place was really small, so he'd have to sleep on the couch. He said that was fine and thanked me. I finished my show and off we went.

I doubt it took William all of six hours to spread to all my friends that there was this cute guy staying with me. Naturally that took off like a forest fire. People were calling me trying to find out who he was. I took it all in stride, but have to say that it was amazing just how fast the story took on a life of its own.

I told Donnie not to worry about anything. I foolishly thought in those days that two could live as cheaply as one. I told him to concentrate on getting work and if he could help me out with some money, fine, but if not, he shouldn't worry about it. I truly was young and naive at the time.

In just the first week I could already see how challenging this was going to be. The washing powder and soap was flying out of the house as if it had wings. To be fair he did provide some of his own food, but that was not much. All other essentials - shampoo, toothpaste, condiments, toilet paper, etc., were taking a real beating.

I noticed that he was going out partying but not much was said about getting work. He had mentioned the company he worked for in California had a plant here in Atlanta and that he intended to talk to them about getting on here. I said fine, but that I didn't think it would hurt to go and try to get something temporary until that came through so he would have some type of income. He agreed, but for the next week or so I heard nothing suggesting that he was trying to do that. Also by this time I was sure that Ernie had returned to town, but any talk of Donnie moving in with him was showing up in the conversation less and less these days.

Then one morning I awoke to find a strange guy in my bathroom. This would not have been so much a problem, as I assumed correctly that he had come in the previous night with Donnie. But the guy was obviously really rough and probably a street hustler. I'm no prude, but I am particular about who I let into my home. Additional problems came when I went to do laundry and found that they'd made quite a mess of the linens that I'd loaned Donnie to use. One piece of which was a satin bedspread. Donnie didn't even bother to mention the mess, much less offer to take it and get it dry cleaned. He'd just balled all the linen together and stuffed it in a corner. All the stains had set in the spread and it had to be trashed. I was livid and disgusted.

I decided that I needed to have a talk with Donnie about the types of guys he was obviously interested in. He told me that he liked the rough boys and that's usually what he went for. I told him that was his choice, but they wouldn't be welcome in my house. He said ok and I thought that was the end of it.

All went ok for a while but by now I was more than ready to have my place back to myself. From time to time I saw evidence that things were happening when I was not home that I probably wouldn't have approved of, but there was no proof so I held my tongue.

Then on Labor Day weekend of that year I went to Chicago for the Ms. Continental U.S.A. Pageant. I was to be gone for a week and I left Donnie there in the apartment. He had begun to work by that time and was telling me in fact that he was working two jobs, though I had yet to see any money. I kept telling him to get himself together so that he could go on and get a place of his own and that would be thanks enough.

The afternoon that I returned from Chicago Donnie was not in the apartment when I arrived home. I assumed he was at work. I went into the bedroom and was instantly aware that someone had been in my bed. This was bad enough. I consider my bedroom really personal space; Almost sacred. No one is to enter without invitation from me. But then I found evidence that not only had he been sleeping in my bed, but he'd been having sex there as well. I lost it and went ballistic. It was all I could do not to throw his things out into the parking lot.

I paced the floor that evening until he came home. He took one look at me and was instantly aware that something was up. I took a deep breath and promised myself that I would handle this like an adult. I told him that I knew he'd been screwing in my bed. He of course tried to deny it, but the evidence pretty much trapped him. I told him that I would under no circumstances tolerate that and if he couldn't respect my wishes around the subject he'd have to leave. He said that he understood and that it wouldn't happen again.

That night I was planning to go out to the bars and he asked if he could get a ride into midtown with me. I said sure and shortly after that we dressed and left for the evening. I headed to Mrs. P's, a popular leather and Levi bar on Ponce de Leon Ave. I have no idea where he intended to go, but when I let him out of the car, I said that I would see him later.

Usually in those days when I went to the bar it was never just to drink. I generally went to see if I could meet someone and that night was no exception. Oddly enough, I did meet someone right off the bat when I walked in. He and I talked for a bit and had a couple of drinks. Pretty soon we decided to leave the bar. I told him that we could go back to my place and have a drink there. He was cool with that, so off we went. I had not been gone more than an hour, but sure enough there was Donnie when I walked in with a date in my bedroom laid up on my bed. My date, seeing that something was amiss, immediately started making noises about leaving. I convinced him not to. I assured him this was my apartment, and that if he'd give me a few seconds I'd get this sorted out. Once in the kitchen I flew all over Donnie. I told him that if he didn't get the hustler out of my house, I would. And I promised him it would not be done tactfully either. And furthermore if he didn't want to do that, he could get the hell out with the guy!

He went back into the living room and told the guy they'd have to leave. Gratefully he had the good sense to stay away the whole evening.

The next morning upon his arrival I told him straight out that he'd have to be gone by the end of the week. It crushed him. He did as I asked and found somewhere to go, but within a week was back asking me to consider moving into a larger apartment. He wanted me to consider us becoming legitimate roommates. It was then that we had a long talk and I realized that he'd never lived alone. He was just not equipped to handle it. It was like the guy needed parenting or something. He begged and pleaded but I'd had enough. I told him that the reason I didn't have a roommate was that I never wanted one. My intention had been only to help him through a rough time. He had moved in around May, and it was now nearly October. Really I was sorry for him. I never saw him again after that. I don't know if he stayed in Atlanta or returned to Rome, GA. I wished him well though. I had my own issues to deal with, and they were beginning to heat up a bit.

That was my one, albeit unplanned, experience with a roommate, and it taught me a good bit about my own limitations with setting boundaries. It's a lesson that I still have to work on today. The other side of the whole Donnie fiasco was that my parents now thought they had something tangible that they could point to as a bold statement from me about my sexuality.

When they found he was staying with me I was called on the carpet. My father made this call to my job and left a message that I needed to call him immediately. When I returned the call I was told in no uncertain terms that I needed to come to their home the next day.

Upon my arrival I was immediately reprimanded for my obvious inappropriate behavior. It was insinuated that there must be something unsavory going on, or surely that's how it would appear since the apartment was so small. It was obvious that they were convinced that we were sleeping together since they had seen the apartment and knew its size.

Since there had been no conversation about my personal relationships since I'd told my mother and sister that I was gay, this forced their hand and made my father decide that he needed to talk to me about it. I saw red with rage. What I think angered me so was the fact that never before had he and I had an in-depth talk about my sexuality, or much else for that matter, and now he was accusing me of doing something that would "look bad to people". Maybe I wouldn't have gotten so angry if I had been sleeping with Donnie. But the fact that I wasn't, and that I was in my own apartment. I was an adult paying my own bills and making my own decisions. The incredulity of the situation was the catalyst that pushed me over the edge. I stormed out after telling them as much. Just then, the strangest thing happened. My car had been working perfectly fine when I got there. But for some reason when I was leaving I could not get it to start. I don't know whether I flooded the engine in my haste to start it or what, but I was stuck in the driveway. That gave my mother just enough time to come outside and try and calm me down. She asked me to come back in but I said there was no way I could go back in there right then. She talked to me for a bit and finally I calmed down some and the car started.

It was a while before it dawned on me, but during the entire six months that Donnie was there my father came over only once or twice. After he left, when my dad did come over he would walk through my apartment like he was doing an inspection or something. This only served to enrage me further. It was one of the most difficult times I ever had with my father and I think if things had continued along that course we would probably have ended up with a severely strained, if not severed relationship. But as we both soon discovered there were other issues on the horizon that would overshadow all our issues.

By now it was 1982 and the money in the downtown hotel business was not at all as good as it had once been. It looked as though it would all but dry up. I was not prepared for the near dead holiday season that the hotels always went through. No one stays in hotels during the Thanksgiving and Christmas holidays. If they're traveling at all, it's usually to family or friends where they'll be staying.

It didn't help that there were newer and bigger hotels downtown now. So the regular conventions and customers that we once had were choosing to go to other properties. There was much more competition for that slice of convention pie that up to that point, Marriott and Hyatt downtown had controlled . Nights that most waiters could average $65-$90 in tips, suddenly became $35 nights. Just as I'd feared when I went out on my own, the financial bottom was falling out of my world. With the funds drying up I was afraid that I wouldn't be able to meet my responsibilities and I felt more depressed than I had in a long time.

Suddenly the drag work was much more than a pastime. The pressure that I felt when doing shows was now increased. It was imperative that I book show dates, and that I was successful when entertaining. I needed these funds to keep going. They had become a very necessary part of my income.

That made it all rather difficult. My attitude around drag had always been that I could walk away whenever I wanted. It had not been what was paying my bills. That took some of the pressure away concerning whether I was making a good impression on my audiences. I now had to really consider whether I went on bookings, and even the amount of salary I was willing to accept. Now it HAD to be within a certain parameter.

The psychological trauma that I was going through trying to juggle acceptance of who I was, the fear and pressure of stage work, money problems, and the health and well-being of aging parents was becoming just a little too much.

I was beginning to panic. I found myself in a position where I felt things were closing in on me. I was desperate to stay in my own place, but could not for the life of me see how that would be possible with things as bad financially as they were. The checks were bouncing and the rent was due.

I went to the landlord and told him that while I may be able to make the rent for the next month, beyond that, I just was not sure.

I don't know if it was youth, fear, or Divine Intervention, but the only solution I could see was to go home to my parents. I would have rather done anything to keep from doing that, but at the time it seemed to be the best I could come up with.

It turned out to be a timely decision for it was around this time that my mother, having been diagnosed with multiple myeloma some years earlier- began having some difficulties. To my knowledge she had been in remission for the last five years or so, but the difficulties had returned.

She was very weak and was also having some problems with bleeding. I'm sure there were other difficulties of which I was not made aware.

Both my parents were beginning to get up in age and with me being the youngest kid in the bunch I guessed that even if I were not having money problems it still would have fallen on me to go home and be there with them. All the others had kids or spouses or homes with mortgages.

So with much misgiving and a true sense of having failed miserably, I packed up all my belongings and trudged back home to the folks.

A great deal of that time is really foggy. I was extremely depressed and pretty much just floated through from day to day on this cloud of discontent. Here I was once again in the bedroom that I spent so many miserable hours as a teen hoping to flee. I felt that all the work and struggle to get out and gain my independence was a failure. It didn't take long for my spirits to plummet to the lowest depths.

My room was a complete mess. There were food wrappers, dirty clothes, and all sorts of junk all over the place. You couldn't find a clear space on the floor to walk on. It was a testament to my inner state as well. It was clearly a visual homage to my emotional disposition.

I remember one night I was sitting up in bed attempting to read a book and suddenly I heard something scratching in the walls. I freaked out! I had no idea what it was, but it sounded like it was coming through. As I listened closer I noticed there were faint scuttling sounds all over the place in the dark.

My bedroom was in the downstairs portion of the house, just off the family room. It had always had a somewhat 'dungeon - like' feel to it. It could also be damp and could show signs of mildew at the best of times. In the past I had really liked that it was removed from the rest of the house even if I didn't like having to deal with the obvious problems it presented. But this new addition of scuttling sound effects was just a little too much even for me.

The next morning I asked my dad about it and he said they'd had some problems with some mice. Well that was just about it for me. I lost it. I told him if necessary I would go out and get another job if he couldn't handle the expense, but we would have to do something about this. I would NOT stay there with rats! Like most men he told me I was overreacting. He assured me they were only little mice. Mice, rats, it was all the same to me!

As I look back on it now, this drives home to me just how difficult it is for older people to cover all life's incidentals when living on a fixed income. It really pains me that they were struggling that badly and at the time I was too naive or self-absorbed to see. With a sick wife and being retired himself it's no wonder that he couldn't get all that needed to be handled there under control.

With a little effort we were able to make the little night visitors get gone, but that still didn't make me happy to be there. My dad tried everything he could to figure out why I was in such a bad mental state. I could never make him understand that it was not about anything that was necessarily wrong with home; it was that I just didn't want to be there. I wanted my own place very badly and having to give it up felt like failure.

Also that little taste of freedom from my family had given me a chance to see what it could be like to not have to hide. It let me see how it could be to begin to accept myself for who I was. For once I didn't have to be so secretive about what I had in my house or what I did in my house. And now, once again I had to be clandestine about my life. I think all gay people will agree once you've begun your coming out process no matter how hard you try you can't put the genie back in the bottle.

Much of that time I spent just out in the streets. I would leave home to go to work, always carrying extra clothes with me. Afterward, I would change at work and head out to the clubs. I would stay out until it was time to go home and to sleep. Once home I would sleep until just about time to take my shower for work and then start the cycle over again. I was only using the house as a place to sleep. I had no relationship with the place because I really didn't want to be there. Many times I stayed out at the clubs or visited friends when I didn't even want to just to keep from going home. I actually had proven to myself when I was in my apartment that it wasn't necessarily the clubs and the streets that were priority to me, it was my privacy and space.

Of course the family wasn't pleased with me. Mostly because they assumed that all I was interested in was party-ing. And I wasn't pleased with them because I knew that they couldn't accept my sexual orientation and thus would never be satisfied with me. The whole scene was just BAD.

Factor in the guilt that I felt about being a disappointment to them, the lying about places I was going and things I
was doing and then put in the worry about my mother's health
and it's a wonder I could function at all.

I would feel so guilty about having to lie when I would
go out of town on bookings.

Add those feelings to the actual fact that a lot of the
bookings that I was doing at the time were indeed in very small
towns in Georgia, South and North Carolina, and Tennessee.
In many of these places the people definitely had issues with
people of color, not to mention gay people of ANY type. Also
a lot of the towns still had laws on the books making men
appearing in public in women's clothing illegal, though they
rarely enforced them. Still, on occasion they would get the
wise idea to go and 'hassle the fags'. Looked at from this view-
point it's no wonder that my stress level was off the charts. I
thought it was a surefire recipe for disaster. I still marvel at the
fact that I was able to keep it together enough to walk on stage
anywhere.

My obsessive nature was running unchecked then too.
One time in conversation someone told me a strange story
involving the SweetGumHead Bar. They told me that in an
earlier incarnation, someone had walked into the place and
shot some people. He supposedly killed many people including a performer onstage at the time. It supposedly happened
back when the place was a straight club. I never knew if this
was true but I worked that bar often and became obsessed
that the same could happen to me since it was indeed pretty
much a direct shot from the door in the lobby to the stage. I
mean, what would it take for some fool hating gays to walk in
and just start shooting? I never did find out if anything like
that had happened in the buildings' history, but I never again
walked on that stage without that fleeting thought running
through my mind.

With all the stress I was under, I was pretty much an emotional wreck. When I factored in the very real fear that the likely conclusion to my mom's situation would be her death, it seemed anything was possible.

It was also just about this time that AIDS became a true reality for most of us here in Atlanta. Up to now it had been real, but distant. Other than the tales from people who had friends in other places sick there hadn't been any cases here where someone had died who was known to everybody in town; So there was still a surreal feeling about the entire thing. There were the rumors that this person had it or that person had it, but most of the people who actually did have it were 'disappearing' by going home to family or were so sick that they ceased going out in public or whatever. All anyone really knew was that they just were *'no longer there...'*

It suddenly became the norm for the gay community newspapers and magazines to run an obituary section in every issue. Prior to this crisis that was virtually unheard of. We were all young and going to live forever. I remember there was this kid a few years earlier that had been jogging around the lake in Piedmont Park and had a massive coronary and died. The shock of his death was so astounding to people that even folks who didn't know him were coming around asking who 'the guy that died' was. That's how foreign death had been to most of us. Soon it became such an everyday occurrence that we reached for the obits like many of us had seen our grandparents doing when they got so old that they expected to find their friends there.

The first person that I knew that succumbed was a fellow entertainer named Alan. He had been one of those people who'd had the 'flu that he just couldn't shake'. He then went home to his family and not many reports came back. Every once in a while I'd hear from mutual friends that they'd talked to him but the reports I was getting was that he was doing ok and nothing more.

The real blow for me came when this guy named Bill who was one of the most popular bartenders in town died. I was out one day and heard a couple of guys that I knew talking about someone that had died and how it was a total shock. Apparently very few people even knew he was sick. They were saying that the funeral was to be held by the end of that week at Spring Hill Mortuary just off Tenth St. Usually I don't make it a habit of listening in on others' conversations but curiosity was getting the better of me. So I asked one of the guys who they were talking about. He told me it was Bill. I almost fell over. I remember it was early in the year; Beginning of spring actually. I was so stunned because though I had not seen Bill since the preceding fall, it was just as these guys said; not many (including myself) had known he was even sick. He had looked just fine a few months earlier and here they were talking about his funeral.

I had last seen Bill the preceding October at a theater at Peachtree and Roswell Rd. Back then, the place was named the Buckhead Cinema and DraftHouse. He was there working a benefit. Almost all the entertainers in town were performing and the bartenders and waiters were donating their time and energies working as servers there. The thing was being held at a theater so it was not staffed. That was why all the bars had pitched in to help. It was one of the first of many such benefits that would be done in the fight against AIDS and Bill had been there working as a waiter in the crowd. He looked not only fine and the picture of health- but indeed looked wonderful that night. I was with Ernie and was in the audience. I can't remember why I didn't work the thing now, but for some reason I wasn't performing. I remember remarking to Ernie how hot Bill was and sharing with him that I had great memories of a night not too long before that he and I had been together sexually. It had been quite a fluke and not planned at all. I knew him from my time of patronizing his bar. It was one of the few bars that I went to when I wanted to meet guys and wanted to be far away from drag. Nobody knew 'Adrienne' there. To them I was just Tony. I had always thought Bill was sexy, so the night that we ended up together intimately was really special to me.

So now the information that he was dead barely six months later left me totally floored. Though it had been only the one time we were together, and it had been a bit of a while ago, I was still quite concerned about what that could mean for me. In those days we all were so worried about getting sick, anything could set off the panic. And on top of that the use of condoms was just starting to be talked about as a viable pre-caution. If you caught a cold you instantly wondered; "is this it"? If a bruise appeared on your body and you didn't remember how it got there you freaked and thought about calling the doctor. So to be told that this man, with whom I'd been intimate less than a year ago, was now dead was like someone throwing a bucket of ice water on my head.

I knew I needed to do something. I was freaked out, but I couldn't bear to not know. There was no way I was going to tell anyone what I was thinking. I had to get to someone and try and get some answers however. I decided to make a run to the Dekalb County Health Department. A friend had told me that they were doing a survey style anonymous interview with gay men in the community trying to learn as much as they could about behaviors and trends. It was their effort to try and get a handle on this thing. So I decided to go over and talk to some-one. I mean what the hell; it was anonymous and just maybe they could give me some answers. The friend told me that they would want to do some type of physical test as well as the interview, but the physical part was very simple. The interview would take most of the time.

When I got there and told them why I was there, the people could not have been more cordial. I'm sure they could tell that I was as nervous as hell, so they really went out of their way to put me at ease. They told me that the first thing that I needed to do was submit to a blood test. I submitted, but not before once again having them assure me that it would be anonymous. Then they proceeded to explain the skin test that they would need to do. I found out later that it was a standard TB test. There was no specific AIDS test developed yet so they would take this strip with sharp little spikes on it and press it into the skin on your inner forearm. I was told that each one of the spikes was tipped with different types of bacteria. The idea was to test to see if your immune system was functioning properly.

As I remember it they pressed the thing into your skin, and you were to go home and return a few days later to see if there was any reaction. When you returned depending on your results to the skin test they would do the second phase of the test.

The interview phase was by far the most strenuous of the entire thing. I have never been asked so many questions in my life. They left no stone unturned. They wanted to know ALL about your sex life. When you started having sex, whether you only had sex with men, whether you had sex daily, weekly, monthly or what. Then they wanted to know how many times per day, per week, per month, etc. And then how many part-ners you had in each designated time period. As the questions went on they even began to sound ludicrous to me and I remarked as much. The doctor assured me that I was not the only person who thought this was absurd, but he said that they were trying to learn from the ground up and that was why it was so important to get a feel for the sexual habits of gay men. He said the information about this section of society was so limited that they really had no idea how to deal with this thing. So the information that we were providing was priceless to them. He explained that for that reason it was imperative that people be as truthful as possible no matter how crazy it sounded.

So I answered him truthfully. Many of the time frames that he was questioning me about I had NO IDEA how many men I had been with. Hell, I couldn't even tell him in the last six months for sure, much less the last five years! We were coming off the seventies! Sex had been something you did like brushing your teeth every day! The doctor told me that from what he had seen so far my responses were not at all unusual. He told me to just estimate. When I gave him my numbers I fully expected his eyebrows to shoot up. He told me that he'd heard numbers that dwarfed mine. And I was pretty sure that what he was saying was true. I knew that we were all pretty promiscuous in those days.

I think the questions went on for about thirty or forty-five minutes. Finally I told him that I had a couple of questions for him. He said that he would answer if he could. I told him that it pertained to his study and perhaps it could help him out. I said that I could not remember and in some cases didn't know the full names of some of my former partners, but that I could give him at least one name. He said ok. So I told him about Bill. He said that he could not confirm or deny that he had been involved in the study. He told me however that he was one of sixteen people in Atlanta at that time "to have died from a condition that was recognized as being commonly found in patients with this apparent illness". Of course he didn't specify the condition that Bill had died from.

I was just happy to have the thing over and the result of my skin test found that my immune system seemed to be working fine. I didn't know it yet, but Bill's death was like that first big rain drop that hits you smack on the forehead when the sky gets dark and the wind starts blowing like crazy. It heralded a coming storm that would nearly sweep us all away in tsunami-like fashion.

About the same time that all this was going on, my mom's health was taking a negative turn. We were all very keyed up about it because the illness had been so elusive and mysterious to us. None of us really knew anything about having to deal with things like this. We had all pretty much been a relatively healthy bunch up to now with minor issues along the way, but nothing of this magnitude. While there was some nervousness we were all trying our best to just go on as usual with not a lot of emphasis put on the obvious. But no matter how you try when something like terminal illness happens, it's always there in the room with you.

Personally I was sort of frozen in time. There was so much shock and despair in the gay community that my social outlet was no longer much of a comfort. Along with the situation in-volving my mother there were still the other family issues that existed within our ranks. I felt that chief on that list was still the issue of my sexual orientation and the discomfort caused by it between my siblings and me. My relationship with my brother still felt like Russia and the United States during the cold war. We acknowledged each other but it didn't feel like there was any real communication there. Though he said that he was ok with my being gay, I never really felt like I could be-lieve that. It felt as though because his wife and I were friends that he tolerated it as the popular position. But I felt that in his heart he didn't really mean it. Meanwhile, the relationship with my sisters didn't even feel that honest. With my younger sister it felt as though she was forever trying to 'trap' me in some fashion. Though I was sure she knew all about my life, we played this game as if she didn't. She knew what the deal was, and I, out of respect for her feigned ignorance. I went through the motions of hiding who I was from her. Remember this is the sister whose kids had; A) found pictures of me in drag in my bedroom, B) found porn magazines filled with nude men in my bedroom. And she herself had intercepted mail from my parents' mailbox years before with my stage name on it. And rather than assuming that mail was addressed incorrectly, brought it straight to me and questioned me about it.

With my older sister to whom I had first come out, it was just as bad. She was now 'saved' and was now from time to time telling me about how she now didn't approve of my life and that she knew I could change if I really wanted to. These were not people with whom I could relax, be myself, or go to for warmth and comfort.

However, even with the distance we all came together wherever we needed to in the effort to meet this challenge with my mom head-on. We began doing things that were totally out of character for my family. We gave mom a surprise birthday party at my sister's and all of us pitched in to make it a nice evening. It was funny because my mom DETESTED surprises like that.

That same year my dad made arrangements and took her on a long trip out west to California to see her niece and just to see Hollywood. She had always wanted to go out west and he wanted to make sure that she did.

Without any of us saying one word we were all circling the wagons for what we anticipated would be the roughest ride of our lives. At that time she was maintaining day to day but we could see that her body was beginning to show signs of the cancer advancing.

As the days went on she was becoming frailer. My mother was a robust woman and a definite presence. Watching these changes in her was traumatic for all of us. However through it all she continued to be the strong woman that I always knew.

As for me I was spinning and running as fast as I could. Trying to continue with life as I always did just didn't seem right but I didn't know what else to do. I felt guilty about going out clubbing and staying out late during that time, but most nights I just couldn't face going home. Not only was there all the past reality to deal with but now the current reality was even bleaker. I was in no shape to even think about dealing with it all so I hid out in the bars, drank and continued to eat myself into bad health.

I did have the presence of mind though to make sure that anything my mother asked me to do - no matter how small- I knocked myself out to do for her. I had always been taught that the absolute worst experience in one's life would be to end up regretting not doing whatever you could for your people when you had the chance. That guilt would kill you like nothing else. I loved my mom fiercely and whatever our outcome I wanted to make sure that I helped her anyway that I could.

I'll forever be grateful for the willingness to go to any lengths to do whatever she asked. I only wish that I had not been fighting so many of my own inner demons. Then I could have been even more accessible. Sometimes not knowing how to cope with the pain and disillusion of the situation sent me spiraling in spite of myself.

There was one night where my mom had an episode that sent her to the hospital for a couple of days. She got sick at home late in the evening and no one was with her. I think my dad was out of town at the time, but I KNOW I was out at the clubs after work as usual. Even though there probably wouldn't have been anything that I could have done to prevent what happened, the feeling that rode along in my head after that was immense. From then on I never let myself be too in-accessible for too long. I tried to make it a point to check in at home when I would not be there for extended periods of time.

My mom made her transition from this life on March 23, 1984 and from that moment on my life has never been the same. To say her passing was devastating to our family would certainly be an understatement. No matter what our differences, the underlying cohesion was undeniable. She was the first passing from our immediate midst and even though it was somewhat expected I learned that you're never really ready when that time comes.

I just sort of floated through it all in shock. Not only was it the most intense sense of loss that I've ever experienced, it brought on a whole new level of consciousness surrounding the subject.

Even more so, her death seemed to open up the floodgates. Within a couple of weeks of her passing, word came that Alan; the entertainer that I mentioned earlier and my dear friend; had also passed. All the pent up emotions that hadn't managed to make it out when my mom died suddenly bubbled over when Alan died. I completely lost it and just fell apart. The days all felt very dim and bleak.

Although he was a very vibrant and energetic man, I watched my dad quite literally fall apart. He and my mom had been together for over 40 years, and quite frankly, I don't think he knew how to go on. He would sit in a wing chair by the picture window in our living room for hours on, and days at a time. This was unheard of behavior from a man that had been on the move in one way or another for as long as I'd known him. For years he had been a cardiac patient. He had fended off at least three heart attacks and a mild stroke. None of this did to him what my mom's death did.

Through all of our suggestions for him to rejoin the world, he just sat. He once said to me, "you can't understand how this feels. You just lost your mother I know. But when you've been with a person for this long they become a part of you." And though that was true- I didn't know how it felt to lose your life partner- I did understand that our little corner of the world had changed forever.

Apparently the shift was not over. On December 7, 1984- just nine months after the passing of my mom, my dad followed her in death. His was a sudden heart attack. We all believed - and I still do to this day- that he just couldn't make the adjustment to being here alone without her.

Though this all seemed to be the worst imaginable I soon discovered the reverberations would carry on for years. My oldest sister decided that she would rent her home and move into the family home with me at the time. Originally I could not have been more accepting of the idea. Things were still very difficult for me in more ways than one. Along with all the emotional issues my own finances and my work situation was all a mess.

As I mentioned earlier I had moved home to help my parents and also because my own situation felt tenuous. During that time my work life had not gotten any better. I was still working for the hotel but the business was so bad that many hotels had begun to use some people on a day labor basis. I was barely clearing $30.00 a day in tips and didn't feel that I could maintain the house alone. I was also on a hiatus from doing shows. My heart wasn't in it. The reality of life was coming down hard on me.

Tips are never certain and I was panicked and convinced that I might lose the house or something. My sister's input seemed a welcome relief. However, upon her entry all seemed to change immediately. She moved in many of her things and started to take charge of everything. This was not what I'd expected and certainly not what I wanted. Pretty soon she started trying to tell me when I could come and go and what I could and couldn't do in the house. It was becoming a real nightmare. While I appreciated her help, I had never wanted a surrogate parent. I was 26 years old, and felt I was more than adult enough to make my own decisions about the life I was to lead. Here I was thinking of her as a roommate and she was thinking she needed to manage my life.

It didn't take long before we were having major disagreements about everything. I can remember one night in particular that I had planned to go out clubbing. During my parents' lives, none of us would ever drink at home because they didn't drink and weren't comfortable with alcohol around. Oddly enough, this particular sister had been the exception to this rule. She had gone through a really bad divorce and had moved back home some years earlier. During that time she had battled a problem with drinking and prescription drugs. So imagine my upset when she met me at the door that night and told me how much she didn't approve that I had mixed a cocktail from my room and was headed out of the door with it in hand.

This was just one of many such disagreements that were to follow. It soon became apparent to me that I needed to make some things happen if I were to get out of this rut. At the same time I seemed to be going through some type of transformation. I had no idea why, but I no longer even wanted to work onstage. It would have been the quickest, most lucrative method of getting money quickly available to me, but I just knew I needed a serious change. I needed to find legitimate and financially supportive work and soon. I was terribly unhappy with my whole life and just wanted things to change, though I had no idea how to make that happen.

I decided to enroll in the Art Institute of Atlanta to see if I could make some things happen. It was very frightening for me. I had not even considered going back to school of any kind since high school. That experience had been so bad that as far as I was concerned it had been all the schooling that I could stand. Just the thought of going back into an environment where people would look down on me or be abusive to me as a gay person again was damned near paralyzing.

Looking back now I can see just how screwed up I was. I chose art school because I thought maybe I could go there amongst liberal minded individuals and not be ridiculed.

However when I went to register I was freaked at the thought of even looking into anything to do with fashion. I was sure that if I did that I would be labeled queer right out of the starting blocks.

I also thought that I'd done a good bit of on-the-job training in that area as anyone could imagine. I had been sewing for other people by that time for many years and felt that most of what they would probably be teaching about garment construction I had already learned through practical application; through trial and error. I now know that this was partly true, but I'm also aware that I could have benefited greatly from as much study as possible. It would have helped me get places faster, but alas, that was obviously not God's plan for me.

Fortunately I did have the presence of mind to try and think of where my skill set was lacking around the art form, and to try and see what in the curriculum might benefit me. When I looked there didn't seem to be much. Also, I needed to remember that whatever I studied must be offered in the evening since I still had to work. Ultimately, I chose photography. The thought was that I knew I needed to put together a portfolio of work that I'd done, yet my sketching was so poor that I was ashamed for anyone to look at it. I didn't see any drawing or sketching courses that I could attend at night. All those were daytime classes. Also, to be totally honest, daytime school felt too much like school had in the past, So I opted for photography with the thought that if I couldn't sketch my ideas I could at least photograph the finished products and put the book together that way. It turned out to be an inspired idea and I'm grateful that I took those classes. I'm not a great photographer, but I did learn scale, composition and a lot about lighting. I also learned a great deal about doing business as an artist. I simply took what was taught to photographers and applied it to my dealings with my clients in fashion and garment construction.

The entrance to art school was as terrifying to me as anything else that I've started in life that was unfamiliar but I was determined to make an honest attempt at it. When I think back to how I perceived the students there and how I expected them to see me my naiveté is astounding. All the paranoia around my sexuality followed me into this environment even though this particular type of school was chosen specifically to combat that. Add to that the discomfort because many of my fellow students were so much younger than I. Night classes did help this out some.

I had an incident where a young guy in his late teens/ early twenties was doing everything in his power to get me to notice him. Even though he was quite attractive I had so many issues that at first I couldn't believe that he wanted to know me and that he was being so open about it. And then when I did become aware I was so unskilled at making connections outside of the casual sex in public or in the bar atmosphere that I couldn't work out how to make the connection with him.

One evening we were both in the lab doing final assignments. It was a Saturday evening and it was highly unusual that there were not more people around. With a golden opportunity I was too socially inept to take advantage and get to know him better. I just clammed up with a burning shame.

That was pretty much the case with all my social experiences there. Here I was in the company of some of the most creative, liberal and accepting people imaginable and because of my own internalized homophobia; I felt totally isolated. It reminds me of the saying, "water, water everywhere and not a drop to drink!"

Still, with all that going on I consider the time that I spent in that school some of the most valuable growth time I ever spent. The most important thing that happened there was that it was the very first time I ever set out to do something that I completed. That went a long way toward helping me to start building some self-esteem. The sense of accomplishment that I felt on the night of graduation was enormous.

Even though I had no idea what the hell I would do with the training I suddenly understood how priceless the experience itself had been. I had proved to myself that against some pretty daunting odds I could do the things that I wanted if I tried hard enough.

Now came a real transitional period and a wealth of understanding which changed my life and the way I would approach it from then on.

Chapter 6

Chapter 6

Chapter 6

Even before I finished Art School I knew that I had a position waiting for me at the Postal Service. I had been contacted just shortly before graduation about coming in to interview, and since things were not at all well for me financially, I knew this was a true blessing.

Though I really liked working in hotels and meeting different people, the money was just not there any longer. I was falling further and further behind. Since starting Art school, I had dropped to part time at the downtown hotel where I had been for years. That hotel; which had previously been owned by Marriott, had been sold to Radisson just a short time earlier. Just before that sale had taken place I had the forethought to go out and get a morning job at a smaller Hilton hotel just north of the city. This meant that I was working full time at that hotel in the morning, part time at the Radisson downtown, and going to school part time. All this and I was still struggling financially.

Through politics, it was brought to my attention that management at the Radisson was not happy with the fact that

I was only working part time now. I was given an ultimatum of either going back to a full time status, or I would have to leave their employ. Needless to say, I was not about to quit school for them, and since there were other people on staff going to school and working part time, I could only surmise that it must have something to do with my working full time at a rival hotel.

The day that the ultimatum was given, I was told that I had to make the decision by the close of that day's shift; no warning, no time to prepare. After 14 years at this property this was what it came down to! For me, this was a 'no brainer'. I told the manager I didn't need to wait until the end of that evenings' shift. Hell, I'd go to Personnel and resign that instant. I figured I might as well get an off day out of it! I sure as hell wasn't going to give them a nights' work and then get booted out!

Now that the part time work at the Radisson Hotel Downtown was gone, I was really drowning.

I had been making the rounds to different photography studios in town, but so were all the other photography graduates. We were all battling for the same few positions. None of what was happening on that front looked promising. I was becoming more and more stressed since my finances were in such shambles. There's that saying; "Things are always darkest just before dawn". When word came that I had the postal job, ironically, I had a call on the same day telling me there was a position at a local paper; The Gwinnett Daily News. It was a division of a larger area newspaper and they were looking for a photojournalist. They needed someone "like yesterday." The pay would be entry level, which was little more than minimum wage, and the area of interest was not one that I'd felt strongly about whilst in school. I had tended to lean more toward product and fashion photography, not photojournalism.

It was a big decision and I had no idea what to do. I was torn between whether to go for the sure money that the postal service was offering, or whether to stay with the path of training. I had spent all this time and money learning a craft and now that I was being offered a position; ANY position in the arts field, I was thinking of turning my back on it. One minute it seemed I didn't have any prospects, and now I had too many! At the time, I didn't do much praying but I gave it a try. I figured it certainly couldn't hurt.

What ultimately came to me was to take the job with the postal service and continue to do what I had been doing with the sewing machine for years, which was to do independent contract work. Now the difference would be that I could add photography to the list of services offered.

I called the Gwinnett Daily News and thanked them for the offer, but informed them that I had already taken a position. I then called the Postal Service and asked if I could push back my start date by one week because I was graduating from school and needed to concentrate on my final projects. They said yes, and I was in!

So as history would have it, I had started at the Northwest Atlanta Hilton Hotel, which was the hotel just north of the city, on October 12, 1986, and left their employ on October 13, 1987. Talk about 'things that make you go,'Hmmmm'... And that was only the beginning.

Trying to tell someone about working at the Postal Service is one of the most difficult tasks that I've ever undertaken. It's like no other work experience that I've ever encountered at any time. From the initial interview, to the scheduling, it's just downright strange.

When I was sent my startup documentation, I was told that I needed to have a physical exam. After having that done, I was to report to Norcross Post Office, main branch at 03:00 on Saturday, 10/24/87. Now, even though I had not been in the military, I was afraid that I knew what the time meant. Surely this had to be a mistake. I called the number on the letter to confirm, and the lady assured me with a little chuckle that the time was indeed correct and I was to report at 3 o'clock in the morning.

That was my first real clue that this was to be a wild ride. I mean, most of the world thinks the Postal Service operates Monday thru Friday, 8 a.m.-5p.m., with holidays closed.... Not so. It actually operates 365 days a year, 24 hours a day; with some of the strangest scheduling that you'll encounter any- where. While I had certainly experienced needing to be present when business demanded in the hotel industry, I can't say that I ever thought that anyone reported to work for the start of their shift at such an odd hour.

The night/early morning that I first walked into the place, I felt as though I'd walked into another world. I've got to say that having been in the workforce since I was fifteen years old, I was already somewhat jaded as to what I could expect from any job; and the fact that the starting pay was so good (about $12.00/ hr.) for unskilled labor, made me instantly wary of what I would find. I had actually tested and applied for this job about three years prior, and I was reasonably sure that min- imum wage in Georgia at the time was an unthinkable $1.25/hr. In the work world I was accustomed to, even the hotel execu- tives were impressed and curious about that type of salary.

I can remember thinking when I took the test, "ok, if this is what they're paying as a starting salary, they are either going to: 1.) work the living hell out of me. 2.) Stress me out totally with a crazy and hostile work environment. 3.) Bore me to complete tears, and the actual job will be the true test of endurance just to stay there."

It's still amazing to me that I could have been so cynical in the face of such a good salary, but I was coming off hav- ing worked for some situations where the organizations were anything but fair to their employees and had treated them like used garbage in tossing them and their loyalty away when done with them.

My years working with certain hotel chains had left me embittered and not at all forgiving of big business. And I have to say that now after many years in the government, that my initial assessment of the situation was practically spot on.

That first night, I walked into a place that was devoid of any conversation whatsoever. All the people were sitting at letter cases sticking letters into these honeycomb style cubicles. No one was saying a word. The cases were set up in a square shape, and as I walked in, a short, rotund man walked up to me and introduced himself as the shift supervisor. He asked me my name and then brought over a young woman named Alice and introduced her. He had her take me around and introduce me to all the employees there. We went from case to case and she introduced me, they all looked up, said hello, and then went right back to what they were doing. I remember thinking, "What the hell have I gotten myself into here?" The tension in the room was so thick I could have cut it with a knife. Before long, I would come to know that underlying tension was the normal state of affairs. However that night all I could do was think that I needed to adapt. If this is what's to be, then so be it....

Until now, I'd never worked in such a closed environment. My work experiences had all included the public up to this point. This would be the first time that I would have to deal with the same set of people each and every day, with the dynamic almost never changing. Between the rotten graveyard hours, the feelings of isolation there and my own insecurities it was a very difficult time for me. I felt miserable. There was so much closed-mindedness around. Being a gay black man in a rural area in Georgia was not the thing to be. Norcross, GA was basically a small, country town; about 25 miles north of

downtown Atlanta proper. Many of the fears that were cours-
ing through me would serve to inhibit me greatly where my
fellow co-workers were concerned. Meanwhile, there was no
way for me to continue to socialize in the arena that was most
familiar to me. My work hours prevented any bar life, and at
the time that was pretty much all I knew as far as mixing with
other gay people.

Also, even with the new job things had not really changed
that much with my sister. We were less at each other's throats
because I was trying to get a handle on the work. Just before
starting to work there my car had started a very slow and
painful death. The transmission was all but gone, and had it
not been for a very shaky patch-up repair to it, I don't know
what I would have done. The job was close to thirty miles
away from my parents' house and with me going in late night
I was a nervous wreck trying to drive the thing that distance
nightly. I was living on borrowed time with that situation and
I knew it. Since there was literally no time in my life for play or
leisure, there was nothing immediate for my sister to object to.
Therefore there were less 'in your face' exchanges between us.
However, she was still determined to tell me what she thought
I should be doing with every aspect of my life.

The adjustment to the workplace was the most drastic
that I'd ever undergone. Up to that time I'd worked in hotels,
bars, restaurants and the like. There's a saying that approximately one in every six people is gay. I swear, in the Norcross
Post Office I had yet to find those others and there were about
thirty to forty clerks on the staff there alone. Not counting
management and office staff. Reason told me that I could not
be the only one, but that's sure as hell not how it felt. If there
were others, they were WAY undercover. To add to the stress,
there was a guy there, John, whom I'd known since kindergarten. People from my past always freak me out a bit. I guess because I think they can't possibly really know me. I constantly

think that I'm in no way who I was when I first met them. I know, it's probably crazy for me to think that way. Nevertheless there it is. John was nice, if a little guarded. We'd also worked together briefly at the Marriott downtown, so it was not the first time that I'd seen him since we were adults. That made me even more curious about what he knew; or thought he knew about me. Had he heard anything or drawn any conclusions about me when we both worked downtown? Actually it was not likely. We worked in totally different departments, and rarely encountered one another. And even though it felt strange, there was some comfort in a familiar face being there.

I had to settle in there but my idea of how I should handle my co-workers had always been to hold them at arm's length. I had never really been the buddy-buddy type. What happened at work, stayed at work... These were not the people that I partied and socialized with. So I was somewhat surprised when the supervisor pulled me aside one night and told me, "you know Tony, we're all family here. You can lighten up and mix with the others." My response to him was that I appreciated that, but I'd always in the past kept to myself where work was concerned. I didn't usually mix socially with the people that I worked with. I explained that I kept my personal life separate and that work was just that. We weren't buddies and we weren't pals. In the past I'd found that to blur those lines usually meant trouble down the line should there be any problems. He looked as if I'd slapped him across the face! I honestly couldn't figure out at the time why he was so shocked. I mean, that was the way work was handled on my jobs in the past. In fact the few companies that I'd worked for actually frowned upon fraternization. Once again I saw just how much the Postal Service was truly a world unto itself. Funny thing; when I think back to that conversation with my supervisor that night I can now see just how inhibited I was. My response to him in that conversation was just as 'clinical and frosty' as it reads here on this page. No wonder he had a shocked look!

In Norcross there was some carrying on. I soon found out there were people having affairs with co-workers, and one or two cases of people's spouses working within the postal system. But nothing like I would find a few years later when I went to the big North Metro facility. However even in this tiny office I would soon find out there was dirt and people most definitely talked. My own issues found their way to the surface and soon. There were a couple of guys in the offices that I thought were really hot. One that worked the day shift and one that worked nights with me. The only problem with the one that worked with me was that he was a MONUMEN-TAL asshole! I mean the type of guy that EVERYBODY hates. Alan was a whiner and complainer. Physically, he was not bad looking, but his personality would run Mother Theresa off. Not only was he a whiner and complainer, but he was the type of white guy that displays that misplaced sense of entitlement. It's as though he thinks it's HIS world, and the rest of us all owe him something for living here. He actually had it so bad that he even put off other white guys who normally you would expect would relate to him on his level.

Needless to say I was well on my guard the night he came sidling up next to me talking about how I could trust him. How he was from Decatur, and went to Decatur High School. All this was to convince me that he was hip to "in town living" and all. He hinted around at my being gay and how it was cool with him, but he never really came out and asked me directly. I think I was supposed to get comfortable and confess or something. All the time I'm standing there thinking, "This guy must be a complete fool if he thinks I would confide ANY-THING to him!" He would be in the lunchroom giving blow by blow details of the conversation before I could finish the last statement. All these people were largely cut from that type of cloth. Most were not as bad as him; but still the generality fit. The image they presented was supposed to be friendly and accommodating but most of them couldn't keep up the facade long enough for it to even be mistaken as believable.

The funny thing is that if I had to vote on the person in the bunch that I thought was most likely to be a closet case and shaky in the role as husband/father/straight man, it would have been Alan!

By now the holidays were upon us and the place really cranked up then. There was a noticeable increase in the work-load, so there were more hours to be worked. The supervisor and manager told me and one of the other new guys we would possibly be moving to a 5 a.m. start time after the holidays. While that never happened, what did occur was that in early January my car finally bit the dust. I got up to go to work one night and it wouldn't go into gear. I was due at work at 2 a.m., and the only person I knew that I could call for help was my sister. She was working graveyard as well, and had left going to work at eleven that night. She told me that she would take an early lunch break and come take me to work. I was grateful to her, I still hated having to ask her for a favor. By this time almost anything that I needed to ask of her felt like an imposition. I just didn't like having to go there.

She picked me up , took me to Norcross and came back to get me the following morning. I asked her to stop by the Toyota dealership on Buford Highway on the way home. She complied. And while she slept in the car I went in to look at some of the pickup trucks that they had. In my mind, I only intended to look that day, but by eleven o'clock that morning, I had been talked into leasing a half ton pickup. A few weeks before ,I had joined the credit union at work; so now I would be putting them to the test with this loan. I'd always had good luck with the Marriott Credit Union, so there was no reason to believe there would be any difference here.

There was, however. The Atlanta Postal Credit Union had a policy that all new members had to have co-signers on their first loans. The number of signatures was determined by the amount borrowed. The hook was that you could ONLY use fellow postal employees as co-signers. So here I was, with people that I barely knew, asking them to co-sign with me to get a vehicle. I thought the whole idea was ridiculous. The saving grace was that many of them had gone through the same thing. A lot said no, but all I needed was three. I found them and was on my way. I do understand why the rule was in place and the reluctance of people to comply. While there, I saw people overextend and default on loans for cars and homes. That meant that all those people who had signed with that person were then liable. Because there were people willing to trust me, when someone finally came up to me asking me to cosign, I felt obligated to do it for the same number of people who did it for me. Were it not for those three people, I don't know how I would have continued to work there. The distance was too great and I had to have transportation. I was not even through my 90 day probationary period, so not getting to work or excessive late arrival would have cost me the job.

For a while all went along smoothly. The manager did finally move my shift, but not to 5 a.m. Stan, the other new guy and I were moved to the afternoon shift. We were scheduled to come in at 3:30p.m. I loved it! I had worked these hours for years, and it was my favorite shift! The girl that had introduced me around that first night had also been moved to the afternoons. Alice would work as a relief supervisor over the afternoons. She and I had become really close. I felt it was a stroke of pure luck that I was able to move to that shift.

The change of time also allowed me to take a much needed breath. Late Nights didn't give me much of a chance to do that. Even though I had spent an awful lot of time in the nightclubs in the past, it was not the same as having to show up for a job overnight. That shift had been really taking the starch out of me. With the new hours, by March I was beginning to feel more stable than I had in years. I was through my 90 day probation with the Service. I had met the requirements of learning route schemes, and had proven to be so proficient at it that they had assigned me all three to learn. I passed them. There were only four zip code zones in Norcross, GA at that time. The fourth, 30091, was the P.O. Box section. As with previous jobs I was proving again that while I may be slow out of the starting blocks, once I got going I would become superior at whatever task they assigned me. I was adapting to the work finally and things were looking up. Now I began to think about getting back out on my own and back to my own life.

I mentioned to Joan, my sister, that I thought the time had come for me to go out and get my own place. She was decidedly against the idea. She said she felt that I should stay there a little longer and get some money saved. While I liked the idea of saving some money, I didn't like the idea of waiting around in any way. It had been my experience that when something felt right for me, I needed to strike right then. To wait around was to invite opportunities for obstacles to enter the picture. Though most of what she said made sense, it was coming from a tentative and cautious place. A place that I felt we'd all lived in for much too long. I think all of us; my brother, my sisters and I had lived that way for so long- expecting hardship- that pessimism had become a way of life. I think that all of us had begun to believe that we couldn't have good times and good things just weren't going to happen for us. Some of this was due to the trauma that we'd all faced with the loss of our parents. But some also was due to the fact that we'd been raised living as though we were always in crisis. Never enough money, food, etc...

Hell, for the first time I had a steady salary! I had held on by the seat of my pants for so long that KNOWING there was a check for a certain amount coming every other week felt like heaven. Every time I brought up the idea of my moving to Joan however, I got a negative response. I didn't let that deter me. I started just as I had before. I still had some of the furnishings that had been in the first apartment, but there were other things I felt that I needed. I didn't have an upright chest or dresser or anything that would hold folded items in my room. I went over to the antique shops in the Virginia- Highlands area here in town and I found a really nice Art Deco Style armoire. It was the first purchase that I made for my new place. Suddenly I was totally rejuvenated! I had a truly concrete goal and purpose for the first time in years.

Since all I had gotten from Joan was negativity I had ceased to even mention the plan of moving out. When I brought the armoire home she looked at it. She had a questioning look on her face, but didn't say anything more. I was on a roll and nothing was going to stop me. I was determined to get back to my own life. I had been so depressed for so many years that this idea was like an elixir to a dying man.

I started to look at apartments and found that things had changed from what they had been when I was out here before. Prices had definitely increased. In my last place the rent was $175.00 a month. Now it seemed the norm was about $600.00. The five years away from having my own place had definitely seen changes. I didn't let that stop me though. Atlanta was MY city, and after years of helping friends find apartments I was sure I could find something that was more reasonable. The first thing I did was throw away all the Apartment Finder magazines that I had collected. Then I hit the street. I went to all the places that I had liked being in before. I looked at apartments that were NOT in complexes. By this time most of my old friends were established in their apartments and had been in them for a while. We were all much older now and the settling had begun. Ernie and his roommate Michael had been living in Peachtree North Apartments for years. And Greg was no longer renting. He had actually bought a condo on Tenth St., across from the park. Chablis had left Atlanta and had moved to Savannah, GA., and Tina Devore was now living on Buford Highway.

As I reconnected with my friends it seemed that about the only people I knew that were living in a familiar area that was gay-friendly and yet closer to where I was working was the drag queens. Most were still concentrated in the Buford Highway area then. So this is where I decided to do most of my looking. It was closer to work. I could actually come home for lunch at times. But it was still close to town as well. And now that I was working evenings, maybe I could be a little more communicative with some of my friends.

I found a place in a complex named Bryton Hill. It was at the intersection of Buford Highway and Clairmont Rd. It was one of those old apartment complexes that you can drive through. The buildings were made of cinder block. There was mostly parking on the street, and every apartment was a townhouse. They had converted two-bedroom units into one bedroom; which meant that the entire upstairs was the bedroom with a bath off to one side. It was huge and I loved it! It had those old fashioned jalousie windows that you cranked outward. And best of all it was only $425.00 a month.

The place was big enough that it had room just off the kitchen for a washer and dryer. They were in a closet to themselves. I had an end unit with a little front yard and a back patio. The one thing that I'd disliked about my first apartment was that it lacked a sense of privacy. My front door had opened directly across from someone else's. There was no back door at all! Here, each unit, in true townhouse fashion, was really a unit unto itself. Sure, there was someone on the other side of the left wall, but with a little effort I could ignore them. Or so I thought.... Either way, finally I felt that once again I had a home.

To avoid the negativity and drama of having to even discuss this with my sister I went ahead and put a deposit on the place. I didn't tell her until the last possible minute that I would be moving out at the beginning of the month. As it turned out, she would be out of town at that time, so I would be spared the scene of anything she might want to add on my actual moving day.

Yes, it turned out that the times had CERTAINLY changed. Many of my friends that I helped move over the years had graduated from doing things that way. No one was eager to sign on to help me with it, and it was even difficult for me to ask. So without a great deal of friends and not very much money, I decided to move myself. I really didn't have much stuff. What little I had was cumbersome, but not really all that heavy. The biggest items were my king sized bed, the sofa and the armoire. Everything else was small enough that it would just take a bit of muscle. I managed, and at the end of the day was quite proud of myself. The only thing that I'd had to leave was my mother's china cabinet, which I had every intention of returning for just as soon as possible.

I got the stuff in and positioned on my two off days and was happy as a clam once I returned to work. Things were finally happening! I knew this new beginning was just the thing for me and I wasn't looking back.

It was April and the days were becoming more and more beautiful and fragrant. I was happy to be in my place and was settling in just fine. The only thing that I had not counted on was that it was very close to my younger sister's job, and she took to just dropping by unannounced. Pretty soon, she found that she could park her car in front of my place and take the bus a few blocks to work. That would save on parking. I would have had no problem with this, but as I've said my sisters both had a way of trying to mother me. In fact, one of the things that most bothered me about my family was that the entire lot of us had issues with boundaries. We were not very good at respecting one another's privacy. With the religious aspect thrown in my sisters had a misplaced sense of responsibility. They felt that now that our parents were no longer alive it was their duty to "straighten" me out. Neither missed an opportunity to let me know just how she felt and what she thought I should be doing. For my part, I didn't help matters. I soon noticed that every time something became troubling to me I called them to talk about it. They of course took this to mean that I was asking them for help. And I guess in a way I was. The truth is, though I didn't know it yet, what I needed was a more positive support system. When I solicited their opinions or counsel they would take that opportunity to tack moral judgements onto whatever the issue was. That would of course make me angry.

Fortunately, it didn't take me long to sort out that if I were to grow beyond where I was, I would need to stop this behavior. It was sabotaging everything that I was trying to do for myself.

As painful as it was, I decided that I would not have contact with my sisters at all unless they initiated it. As for my younger sister dropping by daily, I would just have to deal with that for now. I took to making sure that I was not home at the times that she came by to pick up the car. In the mornings when she dropped it off I was usually asleep and she would be running to catch her bus. She was a very intelligent woman, so I'm sure she figured out that I was avoiding her.

Around that time I met a man who would become one of my best friends. I first met Tom at Bulldogs, the bar in Mid-town where Ernie worked. It was a Saturday night. During that time it was still difficult for me to go out even though I was working the evening shift and off by midnight most nights. They had me working six days sometimes and I had really crappy off days. I was off on Sundays and Wednesdays when I did get two days, so the timing just felt odd. With the split, I usually had to do laundry and all the other home chores on that first day and on the second day I would be so tired I'd just try and get some rest. But that particular Saturday night I was out there.

' Bulldogs', as we called the bar, was a very different place back then. It was still primarily a white bar, but was one of the most patronized cruise bars in the city. And by now my friend Ernie was one of its premiere bartenders. He usually worked evenings, from about 7pm until midnight, so he wasn't there the night that I met Tom. I have no idea what was going on, but I remember when I met him I was seething. I was standing in line for the men's room and he was in line behind me. Some guy had done something to piss me off I remember, but I don't even remember what it was. Anyway, Tom said something to me. At first I didn't acknowledge him. I wasn't sure that he was even talking to me. Then he said something else. Well I was so pissed that I was immediately suspicious of what his motives were. I'm sure my reply to him couldn't have been very pleasant. He was just making conversation though, and soon that became apparent. Then I really looked at him for the first time. I believe that people have auras that most of us are unconscious of, but they penetrate our subconscious. Think about the times when you've met people, and for some reason you were drawn to them even though you couldn't pin down why. And vice versa those people you've met and were instantly repelled by, even though you didn't know them and hadn't even spoken to them. I think we all carry those auras about us. I've heard the idea expressed that they even have colors. I don't know about that, but Tom is an example of a person for me that once I really saw him I was instantly drawn to him. It's hard to explain. Yes, he was quite handsome, but it was more than that. I had long before learned that just because a guy's handsome doesn't make him personable. In fact, often just the opposite is true. No, there was clearly more to this man. And as we exited the men's room and continued our chat this was becoming more and more noticeable by the second.

As we talked, he told me more and more about himself. It was a feeling that I hadn't experienced socially in the gay community very often. The art of conversation and getting to know people does not rank very highly in the bar crowds. He talked of his work as a contractor and his passion for re-modeling. He talked of his roots as a West Virginia farm boy, of which he was quite proud. And of his love for music, which was his major in college. Even though this was during the time that people were doing everything in their power to hide the fact that they were HIV positive, he was very upfront about his status. He said that he had just tested and suspected he was positive,(since his boyfriend at the time was) and he was only awaiting the test results to confirm his suspicions. This was back during the time that it would take about two weeks to get results.

His candor and openness only drew me closer to him. I was in awe of him. He was so genuine. We became very close in record time.

Tom was that type of person. He was one of only a very few people that I had met in the gay community in all my years out here that I felt had true integrity. He was a genuinely sweet, considerate, and loving person. Humble in his approach to life, love and all those he cared about. It was the part of him that touched me so deeply. He was very open to the world. We talked for hours about his growing up in West Virginia, and how coming from a farming community, however nice, had not allowed him to really grow at all until he left home for college.

We talked about so many things. He was my angel in many ways. It was because of him that I eventually had a turnaround in my thinking about love and gay men. I was just at that place where I was poised to become a very jaded queen. Almost all my dealings with gay men had been bad ones. From what I could see most were selfish, mean spirited, bitter, vicious people and were largely only concerned with self. Tom helped me to see that though most of that was true, I shouldn't write off all gay men because of it. He believed in never giving up on love and helped me get to a place of trusting the social process. He never tried to deny that black gay men, myself included, had a rough go of it at the hands of white gay men in this city, but he never apologized for it either. He was very aware of who he was, and made sure to uphold his own principles. He was not attempting to advocate for the world, or for all white people in it. What he brought out through his example was that there is a little bad in the best of us and a little good in the worst of us. He made it his business to try and always concentrate on the good. He believed the only way for any of us to get along in this community was to try and look past those negatives to the person underneath. I have a slightly different spin on that. My own method is to try and take people on a case by case basis. Sadly, there are some people that are just so filled with their own bitterness that you just cannot simply "look past" it.

Suddenly, I found myself with a really good friend. In fact, I think, the first I'd had in years. I told him that the one thing I was really excited about was finally being in my own place again. During our talks I told him of the deaths of my parents and of the last five years overall; About living with my sister and all that had entailed. He offered to come with me to retrieve my mom's china cabinet. We spoke just about every day, and began to spend a great deal of time together. He was having some health problems, and it wasn't long before the positive diagnosis came back. He had been running fevers and losing weight. This was before the days of the drug cocktails.

Even though Tom was a music major and held a degree in that field, he had chosen to work with his hands because that's what he loved. And he was quite good at it. Unfortunately however, the work was very physical. So when he got sick he couldn't do very much anymore. Also he had started the business renovating houses with a partner. His partner was a gay man as well, so the fact of Tom's illness was not something that he felt he had to hide, but for insurance reasons they really couldn't afford to have him on the job site. So for a while there he wasn't working at all. When he was able to return it was in a consulting capacity only.

I did have the opportunity to see a couple of the projects they collaborated on. These guys were spectacular at their craft. All that made the pain just that much greater for him that he was not able to do what he loved any longer.

By now, it was well into the summer and I had been with the Postal Service now for about nine months. I don't know if it's still in effect, but they used to have a rule that was called the 90/10 ratio rule. And what that meant was that a facility the size of the one that I worked in had to keep a ratio of 90% regular full time employees and 10% part time flexible employees. At that time whenever a person was hired into the clerk/carrier craft they came in as what is called part time flexible. Meaning you were a career employee after your 90 day probationary period, but you stayed at part time status until they needed to promote you to full time. The time period could vary depending on several circumstances. The "flexible" part meant that they could change your hours at will. They could work you as few as two hours per pay period, or I believe as many as 120 hours per pay period. Though the latter involved penalty pay or whatever.... Either way, the Norcross facility was out of ratio, so they had to convert all the part time flexibles or "ptf's" as we were called, to regular full time.

I was totally destroyed. What sounded like a good thing was really going to be rather challenging to me. The problem was that while I was happy to be going to full time, it meant that we now all had to be assigned to bid jobs. In that facility all the bid jobs for clerks were on the graveyard shift. That's when all the first class mail processing was done. So like it or not, I was on my way back to working at midnight. The only thing that was good about it was that I would save more money because once again I would not be able to go much of anywhere or do much of anything.

The isolation during this period was pretty harsh. I also had no choice at that time but to deal with a couple of really crazy neighbors. A couple living next door to me who were very abusive and destructive to one another.... The girl had moved here from another state to be with a boyfriend that she hardly knew and he was knocking her around continually. Try sleeping during the day with screaming and fighting going on in what's practically the next room!

I have to applaud myself for that time inasmuch as I didn't once think of quitting. I just hung in and did the best that I could to keep going; Broken sleep and all.

As I think of my life and growth during that period, what I see is very telling. Much of the way that I functioned was about my obsessive and compulsive nature. The fact that I immediately went into social shut down at work was due to my being gay and not at all aware what would be made of that fact once it became known to the people that I worked with. That along with the stress of practically starting my life over again at that point was a huge adjustment for me. Nothing was familiar to me. I was living in a new place, my family life was changed forever (it had only been three years since the deaths of both parents), there was massive strain in the air between both sisters and myself and the people that I was now working around didn't think about anything the way that I did. I was this totally liberal and progressive thinking person surrounded by staunch, conservative, "family oriented" folks. Granted, the types that were all either sleeping around on their partners or at least thinking about it, but nevertheless outwardly they wanted to portray fine upstanding citizens. There was just no way that a gay, black; club kid was fitting into that picture!

In time, I did manage to find some boundaries with the work environment, but not without an emotional price being paid. While on the job, we were allowed to wear headphones and listen to music or audio books or whatever. I practically lived with my headset on at work. That way, I didn't have to communicate with anyone. They grew tired of having to wait for me to remove them, and then repeat what they were saying, so they just started to leave me alone. And believe me that was fine with me! My obsession with being able to hide out with the headphones was so severe that if a pair were broken or malfunctioned in some way, I would not go to work the next evening until I acquired new ones. So basically, I was listening to only music and talk radio at work, not talking to my neighbors who were crazy as far as I was concerned, and had practically no contact with other gay people. Not good! No wonder I began to show cracks in the armor.

It was during this time that I began to notice that my breathing was getting pretty lousy. My intake of breath was very shallow and I would have fits of coughing that would go on for several minutes whenever I entered a closed environment. Any room or closed space where there was not good air circulation would have me coughing like crazy. It never occurred to me that this may have had something to do with the fact that I was smoking nearly three packs of cigarettes a day, and my weight had ballooned to beyond 300 lbs. At that time there was no machinery running in the office where I worked. All mail processing was being done by hand. This made for a very quiet room. But it also made for a very dusty area. Paper creates tons of dust. When I would start coughing it was very noticeable to others. Finally someone brought it to my attention and asked if I was all right. It was such the norm for me that I didn't even notice I was doing it. It's funny how we adapt to our circumstances and make allowance adjustments for our developed disabilities.

Once I was made aware it did seem a little strange. Of course I went about for a little while longer saying, "I need to quit", but didn't make any move in that direction. Then one day I was coughing heavily and coughed up what I thought was phlegm. I spat into a waste basket and it turned out to be a wad of phlegm mixed with blood! When it came forth, there was a wracking pain in my chest. That was it! I decided that day to quit smoking and did so cold turkey!

There had been many attempts and by that time I had stepped down to a cigarette that was so low in tar and nicotine that it was practically like smoking air. However what that did was make me smoke more and more to try and 'get the fix'.

I had just purchased a brand new carton and had only taken one pack out. I challenged myself to leave the remainder of that carton on my nightstand in plain view. My thinking was if I could maintain my abstinence from the smokes with them right there in sight, then I could do it permanently.

Having always been a practical thinker I remember some of the thoughts that went through my mind were, "Okay, be prepared because you'll easily gain another twenty pounds now that you've put down the cigarettes." But that didn't matter. I knew that I would need to deal with one thing at a time. The second thought was, "How will I ever have a cocktail without a cigarette to go with it?"

I needn't have feared. This was to be the beginning of a whole new chapter in my life. "A new way of thinking and living", as some good friends of mine now say. Only, I didn't know that yet...

When I look back on those first tentative steps I can now see just how guided my life was up to that point and beyond. I now truly believe that I was moving into the next phase of a predestined path. I now believe that things were happening just as they were supposed to.

Just as I predicted I did gain maybe another 15-20 lbs. By now, I had been off the cigarettes for about a year, and the cravings had all but disappeared. A funny thing that I learned over that year was that the cravings disappeared early on. It was the HABIT itself that stuck around and was so hard to break. That desire to reach for a cigarette when driving the car, after a meal, upon waking, etc.... That's what I had to watch out for. It meant learning a new way of doing things. However, just as planned, I now knew that it was time to start looking at the weight. I should no longer put it off. I was beginning to experience pains and numbness down my left arm. Having read a lot and coming from a family where heart ailment and stroke were common, I knew these were warning signs. What I didn't know was that I was about to open Pandora's Box here.

I had been heavy for as long as I could remember and the only time I had really been able to really slim down and maintain worth anything was near the end of high school when I had done the aforementioned stint with over the counter diet pills.

Oh no! I had enough sense to know that I couldn't go through that drama again. I had to find another way to lose weight. I felt that since the diet pills had been the culprit I needed to find some way that was 'natural'.

That's when I discovered the Dick Gregory Bohemian Diet Plan. When I looked at it, I saw it was basically a fast and liquid diet. I had no experience with doing anything like that and was sure that it was the way to go. I skimmed the leaflet that was enclosed and from what I could see the mix was made up of all natural ingredients, and it looked easy enough, so why not??

I laugh now at the way I read the literature and took the meaning that I CHOSE to take from it. I just wanted to lose weight. Forget about all that 'spiritual stuff' that went along with fasting! Who needed that?? I didn't care about getting closer to GOD, I wanted to get skinny!

So off I went, embarking on self-imposed starvation. And much to my credit (or detriment), I managed to lose a great deal of weight in a somewhat reasonable period. I started working on that plan in August 1990. At that time I weighed 298 lbs. Then, I would go on and off my starvation routine from time to time, alternating with always eating foods that were steamed, and skinless fish and poultry, for lowest caloric content. Of course I would allow myself little 'treat' periods. My routine was that if I stayed on my diet all week I could then have whatever I wanted on the weekend. There was a Baskin Robbins Ice Cream Shoppe on Buford Highway quite a ways from my apartment. I had purchased a bicycle, and would take the back roads from my complex through a neighborhood, up to the shop on Saturdays to get my treat. Naturally those little 'treat' periods would grow and soon I'd find myself packing on pounds again. Then I would go back to the liquid program: Two drinks from the powder mixed with grapefruit juice and a meal in the evenings of steamed veggies, and skinless steamed chicken breast.

In about two years' time I managed to go from that high weight to the low weight of 232 lbs., but it was anything but a smooth ride or a direct descent.After prolonged use (or misuse) of the liquid diet I was beginning to experience excruciating stomach cramps and bloating. That told me that I couldn't continue the behavior indefinitely. I also knew deep down inside that the minute I stopped this ritual the weight would find its way back. I was so convinced of this that the night I decided to stop, I came home from work and set up my camera equipment to take self-portraits. My thinking was, "well take a picture of this because you sure as hell won't be this size for long".

And sure enough practically the moment I got off that routine the weight started to come back. It was not a total loss however. I learned a lot in the experience. Up until that time on some level I had allowed myself to believe that there was some physiological reason that I couldn't lose weight. Well, the experience of those last couple of years of dieting had shot that theory full of holes. And that started me to wonder what was really behind my weight fluctuation. Why was I eating and what could I do to get it all under control?

Of course the very next thought was that I needed to do what most people needed to do. I just needed to get in shape! The apartment complex that I lived in had a health club for residents. I went in and started attacking the weights. Since it was during the day, there was no one around for the exception of the management personnel of the complex. The office was just across from the weight room.

After about three mornings of my coming in and banging around in there, one of the ladies in the office came out and told me that I really shouldn't be doing that. Resistance was the key, and if the weights were slamming down as they were, then I really wasn't achieving anything.

I realized that the reason she was saying anything at all was that the noise was disturbing her, and the reprimand embarrassed me. It also did me good. I knew that she was correct, whatever her reasons, and that I needed some guidance in this area. The funny thing was that I was too ashamed to ask any-one for help. I felt that I was a fat blob and would be ridiculed if I even asked for someone to assist me. Furthermore, the thought of being seen by another person as I embarked on this seemingly hopeless task was horrifying. I was still so ruled by shame in those days.

Fortunately I was able to re-organize my thinking. I decided to come at the problem from the standpoint of, What is it that I like doing that will give me the workout that I desire, that I can do in private and yet get the sought after results? The first thing that came to mind was dancing. So I started off just dancing around my apartment in the mornings when I got off work. That worked for a while, but then it didn't really feel directed enough. So I started to watch some of the exercise programs on television.

While I knew from the start that I was not interested in trying to follow these shows, what I did was watch them long enough to learn the structure of their aerobic plans, then I put together my own using my own music. Step aerobics was very in fashion then and my townhouse had a lot of steps! So using those, I began to work out. That was a terrific starting point for me to get into some type of exercise. It got me going at least.The most important thing was that I needed to sweat. There was still the problem of my food intake though.

Even though I'd left the Dick Gregory Plan behind, I still tried to follow the basic structure that I employed while I was still using that; modified of course. Instead of the two drinks and then having one solid meal, I attempted to do two sub-stantial "snacks" and then a "modest" dinner.

Can't say that worked well for me at all. Having eaten so outrageously for such a long time, all this round of fasting and dieting did was shut my body's natural detection system for weight gain and loss down. Our bodies have a natural system for determining the need for nutrition. When we have eaten outrageously or restricted our food intake, we sometimes throw our systems into chaos. Since I had practically been starving myself for some months, my body was detecting any removal of nourishment as a message that it should conserve. So if anything, my weight hit a plateau and just sat there.

Meanwhile, I was still in the habit of doing the diet plan Sunday through Friday and on Saturday eating anything I wanted. As I'm sure many people have experienced, that lasted about 2 weeks. Before long, I was eating the bland skinless fish and chicken, and steamed, plain vegetables for meals, but then doing all sorts of sugary treats in between all day every day. I had not realized yet that for me, a diet is a short term fix for a permanent problem. I needed to learn how to manage my food intake and exercise on a daily basis for good. My problem really had nothing to do with food, but I didn't realize that yet.

Eventually with all the snacking in between meals, my weight started steadily going up again. I convinced myself that now that I was exercising I could manage that if I exercised more. I began doing my step program for sometimes two to two and a half hours at a time. When I would finish, my legs would be so rubbery that I could not support myself on them. And still the weight would sit in one place for a while and then increase.

Also, though I didn't really see it at the time, I began drinking like I never had before. I was purchasing alcohol at the rate of about three quarters of a gallon or more a week. I would buy a half gallon of Vodka on Tuesday, along with a 1.5 liter bottle of wine. And by Thursday I'd be afraid that I wouldn't have enough to make it through the weekend, so I'd return to the store and purchase either another half-gallon or at least another liter of Vodka. By Monday it would be time to start the whole cycle over again. As I tortured my body with the insane exercise routine, binge ate, and drank uncontrollably, my life was spiraling out of control. Then I met Gunnar and the shit

REALLY hit the fan! He was the type of man that I'd always thought that I wanted in my life. He was from Sweden, and worked in government, so he was in and out of the U.S. on a regular basis. He was the first European guy that I'd ever been involved with and for that reason, I think I fell madly in lust! However, I convinced myself that it was love. For him, I think it was anything but. He was out for a good time and after our initial meeting told me just about whatever I wanted to hear when we corresponded. I now know that what he wanted was some place guaranteed to stay when in town so that all his travels wouldn't show up in his expenses. The Swedish government would allow him to travel to the States unchecked, on a regular basis, but would only cover those expenses that had to do with his work.

Being mentally young and gullible as I surely was back then, I just knew he was the ONE! I began making all these plans for his next trip over and wondering how I could work it so that he could always have a place here with me. I also was thinking that maybe if I were very frugal with my vacation time, I could spend large parts of the summer there with him. I was one step away from declaring undying love and tattooing his name on my body. Whew!

Well to sum up and otherwise very long and boring story, he came to town on his next visit, spent all the time that I was out working running around screwing all over town and then for an encore I took him to South Florida for New Year's Eve weekend where he promptly abandoned me to spend time with someone else for the entire trip. I was livid but I now know that I set myself up for that one.

The day we returned to Atlanta I had to go right to work later that evening. Gunnar waited until I went off to work and then cleared out to take up residence with some other guy that he'd been sleeping with while I was working. I had spent lots of money that holiday season on this creep! I tried to blow it off. My dad used to say, "Bought sense is the best sense". Nevertheless I was devastated. I went into a deep depression that found me sitting in the middle of my bed with a shopping bag full of snack cakes.

As bad as that whole scene was, it was still a learning opportunity. Gunnar was the first time that it really sunk in that I couldn't "manufacture" love or a relationship. Truthfully he didn't really try and hide the fact that love was not what he was there for. I was so starved for it though and had such low self-esteem and self-worth that I was willing to do just about anything to have it. I truly believed that a bad relationship was better than no relationship at all.

Now I can see the tie in between my behavior with the food and alcohol and my emotional distress, but back then that was nowhere on the radar screen for me. I just got angrier and more despondent.

The next few months are a real blur for me. I know I was anxious to go into the New Year making some changes, but was so deep into the sugar binges that it's just a huge fog. I do know that I was doing things like waking up in the wee hours of the morning around 3:00 a.m. and going down to the all night convenience store at the end of my block to buy junk food. I would go there and purchase moon pies,twinkies,Little Debbie cakes,etc., and binge in the middle of the night. Then, I would wake the next morning with wrappers and crumbs all over the bed. The sugar hangovers and the lethargy was pure hell. No one had ever told me that you could have a sugar hangover.

As the year rolled on I was getting increasingly messier in my life. My feelings were in the toilet. I was primarily work-ing, going home, eating insanely and drinking like a fish.

Still struggling to find a toehold at work, someone asked me to supervise, and I said that I would give it a try; A BIG mistake. My mental acumen was such that I could no more handle the focus that was required to manage people than a newborn; let alone all the emotional turmoil that was present in that environment. I don't think I've ever known myself less than during that period. And believe me, in an organization like the Postal Service, it's imperative that you know yourself. Management against employees, employees against each other, and the feeling that everybody wanted to use me – the relief supervisor in the middle - as a battering ram against one another.

That was a very painful time but it was the period that I learned the true meaning of the saying; 'to thine own self be true'. I knew that to do the job I would have to forget about what my fellow employees were saying and doing. And also about management's agenda to use a fellow employee in a temporary position to manipulate the people he usually worked alongside.

The guiding light for me would have to be to do what I felt was right. It was not about what I wanted or what either entity wanted. I learned that but was nowhere near strong enough to enforce it. As a result I soon elected to give the position back over to management and let someone else give it a try.

Meanwhile back at home I'd begun to attempt going out on occasion. Even though my schedule was miserable I just could not continue sitting at home rotting away. So some select Saturday nights found me venturing out to the bars once again.

It was on one such night that I met the guy that was to become my very first mature love interest. He certainly was the first man that occupied a huge space in my heart.

The way I first met John was rather comical. It was a case of mistaken identity. About a week before I was in a club called Blake's on the park. It was a Tuesday evening and I saw this very attractive guy sitting there on the side of the bar. He was dressed in black slacks and a red crew neck sweater. It had the design of Mickey Mouse's face practically covering the entire chest and abdomen area. He was obviously part of that white collar after work crowd; A group of men that have always attracted me. I was just about to walk over and introduce my-self when some guys that were apparently friends of his came over to him. They began to talk with him and that stopped me in my tracks. It's a standing rule of mine that I never approach a guy to introduce myself when he's with a group of people. No matter what, if that's the case he must come up to me first. I doubted this was likely since I didn't even think this guy had noticed me. I went on my way and basically put the incident out of my mind. Well, that weekend I went into the Eagle which was more my usual hangout when I was looking for guys to score with. Tuesday nights and Saturday nights were my off nights then. Since I had struck out on Tuesday, I was back at it on Saturday. As I was standing there leaning against the wall in the hallway I noticed this guy that's somewhat diagonally across from me. He was not really looking at me constantly, but rather glancing my way occasionally, attempting to look nonchalant. Damn! I was sure this was the guy that I'd seen in Blake's the previous Tuesday.

I've always hated the mind games that we all play in the bar settings, but I don't like rejection any more than the next person, so I waited until I caught his eye. I then gave him an exasperated look that seemed to say; "Well? Are we going to talk or not?" He had the required unconcerned near smirk on his face that those places usually demand, but when he saw my look he immediately understood and started grinning. I walked over and introduced myself and we began to talk.

Practically the first thing out of my mouth was that I'd seen him the Tuesday before at Blake's and that I'd wanted to talk to him but was too shy to do so once his friends showed up. He assured me that I must be mistaken. He said he was not there, and in fact, almost never went to that bar. I then asked him about the sweater that he'd been wearing. He denied owning a sweater like the one that I described. Well I knew that I'd not been drunk and was so convinced it was the same guy that I immediately became suspicious. Fortunately I decided that whatever his game was, I couldn't care less. I just thought that he was cute and wanted to get him into bed. I certainly wasn't about to ruin that possibility by belaboring the point. Regardless of whatever happened or didn't happen the previous Tuesday, at that moment he seemed as interested in me as I was in him.

Needless to say we left the bar together and went to his place. I had the most incredible time with him. He was just the physical type of man that usually turns me on. It seemed we were compatible on a lot of different levels. It didn't take very long for me to become totally enthralled by him. And of course, the idea of a relationship at that time would pop up almost instantly, obsessed as I was with the idea of having one.

After that night we began seeing each other on something of a regular basis. He was not working just then. It was 1990 and he had been in the mortgage industry. Things were really rough in the housing market then and he'd just been laid off. I was working graveyard still at the P.O. so when I got off in the mornings I would go by his place every morning and have coffee or go out to breakfast with him. I was thoroughly enjoying his company so it took me by total surprise when he announced to me that he didn't want a relationship.

The way he did it left me saddened, but it also made me mad as hell. He told me in no uncertain terms that he was in no hurry to get back into a relationship anytime soon. However he said quite freely that he was more than happy to just keep on having sex! The funny thing is that were this happening today, I probably would have agreed. And I know that I would totally understand the concept. Age and maturity having set in, I get it now for sure. John was ten years my senior, and had already reached an understanding of himself as a man that I had yet to achieve.

At that time however, I was becoming acutely aware of being objectified sexually by myself and by others. I didn't know yet exactly what I was doing to invite that in, or even if I was the cause, but I knew that I was getting really sick of it. Sex just for the sake of having sex had lost its lustre.

The problem here was that he was 'already in my bones' so to speak. I was very taken with him and knew that I liked him as a person. At that time, I believed that if I stayed there long enough he would come around to see things my way. I sometimes think that what developed was just what we both needed, and maybe even wanted at that time. I was still learning that relationships can take on many different forms. They don't always need to be two people in a committed, monogamous bond. I wanted the companionship, the sex and the emotional connection but thought that I couldn't have those without commitment. John wanted the companionship and the sex, but could have given less than a damn about all the rest. In time I came to see that he had a sort of block to emotional connection, and he sure as hell wasn't interested in any type of commitment. Over time I came to know that he'd had the same situation with a few other men that he sought with me. He saw them as friends, but, like me, they wanted more.

Day by day our relationship grew into something that was a respectful fit for us both. We sort of became 'surrogate' boyfriends. We spent lots of time with each other, did all the things that good friends do, went to affairs like the theater, movies, dinners, parties, etc. We did all those things that one will do with a significant other. We helped each other with projects around our respective homes once we both purchased them. All without having sex or mentioning the sex that we were both having with others. There were a couple of times that the old flames reared in both of us, but when they did we either thought better of it, or studiously ignored them; I'm sure for our own separate set of reasons.

We even went to the Summer Olympic Games together in Atlanta. By that time this relationship of convenience had stretched to the seven year mark. I don't know what his friends made of me, but I know that almost all the people close to me that knew him saw him as my unofficial boyfriend.

Around that time, after all those years together, I started to feel that maybe I deserved more in my life. If I were to ever have more with someone it would mean putting some distance between John and me. We still chatted and went out to dinner on occasion, but I also started to look around for others to date and to get to know.

By the early 1990's I had lost two very dear friends. Both Ernie and Tom had succumbed to illness. Though both were huge losses for me, it was nearly impossible for me to be there for them. I was going through huge changes with work and that was overshadowing just about everything else. I was leaving one location within the Postal Service and being transitioned to another. It was right in the middle of this move that Ernie went into the hospital with various complications. He was having difficulty with many allergies to medications and that was thwarting the efforts of the doctors. From what he told me it was really a crap shoot for them trying to find things that would treat his illnesses because he'd always had so many drug allergies.

Through some of his worst days however he stayed in good spirits. It was difficult for him since he had very little energy and was in the hospital for such a long time.

Tom on the other hand had battled long and hard, but had managed to largely stay up on his feet. There were times that were crushingly difficult. He dealt with several bouts of pneumonia, and kept on fighting for a good bit. After things started to get really bad he made the decision to move back to family. He didn't really have much choice and I knew that hurt him greatly. But being self-employed and having no insurance didn't leave much choice for him. Even after his relocation he made it his business to return on a couple of road trips to Atlanta for a visit.

When he called me and told me what he planned to do it scared the living hell out of me! The drive he was talking about making was no short car trip. He was talking about driving alone from West Virginia to Georgia, and he was not in the best shape. Even so, I knew it meant the world to him to get out of his parents' house just to have some breathing room.

He drove into town and told me he would be staying with friends south of the city for a couple of days, and then would head up to Atlanta and stay with me for a couple more on his way back up to his family.

On the day he arrived I could see immediately that he was exhausted. He went upstairs and directly to bed. He was frail and it was very apparent that the drive had beaten him up. I couldn't imagine how difficult it must have been coming all that way. Let alone the torture of driving back.

The day that he arrived at my place just happened to be one of those days that my sister had parked out in front of my apartment. When she came back that evening to pick up her car, saw that my truck was out front and that there was this unfamiliar car with out of state license plates parked there as well. She knocked on the door and when I opened it she noticed the luggage and made some comment. I remember that I totally lost it! I told her that I couldn't go into it right then, but it was none of her affair and I didn't appreciate her meddling. It was just the type of thing that she and other members of my family had done in the past. Once she found that she was right about the visitor being mine she immediately jumped on a self-righteous high horse and jumped to all types of conclusions. It made me livid and I was sick of it.

This incident, along with a couple of others, was what helped me make the decision to finally put maximum distance between myself and my sisters. Shortly after that I withdrew from the relationship with them so far that the only time I spoke to them at all was when they initiated contact. Even then I kept it as brief as humanly possible. I never discussed with them why I had become so distant. I was so tired of fighting. Truthfully I don't even remember if they even asked, but I'm sure they got the message. It was hell, but it was necessary.

I had no conscious thought at the time that this visit would be the last time that I would see Tom, but I was certainly aware that his time seemed to be growing more limited every day. This last visit was in the early fall; I think around September of that year. It was early the next year when he called and told me that after yet another bout with pneumonia he was just tired of fighting. Shortly after that, within the next three months, the call came that he had died.

I'm sure that all those losses packed in together in just a stretch of a few years were partly the reason I was so obsessed with getting into a relationship. I know that a large part of wanting one was this sense within the gay community that if you got into a relationship then you might be somewhat 'safe'. Add that to my already palpable desire to be loved and a crazy obsession was the result. However, it didn't seem that any of that reasoning was going to sway John's mindset one little bit about getting committed. His mind was firmly made up.

The work transition from Norcross Post Office to North Metro Processing and Distribution Center became complete on September 18, 1990. I remember the date perfectly, as it is my father's birthday. It was a new facility that opened on the northern end of the city. Like the opening of any business, it was totally nuts.

We were working insane amounts of overtime, and my issues with getting acclimated to a new environment were every bit as much in evidence as they had been in any other situation to date. The only saving grace was that everybody else was in a new environment too. Still, it was a coming to-gether of employees from all across the state and beyond to work together, so it meant a sea of new people for me. Imagine going from dining every day in the corner diner in a country town to having dinner suddenly in Buckingham Palace. That was the difference in the work environment at Norcross and the work environment at North Metro. Ours was the first group installed in the facility on that night. Since all the equipment wasn't yet in place you could really see the vastness of the space. I had come from a post office that had no mechanized equipment. We still cased letters manually. Here, you had to ride scooters to get from one end of the building to the other! It looked like you could probably land a 747 in the place, and it wouldn't touch any of the walls.

However some things just weren't changing fast enough. We were working all this crazy overtime and I was still stuck working nights. The whole reason I'd taken the bid coming to North Metro was that I saw it as my shot to get off the night run. I was pretty sure that if I stayed in Norcross that I would be on those hours for much of my career with them. Up to that point I'd worked nights for just about three years and it felt like twenty. I didn't think I could take much more. Ultimately, the arrangement was that even though I had been awarded a bid job with the hours 2pm-10:30pm, I'd still have to remain on nights for the next six months to allow the person awarded the bid position I was currently occupying ample time to complete training and assume that position.

I think knowing that I was coming to the end of the night time work made those last six months even more hell than they would have been anyway. The workload was staggering. There was so much confusion with them trying to get routes changed and trucking schedules worked out. Not to mention that all these people from all these different post offices didn't necessarily all work the same way. The place was a zoo! The upside was that I did get to meet some new people and suddenly there were definitely more gay people around. It was easy to see that some were most definitely out. Still, it was the post office and that meant it was stressful.

Despite all that had happened in the last three or so years one thing was undeniable; Like it or not, for better or worse, my life was certainly moving. That was what I'd wanted from the moment I entered art school with the desire to leave the hospitality industry. Now, all I had to do was grab the reins and get it under some sort of control.

Chapter 7

Chapter 7

Chapter 7

The realization that I needed to make a move toward a more fulfilling relationship started much sooner than the 1996 Olympic Games. However, that was when the thought really gelled in my mind. I was spending so much time with John, my 'surrogate' boyfriend that I wasn't really meeting anyone else. It was back in the fall of 1993 that things first started to come to a head for me around my relationships and just about every other area in my life. I felt so insecure all around that I began doubting my own sanity.

I had become very close to my friend Curley at work. Other than my friendship with Greg, it was probably the closest relationship that I'd ever developed with anyone. She became my rock. I had known very few people that I felt comfortable enough to just be myself with. Even so, I just didn't feel I could share everything.

A few years prior she had openly confronted me asking me straight out if I were gay. It was the first time anyone had done that and their approach didn't cause me to run in the other direction. I think the reason for that was the way that she did it. She let me know up front that it didn't really matter to her one way or the other but she was curious and just wanted to know. She came at me head on, in a reasonable manner with no pretense or shrouded agenda.

By addressing the issue that way it gave me permission to consider the question and took the pressure off as to whether I should answer it honestly. Though I figured that she'd already suspected, it meant a lot to me that she had shown no sign of it chasing her away. Nor had she shown any sign that she would ridicule me or treat me badly in the face of others. That was a monumental moment in my coming out process. As a result we became almost inseparable friends. We became so close that people at work - even supervisors- started to ask us respectively where the other was if one of us didn't show up for work or whatever. We would laugh about it and tell one another just how people were trying to get into our business. She would tell me how this person and that person would come up to her and ask about my sexual orientation, and I would tell her about all the guys that would stop me and try and find out if she were single, had a boyfriend or what.

She became the person that I told some of my most intimate secrets to and I think I became much the same for her. We confided in each other when things were troubling us. So it really was no surprise to me when things started to get really crazy for the two of us wanting intimate relationships. Of course we confided in one another. We often discussed openly our difficulties with dating and trying to find someone with whom we could build a life. It was quite painful at times for us both, and I think we were a great comfort to each other. I had the situation with John which was going nowhere and she had just managed to get away from a man who was very abusive to her. We both went through a lot of hurt and healing and were eagerly looking toward the future. We made a little pact which some would probably call a stupid thing. It was destined to set us up for failure. During that summer we both made the agreement that we would be in committed relation-ships by the end of the year. We sort of turned it into a little contest. I had no idea that it would hit so close to home with some of my core issues. In the end it set me off like crazy.

As the year progressed the stress of not being with any-one began to mount on us both. I don't think it was as difficult for her as it was for me, but who could tell? The tension was making me more and more crazy by the day it seemed. It put my food issues right at the forefront of my mind, and kept them there. The closer it got to the holidays and the more tense this urgency to find someone got, the more I ate. The more I ate the worse I felt about myself. The more the bad feelings built up the more I drank and ate to console myself. Before long it was autumn and I was feeling very desperate about the whole situation. I was unhappy about being alone, being fat, being gay and just generally feeling like an outcast. The whole mess had put me into a deeper depression than I'd experienced in quite a while.

I decided to go away for the weekend. Hopefully that would ease some of the pressure. I had just had an altercation with my supervisor who didn't particularly like me, nor I her. I believe that her reason was mostly my sexuality. We'd ex-perienced many tense situations that were only contributing to my overall discomfort and misery. It didn't help that the environment at the job was always very stressful. The govern-ment was coming down mightily on management, and nobody in the place was happy about that.

I booked a flight to Chicago with the hopes of doing a little playing and getting some relief. The last time I'd been in the city had been when I was there with a group of fellow entertainers for a pageant back in 1982. It was now ten years later, and I was far removed from the show life. By now I had no real contacts in the city. I chose it for my destination for largely that reason. It had been so long since I'd been there and when I was there before there had been little opportunity to explore the rest of the gay scene because of all the time spent within the drag community.

Once I arrived it was not the experience I'd hoped for. During that period, most cruise bars in larger cities were about 'hyper-masculinity'. This still exists to some extent today, but back then several of the bars had entrance policies like, "you must remove your shirt to be admitted". The inference was that if your body wasn't acceptable then we don't want you here. And truly some places in the country if you didn't quite fit the ideal of what they wanted you would be denied entry, or at the very least ridiculed. Being overweight and having a condition called Gynecomastia (abnormal enlargement of male breast tissue), I was sure as hell not about to take off my shirt and let someone be the judge of whether or not my body was acceptable.

As a result I had little or no success going to many of the bars in town there that weekend. It seemed all the hottest clubs for cruising had that ridiculous policy. So the trip that was supposed to help me forget my problems only served to magnify them and depress me even further. I wore my misery like a shroud and felt that everyone in the world could see that I felt awful.

There was a small fast food stand across from my hotel that served the greasiest hamburgers, fries and hotdogs you can imagine. They were wonderful! I bought a liter of Vodka, a couple of quarts of orange juice and spent the next day or so bingeing from the fast food joint and drinking myself into oblivion. I don't think I left that room for anything but more food and booze for a couple of days.

When I finally came out on that Sunday it was a beautiful sunlit day. I decided to go for a walk in the old town section of the city and just enjoy the scenery. It was my hope that this at least might lift my spirits. Maybe it would get me moving in a positive direction.

While walking down the street that day I passed a sidewalk cafe. There was a woman sitting right out front at one of the tables and as I passed she visibly blanched and moved away. Truthfully, there's no way for me to know what brought on her action. But there are a few looks and public reactions that most obese people are quite familiar with. Often people will look straight through you and not acknowledge your presence.Or they may stare at you with expressions of shame, pity,embarrassment or horror on their faces. But by far the worst is when they look at you with expressions of disgust or demeaning impatience. They act as if you're taking up space in the world that's not yours to occupy. The thing about the situation with the woman at the cafe was classic. I'd caught her off guard and she didn't have time to arrange her face. As a result, the look that I got was complete and abject horror. I have never felt so devastated in my life. She seemed to confirm my hatred of myself at that moment. I immediately went back to the hotel and shut myself in the room once again.

That day I hit what people in recovery call a bottom. I decided right then that I needed to get some help when I returned home. I knew that I could not continue as I was, yet I also knew that I was terrified to ask for help. Being desperate I could see no other options. I knew I'd never be able to do this on my own.

Upon my return home I wanted very much to go through with my decision. I ended up procrastinating however because I was just plain scared to seek the help of anyone connected with mental health. Much of the irrational fear I'd experienced was from my deep seated belief that if I sought help I would be told that all my emotional problems stemmed from my being gay. I was convinced that I would be told the only way to deal with those problems would be to turn straight and of course, I knew that was impossible. To some this might sound a bit melodramatic but it was very real to me. Talk about feeling helpless! Since that time I've found that I'm certainly not the only person that's felt these things, but back then it felt like the dirtiest secret in the world and people would be shocked if they knew. Those feelings were so strong that it took real desperation for me to finally do something.

I had shut down to the point of only going to work and coming home. I wasn't going out and facing people at all. The depression had become all- consuming and even the ability to carry on conversation felt as though it was eluding me. Greg called me on the phone one evening for a chat. My response was so off kilter that even I could tell something was very wrong. My thought processes were totally disjointed, and I could not string together an intelligible sentence. He immediately caught on and with a very worried tone asked, "Tony what's wrong with you?" I was trying to talk to him and I knew what I wanted to convey, but it was all coming out garbled and confused. It was so bad it scared him AND me!

I began to relate to him all that had happened and all that I'd been feeling lately; My depression over my weight and the feelings of despair over being gay and not feeling acceptable to the world around me. I talked of feeling shunned totally by the gay community. I told him of the pain and anger that I felt and that it was beginning to take over my life. It felt as though all my life I'd been apologizing for who I was. If not to the world and to my family for being gay, then it seemed that I was apologizing to the gay community for being black. It seemed most of the time I walked around playing the role of vertical rug. My self-esteem was in the toilet all the time. And to top it off I was sure that if I expressed displeasure with anything it would mean exclusion from everything.

I didn't feel committed to any part of my life. No one really knew me. I was so afraid to show who I was that I kept everyone at a distance. My thought now is that my demeanor kept people at a distance from me. On some primal level most were naturally repelled and suspicious. The shrouding around my life kept them on guard around me. The more isolated I felt, the more resentful I became about all of life. It got to the point that the only emotions that I felt were fear and anger. After years of bottling up the feelings inside they were now trying to get out but there was no release valve.

I guess this must be what a nervous breakdown feels like. I thought I was going mad. I was so depressed that I couldn't hold any conversation with people. At work it was all I could do to hold my temper. I was sure that it would erupt at the wrong time and get me fired or worse; jailed any day. I knew I had to do something.

There's always been one thing that I could rely on for escape. That was reading. During that time the one thing that I was consistently doing was reading the community papers religiously. I would grab the Creative Loafing and the Southern Voice, two of Atlanta's most widely read free community publications at the time; on my way home from work.

That week in 'SoVo', as Southern Voice was called, I found a full page spread advertising a treatment center which dealt with addictions; Alcohol, Drug, and yes, EATING DIS-ORDERS. Right across the top of the ad it said in bold letters: LESBIAN AND GAY AFFIRMING. They were just beginning a new phase in the treatment process which they hoped would tackle the unique issues concerning the lesbian and gay community and its members as they attempted to get clean and sober in such an adverse climate as the general populace.

This program sounded tailor made for me. As I've said I almost never missed reading the Southern Voice or the Creative Loafing, yet I'd never seen an ad for that program, and can't remember seeing a full page one after seeing that one. For that reason I've always believed that my finding that piece of news just then was meant to be. Call it God, Serendipity, Divine Providence, Psychic Intervention, Fate, or whatever. I know in my heart that I was being taken care of right then by something outside of myself and will forever be grateful.

As scared as I was to take the chance I decided right then that I would go and see these folks. I needed to know what -if anything- they could do for me. So on the following Monday morning I got up and went to see them.

When I got there I had no idea what to expect. I walked in and told the people what I wanted and they directed me to the intake coordinator. They told me her name was Mollye. I walked into the office and the person had his back to me. All I could really see was that the person was slight of build and of medium height- that they were conservatively dressed in a pair of slacks, penny loafers, socks and a sport coat. With mixed gray hair cut slightly in a style reminiscent of the old Beatles haircut. When he turned around I could see he was wearing wire framed glasses. Then with a start I realized that it was a woman! I was floored! It was beyond me that anyone could be so comfortable and obviously lesbian and working in a professional environment. And all the time apparently not being disparaged for who she was!

We introduced ourselves and my reassurance that this might not be so bad was immediate. We started talking and she asked me about all that was going on and how I was feeling. I told her about the ad that I'd seen and the hard time I was having in my life. I told her About my constant weight gain and the constant dieting. I also told her about my losing control of it when I did manage to lose weight.

She started asking me questions about my life in general. Because I now felt that I was talking to a kindred spirit I was ok with being open with her about my being gay and all that was being brought up in me because of it. However when the inter-view turned to other matters I clammed up quick, fast and in a hurry! She asked me if I'd ever worn women's clothes or had any desire to do so, and I lied my ass off! GOD! I'd never talked to anyone outside of club life about doing drag. Not even other gay people who were not obviously a part of the drag scene. And I certainly wasn't about to start now. Besides, what the hell did my doing drag have to do with my food issues?

I suspect now that my strong protest and nervous reaction most likely tipped her off right away that I was lying, but she moved on to other things and before long I was checked into the program as an outpatient.

Once I'd finished the intake interview with Mollye I was sent downstairs to admissions to fill out all the required paper-work. Even though it was a treatment center and I would be attending as an outpatient, I still had to be admitted. Just to show how seriously uninformed the general public was at that time about eating disorders when I gave my paperwork to the admitting nurse she took one look at it, saw that I was being admitted for an eating disorder and commented that there must be a mistake. I assured her that I was indeed there for an eating disorder. She then commented, "Well you sure don't look like you have an eating disorder!" Outwardly, I'm sure I appeared to be what some would consider a reasonable weight for a large man. I've always 'carried extra weight' well. At the time, to most people eating disorders meant teenage girls who were starving themselves or puking constantly. Then and sometimes even now people don't have a clue as to what all the term encompasses. No one even considered compulsive eating back then. Everyone just assumed that if you were grossly obese you just needed to control yourself. And for guys, it was practically acceptable to be whatever size you were. So with no overt visible evidence people just assumed you didn't have a problem. With this problem it's not about what you're eating, it's about what's eating at you. If that intake nurse could have seen some of the ways I acted out with food when I was alone she would have likely been quite shocked.

I checked into Decatur Hospital Treatment Center in November 1993. Today I can freely say that it's probably the best thing I've ever done for myself. In many ways, I consider it a rebirth. Almost at once I was aware that I had finally hit upon something that would move me in the direction of getting my life together. I was barraged by messages that confirmed for me that the decision was the right one, and if I would honestly take hold of the suggestions given me then perhaps I would experience some introspective growth.

I feel that I was guided considerably during this period. For the first time I felt a positive spiritual connection to the world around me and the people in it.

Much of the six week period spent in treatment passed in a blur. There was so much information being given me that the reshaping was having a drastic effect. Sometimes I was very aware of it but often not. Suddenly I was introduced to a whole new way of looking at my life and the happenings all around. Practically everything that I was exposed to and all that I did took on a whole new meaning.

For the first time in my life I was actually talking to people about some of the very real and troubling aspects of everyday life. All the things that we all see and experience, but never talk about because they're either too personal, too provocative, or too disturbing to discuss with others.

During that six week period I got things off my chest about my life, my family, my sexual orientation, etc., that I never thought that I would discuss with another human being , let alone in a group setting. I also heard my life story in the stories of others. We got honest and unburdened ourselves in the sanctity of that group like I could never have imagined.

For anyone that's never been through any type of group therapy or any related situation let me tell you it's exhilarating, embarrassing, exasperating, maddening, horrifying and more; and all at the same time. At the end of the first week I felt like I had been through hell. I finally understood emotional exhaustion. And all of it was from mostly going back over things I'd already lived through! The more I experienced the better I understood that if I wanted to get to the reasons that I was dysfunctional with food and a few other things I had to go through all this to find those answers. The only way out is through....

It wasn't very long before I had settled into the routine at the treatment center. I was very trusting and dedicated to the idea of getting better so I was quite malleable to whatever suggestions that were given me. I felt as if I had my first break-through within the very first week.

When in the group circle the counselors would do their best to make sure that anyone who needed time to process issues had that freedom. On about the third morning in session there was a woman that brought to the group that she had been put into a room in her halfway house with a girl who was a lesbian and she felt that because of that she was being violated. She felt that consideration should have been given to her. She remarked that she felt as though she'd been put into the room with a man.

The roommate in question was indeed a lesbian and was struggling to come to grips with that fact and to be as honest with herself and in her life as she could. She was very young- I think about nineteen or so- and the whole thing was making her feel attacked. She sat there bawling her eyes out.

One of the reasons that you are encouraged during therapy sessions to bring up your true feelings about various issues is to stimulate reaction and discussion about the issue. That way all can work on feelings in a safe environment. The goal is hopefully to allow people to work through their own feelings about the topic. Well the woman with the complaint couldn't have plugged into what was pissin' me off with the world more if she'd tried!

Before I knew what was happening when the facilitator asked how the group felt about what had been expressed and whether anyone had feelings about it, my hand shot up like a rocket. Once I started to respond it was like a floodgate opening. All the pent-up frustration that I had been holding onto about the way society in general treated gay people and minorities came tumbling out. The myriad of feelings inside of having to defer to straight people ; and in my case, white people in just about all situations came pouring onto that one woman. That pain of being made to feel less than by the world at large because it doesn't understand or agree with my life was instantly laid at her door. There have been times that I wish that the facilitator had done more to stop me because although my diatribe wasn't intended as a personal attack when it started, that was the shape that it was taking. And before I knew it I was practically yelling at the poor woman. In an attempt to defend herself she even attempted to make some unsavory comment back at me, which of course only added fuel to the fire.

Needless to say by the end of the session EVERYBODY in the place knew the big black guy was gay and if you didn't like it you sure didn't want to let him know! People were coming by at lunch letting me know just how much they loved gay people.

While it was a very freeing experience for me I don't want to give people the wrong idea about group therapy. Not all experiences are as lively as that one. The fact is generally the people in the group were usually dealing with many of the same issues so often it would cause people to 'mirror' off each other. That could cause a wide range of emotions. There were days when people would leave the room in tears as well as moments of downright hysterical laughter. Lord knows I was far from the only person to ever get mad in the room. But more often than not the hour would pass uneventfully. There was lots of learning about ourselves and our fellow group members that would hopefully help us to get back on track with our lives.

About the fourth week of my time at the center there was a new therapist introduced to the day sessions. His name was Jamie and he was adorable. Although I had only a little while free of addictive behavior by then, it was very apparent to me that my interest in him was not totally about recovery. It had much more to do with his looks than with his talents as a therapist. While I was aware this was going on inside of me, I had no tools yet in place to defend against those feelings. In fact I didn't even fully comprehend the relation between my sexual urges and my addictive behavior. So I found myself going headlong into a fantasy about him.

When we formally finished the six week stint in out-patient I went into aftercare with the center. There it was strongly recommended that we continue to get support for our recovery through 12 step meetings and even individual therapy if we thought we could use it. That was all the prompting that I needed to tell me I should talk immediately to Jamie about taking me on as an individual client. I don't know what I expected but at the time I was so basic in my approach to attraction that I just knew that I wanted to be close to the guy.

Once in session though I caught on that seeing him professionally was not fulfilling those fantasies. When I saw how futile going down that road would be I had the good sense to end those sessions. I now know how detrimental and derailing that could have been to my overall recovery had I stayed in session with my attraction as the motive for my being there.

While it became clear to me that I was reacting to him physically and that was not what should be going on, that doesn't change the fact that the situation was just plain awkward in its very nature. I would spend an hour twice a month sitting in his office chatting about my relationship issues and my feelings about the hypocrisy within the gay community and then that very weekend would run into my therapist in some bar leaning on the wall with his shirt off cruising in the same sex pool that I was complaining about! TOTALLY FREAKY!

For his part I can only wonder at how difficult it must have been for him. He was a young, single gay man trying to work in the mental health field and wanting to focus most of his help within the gay community. It's not an unusual occurrence for a client to become enamored of their therapist. Yet often many gay men feel that the options for finding partners and mates are rather limited. So it stands to reason that sooner or later if he was out there looking for a partner in social settings he's going to run into his clients in bars or whatever. And while he made it clear that once a person became a client there was no chance for socializing, it just didn't necessarily ring true coming from him. What with seeing his behavior in a social setting as contradictory with what he proposed as good and recovering behavior, it undermined any effectiveness that he may have had therapeutically. Of course that confused and affected me as a client.

The fact that being around him socially was off-putting for me was put to the test a few months after we parted ways. I was out on a date with a guy that I liked a lot, but around whom I sometimes felt a little less than. It was not anything that the guy was doing; it was just that he always seemed to be in such a good place with life. He had a very understanding and loving family, a good job, was very even tempered and generally had such a great disposition that it seemed his life was just charmed.

On this particular night it was the first time that I had gone out with him since I had started my recovery so I found myself feeling a little 'broken' around him. I was hoping for a new start with him now that I was sober and he seemed to be such a great catch. It had been a while since he'd been available.

We decided to go to a play and the evening started out fine. However when we got to the theater the place was packed. It was general admission in a very intimate theater and the only two seats were at the very back of the house. This wouldn't have been too bad, but they just happened to be next to Jamie and his latest boyfriend. And of course they were all over each other. The more I sat there, the more I felt like an outsider. Between them being the loving couple and my date looking like the successful model citizen.

Then to add insult to injury during intermission, my date ran into a friend that he'd worked with at IBM. They started talking about internet technology and that conversation was so over my head that I ended up feeling very isolated and shut out there as well. By the end of the evening I felt very low.

I made it through that and I don't blame anyone for how I felt. The experience helped me to see how delicate the psyche can be and how screwed up it really could have turned out if I had continued the sessions with Jamie while harboring that ridiculous obsession for him.

As time went on, I began to relax into a norm with my recovery. I was enjoying the growth. There was no longer so much discomfort within my own skin.

No matter the drug of choice - whether it's food, alcohol, gambling, drugs or whatever - it takes up a considerable amount of time when you're in its throws. Consequently once you become free of its grasp you usually have an awful lot of time on your hands. That time represents the time you spent getting your drug, thinking about your drug, using your drug, coming down from your drug, etc... As a result of all this new-found time, a recovering person can find that he doesn't know what to do with himself. It's widely believed the reason many people become addicted in the first place is to avoid feelings that accompany our emotions. So once we've cleared out the blocking distractions; the drugs, alcohol, food or whatever, the feelings return. We then need to be sure that we're learning proper methods of coping with those feelings. In the first few days we're normally not there yet. That's why the comrades and the support are so very important. We need people around us to guide us and show us the way.

As I became more acclimated to my new blueprint for life there were many changes. I began to lose all the excess weight I had been carrying around for years. This was happening both literally and figuratively. The people that I encountered in the recovering community had a different perspective about what happened in their lives than most others I'd known out in the everyday world. First of all I found people willing to acknowl-edge that they made mistakes in their lives. That they were not perfect and were willing to try and look honestly at their strengths and weaknesses. That alone was a true awakening. I began to believe that life could be happy and fun after all.

By now I had settled back into my work environment at the postal service though it would be quite a while before I would even attempt to do any garment work again. I found that each endeavor undertaken now that I was sober and abstinent from the food addiction was a totally new experience than it had been when I was still using and blocking my feelings.

I spent much of my time now devoted to the remodeling of my little house and not chasing around in the bars. I was meeting new people and though the encounters were not al-ways smooth, I was much more present with people than I had been in the past.

I was starting to get clearer about my spirituality and where my beliefs lie around that subject. No longer did I feel so challenged in the face of others' belief systems. I had begun to develop one of my own. I wasn't at all sure about the things that I'd been taught as a child about God and Christianity, but I certainly did - and do - believe that something greater than myself is guiding my life, and that all that happened to me was supposed to.

When I looked back at all that had happened in my life over the past years a pattern began to emerge. I could see how each event led up to where I had come in life. Still today I believe there is a Divine order to things and that nothing happens in my life incidentally or by accident.

When I went into treatment and even before ,there were things that happened for which there was simply no other explanation. The surfacing of these feelings created a conflict in me. I began to feel that I had been obviously "God Bashed". All my life people around me had fed me a steady diet of guilt about who I was and how I lived. I understood that though my belief in a Higher Power was intact and growing there was traditionally a great deal of negativity and horror that the religious community of my youth connected to thoughts like this. The more I grew spiritually, I simply could not accept those ideas. Christianity as well as many other organized religions hold a sort of "quid pro quo" imagery of Higher Beings that they espouse. They promise that if you're "good" that the Higher Being will be good to you, but if you're "bad", well - you get the picture.... Because that type of thinking had been drilled into me I believed that God wouldn't even want to talk to me. I was made to believe that my 'sin' was the ultimate misdeed. I was surely going to burn in hell.

However, once I got into recovery I found a whole new way of looking at things. I certainly knew that some really good things had happened for me, despite society's view that I was a candidate for the scarlet letter to be painted on my forehead. But because of how I'd been made to feel about this issue I didn't even think I could share those good things with my family of origin. They'd never believe me. I was sure of it.

But this new way of seeing my "Higher Power" was freeing from all that. I love a statement that I heard a young man make one time. I'll paraphrase here; He said that when he'd been out drinking, drugging - and in my case I'll add killing myself with food - that had been the true hell. He believed that something or someone- who he chose to believe was God - had picked him up and sat him on the right path. He then used the analogy of drowning in the ocean and comparing it to drowning in addiction. His question then became, "Why would God save me from hell and a certain path to death through drowning that way just to drag me up on the beach of life and beat the shit out of me anyway?" If I have no worth then why not just let me drown and die?

Looking at this from that perspective I began to believe that I must have some worth and that something out here in the universe must be looking out for me. There were just too many things that happened from the time I'd graduated art school to the present that fit together and made perfect sense when looked at collectively. When looked at separately I'd never understood why they happened or how I even got in the situations.

Still, with all this evidence at hand the imagery of the punishing God of my childhood was just too strong for me to dispel. As a result I began to look about to see the places in nature that I felt certainly had a fingerprint on them other than the fingerprint of man. Those images; that phenomenon became that special ingredient that allowed me to trust. They helped me greatly to release some of the feeling of responsibility that came when I thought that I had to do everyday life all by myself. I began to believe that it was not all up to me.

I soon started to see a clear picture of my responsibilities versus those things that I could not control. That in turn led me to the knowledge that usually my path is to do the next thing in front of me and forget about the results. Just to take it all step by step.

It began to feel as though a tremendous weight had been lifted from my shoulders. I felt good. Life was moving forward positively. I began to see that the thoughts that rambled about in my head were not that different from the questions and thoughts that go through a myriad of peoples' minds; it was just that I'd never encountered people willing to talk freely about them.

I met gay people and straight people alike who seemingly had begun to transcend a lot of the day to day pettiness of life in search of things more substantive. This is not to say that those people couldn't get lost in the day to day drama that we all get caught up in. We still sometimes allow ourselves to be allured by all the gossip – who is sleeping with whose partner, who's doing what at work, who has the biggest house, etc.; but the difference was that now I found people who were making a conscious effort to learn not to live there mentally or emotionally. To acknowledge those things and identify that it was not the path they wanted to take if they were to stay free of distraction in their lives.

Soon I started feeling like I wanted to catch up on all the dreams and desires that I'd previously thought were impossible for me. I had been a prisoner of my fear and naiveté for so long that I now felt renewed. I could see that all the things that I'd only dreamed about before were not necessarily inaccessible to me.

The only problem was that I didn't really know where to start. All I knew was the way I had done things all along. My whole life since leaving high school had revolved around sex and the bars. So naturally I tried to start my social life back where it had left off. I found pretty quickly that those things didn't fit anymore. In just a few months I'd moved so far away from the person I'd been previously! It was phenomenal.

I was invited to dinner at a friend's house one Sunday evening around that time. I had known him from my days out in the bars. He had moved away from town for a while, but had recently returned and was trying to reconnect. It seemed like a really good idea to go, I thought. We both had worked in clubs, he as a deejay and I as an entertainer, so I thought this would be ok. Unfortunately things were a bit shaky when I got there. There were only four people - a couple of other friends of his, him and me. Dinner went ok but they were all drinking and smoking pot, and when I declined I could see it made him feel a little uncomfortable. We did have some good times chatting about all the old times and the people that we'd known. I had gone over about 3:30 or 4:00 p.m. with the thought that I would stay for dinner and then go to an 8pm meeting that I usually attended. Things got just a little tense around seven when I told him that I would have to leave shortly. He didn't understand why I wouldn't stay and go out to the bars with them later on. I tried to explain that I had a previous appointment and when he asked what it was, I tried explaining to him. Not only did he not understand but like so many others in the world, he saw my trying to turn over a new leaf as a criticism of them and the life we once shared ; the things they were still doing.

This turned out to be my first encounter with that issue. I have since found that the biggest problem that I have with telling most people that I'm not drinking or binge eating is that I then have to listen to them defend that they are still doing those things. I now know not to take that on as my issue, but back then it really felt shitty. There's nothing you can say to someone when they're wrestling with their own decisions about their behavior in life. It's the battle between desire and consciousness and all you can do is stand there and be an embarrassed witness to the struggle.

I hated to walk out on his little homecoming, and would have had no problem getting together again to maybe see a movie together or the like, but it was pretty clear to me that I wasn't on the drink and party page in life anymore.

After I left I went directly to the meeting and ironically I ran into a girl that I knew to be a good friend of his. Apparently he had called her and talked to her about the situation. She knew my path, as she was trying it out for herself. She talked to me and told me that she had spoken to him and explained what was up with me. She and I had never really been friends, but I knew she was friends with him so I was grateful to her for attempting to smooth things over. Nevertheless I never heard from him again.

My early attempts at trying to rebuild friendships are full of encounters like this. At first the going was really tough. I didn't know any other way to form friendships or any other arena in which to look ; my life experience being what it was. So naturally it wasn't very long before I would venture back into the bars to make contact with other gay men.

If I thought the atmosphere in most gay bars was uncomfortable for me before I got sober that was nothing compared to what it was for me now. It was as though all the character defects that I saw in my fellow gay men were magnified a thousand times. The problem was that I seemed to be the only person in the place that noticed it. The honest disillusionment that I'd found in the gay bar culture earlier; the blatant hypocrisy, prejudice, sexism, ageism, and overall narrow minded shallowness of it all suddenly morphed into downright loathing.

I need to be very clear here and say that this was not a case of my feeling pious or above anyone. I had no problem with people having a good time and doing whatever they needed to do to have that fun, but there was a definite awareness in me that prevented me from just taking it all in stride as I had for many years. I had not yet realized that bar culture is not and never has been the real world. I was still trying to fit basic principles that were developing in my life into a plan including people who did not share those principles.

The very idea of walking into a bar and having people totally ignore me when I said something to them or have them bump into me (with me well over six feet tall and over two hundred pounds) and then act as if I weren't even there was no longer tolerable to me. Not to mention the seemingly foregone conclusion that has always existed in the predominantly white gay clubs; the ever present idea that black patrons should just accept whatever treatment is given them and should be grateful just to be there and have them accept our money.

Then, beyond the obvious racist stuff is the fact that often gay men don't really seem to respect very much. Not strangers, not those that they call their friends or relationships, not each other as people and often, not even themselves. All the bitchiness and cattiness was just too out there for me now. Angry exchanges that just mere months earlier would have had me trying to feign ignorance, or pretend they didn't matter, now affected me deeply. I was very aware of feeling let down, saddened, and upset. However, the recovery was that I could see clearly that the problem was not me. Before, I would spend hours going over the situations like that in my head trying to figure out what I'd done to make the person act that way toward me. Or if there was something I'd done to offend the person.

I now was very aware of the tense feeling that for years would grip me in my belly when I would venture out to the clubs. Now however I wasn't having three to four drinks before leaving home to steel myself for the onslaught. There became a sameness to it all that was at best depressing. These days

I really didn't feel there was a chance in hell of meeting any-one for anything substantive there. But still, I didn't yet know where else to turn. It was quite the dilemma. I didn't want to start shopping in the recovery arena for a boyfriend, but I was very lonely. Making friends there was ok, but I just didn't want to be looking for partners or whatever. Even in those early years I had an inherent sense that I shouldn't pollute the waters that my life's sustenance was coming from.

I didn't yet understand that developing relationships is a process. There is no 'certain' place to go to meet that SOME-ONE. The reality was that I wasn't far enough along to realize that I didn't know how to be friends with gay men and not bring the sexual component into it. I feel that sex addiction and sexual objectification in the gay community (and maybe in society at large) are at epidemic proportions.

It would take many fitful starts, much pain and a few more years for me to learn that this too was part of the rebuilding that needed to happen in my life. It was very unclear in which direction I should head, so even though I really didn't trust the thought of meeting anyone through the recovery community I was willing to give anything a try.

I met a young guy at the hospital. He was just completing his treatment, and I was doing aftercare. I don't totally remem-ber when I first saw him, but I did think him attractive in a sullen and angry sort of way.

We struck up a conversation and pretty soon I asked him to dinner. I really didn't know what I wanted from him; whether just to talk, a friend, sex, or what. Today I know that I was in no shape to be starting anything new with anybody. No new friendships even. My total concentration needed to be on myself and getting my life in order. But I was still very capa-ble of deluding myself and thinking I would just strike up a conversation and become friends with him. When I asked him out he readily agreed. Pretty soon we were talking on a regular basis to each other and I told him that I'd like to get to know him better. I said that perhaps I was looking to date someone, but I wasn't sure that I wanted anything serious. He said he could understand that, and thought it would be cool to date for a while.

Needless to say it took all of about one more day for us to end up in the sack. Today I think I would see that was probably the worst thing we could have done. However back then I was in no shape to make those type determinations. Even so I was content with going out to the movies, going to dinner and even attending meetings together. It was good to just spend time with him hanging out. He, on the other hand, was anxiously seeking more. I found that as I got closer to him he had some very deep unaddressed issues going on.

There was major tension going on between him and his parents. They were having a tough time with his being gay. They also objected to his not being responsible around work and career. You name it; he was having a problem with them about it.

Another big issue that he had was the fear of being HIV positive. While that was of course an issue for everyone, as he talked I realized that he didn't know what his health status was. There were still people who thought that ignorance around the issue was somehow safer than the stress of knowing. For me, I had for years by then treated EVERY partner that I had as if they were positive; Meaning that my sexual repertoire had become such that if it were not deemed safer practice, I didn't do it. And while it was a stressful nightmare to test, I knew that it was necessary.

So now I found that while I felt like I had a brand new start at life, he was feeling like perhaps his time was running low. Add to that his already low self-esteem and it was a recipe for want and desperation. I could also see that with our age difference (I was perhaps 8-10 years senior), I represented to him a replacement for the father that he hated as well as some type of security.

After a couple of months I began to feel pressured into making a relationship commitment. He wanted that and he wanted it NOW. And the more he pushed, the more I wanted to retreat. Hell, I was just beginning to feel that my life was opening up. There was much that I wanted to see, do and feel.

I can say there are lots of reasons that I was not keen on getting into a serious relationship with him. Amongst them was his fatalistic approach to HIV. Scared, but not willing to do what he needed to for himself. It was somewhat scary to be with him and felt like Russian roulette. I tried to keep abreast of my health and things going on with me. Even so, it still felt like Dodge City out there, with no guarantees.

It's been my experience that many of the people that I've known that had suspicions that they were HIV positive usually have turned out to be so. I think that we know our own bodies. If something within a person is reacting in a way that gives rise to a suspicion of a health issue, nobody knows the inner workings or feelings of your body better than you. After the decade that I'd had prior to coming into recovery - losing parents, friends, etc.- the very thought of getting involved with someone who was feeling and thinking this way; choosing denial over being informed, scared the hell out of me.

My problem was that I'd developed no boundaries yet, and could not tell him that I wanted out. So he kept asking, and I kept stalling. Hoping all the time that he would get the message and move on. After a while I started to think that he had the message all right, but was going to make me say it.

This actually went on for months. It got to the point that it was downright comical. I was dodging him at every turn by now.

I had previously made plans with a friend to go to the Stonewall 25th year anniversary celebration in New York. As we neared the departure date my friend determined that he would not be able to go. I had been looking forward to this trip with my friend Kevin for a long time. It would be the first real break from my routine since I'd gotten sober and abstinent. As it turned out, without my knowing it, Kevin decided to sell his ticket to Johnny, the guy I was dodging; and didn't tell me first! Kevin knew that Johnny and I had been seeing each other but had no idea the state of the affair.

Now I knew there would be no way I could get out of the inevitable confrontation that I'd been staving off. We would be in New York sharing a hotel room over a four day weekend.

The blow up finally came on our second day there. We'd been over to Macy's in Herald Square to do some shopping and were walking along in Central Park when I told him there was something we needed to talk about.

He threw a fit and went totally ballistic. You would have thought he had no idea this was coming, but truthfully there's no way he couldn't have known. I'd been dodging him and his calls for at least two weeks prior and once we'd gotten in the hotel the night before I'd slept so far on the edge of the bed that a breeze would have made me lose balance and fall off.

I offered to give him the ticket difference to fly back to Atlanta, or to get another room there in the hotel. Neither of which was he even willing to consider. I think he was determined at that point to make the trip as hellish as possible for me.

We struggled through the remainder of the days, went to the pride parade, spent some time in the Village and of course had endless deep conversations. He confided in me at that time that all he wanted was to, "get it right just once before he died". Well that was the WRONG thing to bring up if he were trying to get me to stay!

I don't remember much about the final days of the trip; Just that I couldn't wait for it to be over. However, the one thought that kept reverberating in my head was how alive I felt being in New York during that time and in spite of the friction with him, I was feeling free and enjoying myself just being in the city amongst all the people. Not feeling weighed down by family issues or work. The time away helped me feel totally free of day to day responsibilities. Things like, "I should be home doing work around my house. I ought to be saving this money rather than blowing it here in New York". For the first time in a very long time I was enjoying myself.

Somehow by the time we got on the plane to return home he'd decided that maybe a month's cooling off period would do some good. So on the train ride back into the city he informed me that for the next month he didn't want to hear from me, see me, or anything... (HUH?) Hell, I thought I heard myself say in the park a couple of days before, "I DON'T WANT TO BE IN A RELATIONSHIP WITH YOU".

Well, the no contact idea was just fine with me. I was sure that by the end of that month he would have seen that it was clear I was moving on and it was probably best for us not to see each other if we could help it.

Almost to the day of that month, I received a call about 4:00 a.m. The caller said, "why haven't you called me"? I was very disoriented and had no idea who it was, so I said as much. Definitely the wrong response! He went off ; calling me all sorts of names. I could tell he was really in a bad way. There was no telling how long he'd been drinking or what else he might have been on. I tried to calm him down but he just told me to fuck off and hung up the phone. Needless to say that shook me to the core. I was awake and up for the day from then on.

His sponsor called about 9:00 a.m. and told me that he and someone else had gone over and taken care of him. He'd gotten drunk and ripped the phone out of the wall, but thankfully had not hurt himself. They said it was probably best if I stayed away, so that's what I did.

It was many years before I talked to Johnny again, but when I did next speak with him it seemed he'd at least begun to get himself together. I'd heard through the grapevine that he'd gotten into a relationship with a guy shortly after the incident on the phone. When he did finally contact me, it was to ask if I would take some photos of him. He was a musician and wanted me to assist him with publicity pictures so that he could go back to booking work for himself. I don't know what happened. He didn't show up for the meeting that we'd scheduled. I never heard from him or saw him again.

That remarkably free feeling that I'd experienced in New York stuck around however and I began to grow curious to know more of it. I wanted to experience it in as many ways as possible. Between a strong feeling that my life had become very stale and routine and the desire to continue to grow I soon found that I was increasingly curious about the world around me and its inhabitants. I was going to about five or six meetings per week, working a straight forty hour schedule with no overtime and working on my house. That was the extent of my life. Even though I was now comfortable going into bars if I chose, I knew that what I was seeking was not there. I remember chatting with Greg and talking about a recent trip that his employer had sent him on to England. I had always wanted to go to Europe. I began thinking about it more and more. I started to check into air fares and was pleasantly surprised to find them quite reasonable. For the next few weeks all I could think about was how great it would be to get away and finally see the places that I'd heard so much about all my life. I had settled on starting in Amsterdam. A friend of mine had told me that it was easy to navigate, and everyone spoke English, so there wouldn't be a language barrier.

I'd be lying if I didn't say there was some hesitation. After all, I'd heard all the stories that you hear in the media. The drug scene was supposedly rampant. The word was there were junkies practically lying about in the streets, or so the news made it seem. But I had also heard that it was the most sexually liberated place on the face of the earth.

So after much mulling it over I called Delta and booked a round trip flight. It was February of 1996. I can remember peoples' responses when I told them of my plans. Even though I was wildly excited about the trip, more than once I had people ask me, "Aren't you afraid to go over there alone?" Prior to this I had no clue that American people had such an aversion to leaving the country. It was astounding to me. The second most popular question that I got was, "why are you going in the winter?" But I would not be swayed! I was not going to become leery of the trip because of these pessimists!

I boarded my flight on February 16, 1996, at approximately 6:00 p.m. Although it was a night flight, I was hardly able to sleep! The experience was already happening and I didn't want to miss a minute of it.

I had brought my handmade leather coat and a group of doctors from Jacksonville, Florida who were also on the flight were floored by it. They asked if I had a catalog and I had to tell them that I was not really established with my clothing as of yet. They all gave me business cards and asked me to contact them once I was back in the States. I was thrilled at the prospect of the coat being an advertising tool for me on this trip. I'd never thought of it that way when I'd packed it, but now it seemed a good idea to me.

There was a tremendous amount of activity on the plane as it made its way to cruising altitude. I'm not usually a very social person on flights, but this night seemed to be the exception to that rule. I was seated next to a very nice older fellow who was traveling to The Hague to visit his son who worked there. We struck up a good conversation and soon became kindred spirits if for no other reason than we were both virgins to international travel.

Soon the duty free cart was brought around. Wow! This was the first time I was ever on a flight where you could shop from your seat and I truly loved every minute of that. I had run off and left my watch home and that left me feeling pretty naked. This was before everyone had a cellphone with a built-in clock. So of course I purchased a watch from the flight attendant.

Another thing that was new and I must say a little difficult for me was how once the flight got rolling along it seemed that every time I looked around the carts were coming down the aisles offering food. There was the initial dinner service, and then two or three snacks served, countless offerings of beverages as well as the coming breakfast offering prior to our landing. With my new food plan this was making it very tough for me. To this day when I travel internationally the flight length and the changes of time can disrupt my food and my body rhythms if I'm not careful.

Nevertheless, I was not willing to allow that little glitch to ruin this experience for me. I went about my business and watched movies or whatever.

Once we reached Schiphol Airport it was about 7:30 a.m. I doubt I'd slept two hours. I was keyed up. A little nervous and extremely excited, I didn't know what to expect. I had talked to friends who had assured me that there was nothing to worry about. Practically everyone that you'll encounter in Amsterdam will speak English. So I was armed with the assurance when I left the plane and collected my luggage.

Heading through customs I presented my newly minted passport to the officer. He asked me the reason for my visit and where I would be staying in the city and for how long. Upon answering his questions, he looked down again. When he noticed my last name he immediately commented, "Welcome home Mr. Holland, I hope you enjoy your stay!" As he beamed at me, I thought to myself, "I couldn't have scripted this. This is the best moment ever."

Downstairs in the airport very near baggage claim there is the train station and platform. There you can catch the train into the city or wherever your next destination may be. I picked up my ticket and made my way into Amsterdam's Central Station. Once I reached the platform there all my doubts were suddenly recalled.

Once I exited the train, having never traveled by train before, I had no idea that I needed to go downstairs to enter the actual station there. I looked over and saw a man that I assumed was a railway employee. He had on an official looking uniform. I went over to ask him about transportation into the city. Wouldn't you know the very first person that I attempted to speak with in this place clearly didn't understand a word of what I was saying! That immediately flustered me but I told myself to calm down and observe. It wasn't long before I noticed that the people around me were all heading downstairs so I reasoned that perhaps I should follow. That little experience helped me return to what I call common travel sense. Observe the surroundings, stay alert, and think, think, think...

Once downstairs and armed with my tram ticket into the city I was ready to go. Even now I love to travel to foreign places during the off season. This first trip gave birth to a realization that I still use today. Not only are the costs of travel this way more reasonable, but there's no snarl of tourists. You can get a true feel for the place that you visit. It's not dressed for show. It just is what it is. The people are going about their daily business and life there is much more relaxed. It makes for a less rushed feel to the vacation.

When I boarded the tram and headed into the city I was astounded by the sheer beauty and the fairytale quality of it all. My hotel was just across from Westermarket Church and just down the street from the Anne Frank House.

When I entered the Hotel Aspen it was like entering a different world. I was totally enchanted. The hotel itself was tiny. Maybe a dozen rooms at most. I rang the buzzer and was let in. The first thing I saw was a long staircase of at least eighteen to twenty steps. I was at the very bottom and lugging three pieces of luggage. The proprietor looked at me like I was crazy. I schlepped the bags up to the landing where he waited and was checked in. And then of course I found that my room was on the very top floor! Lesson number two of international travel: Learn to pack tightly! Well, off to climb even more stairs. Once in the room I found that a single room by European standards means a bed that's practically the size of an army cot! Not the best news when you're my size.

Despite all this I could not have been more excited. Once I got settled in I knew that in order to have the best experience possible I needed to take care of myself. So right away I lay down to take a nap. I set my alarm to sleep for four hours and was out almost instantly. My room had ceiling skylights and just before I went to sleep a motion caught my eye. It was a seagull flying over the roof. I was immediately reminded of the opening scene in the movie, "The Diary of Anne Frank"(Shelley Winters Version). As I pulled the duvet up over me that morning I was more content than I had been in quite a while.

When I awakened a few hours later the first thing I did after showering and dressing was dig out my map of the city. I wanted to get my bearings since it was my first time there. Whenever I'm somewhere new that's what I try to concentrate on the first day; walking the neighborhood and checking out the landmarks, the attitude of the people. I like just getting a general overall feeling for the city. From the moment I started walking through the town I felt as though my senses had been plugged into an electrical outlet. Just the experience of walking past buildings and knowing they had been there since before the turn of the century. I've never felt so inspired. Though I was never a great sketch artist, the architecture, the crisp air and the love of art and culture all inspired me tremendously. Before the day was over my mind was reeling. I had definite imagination overload. Artistically my focus at the time was outerwear and the designs were coming so fast that I was sketching on the backs of paper bags, magazines and anything handy that I could draw on while the ideas were hot.

At the time Amsterdam proper was still chock full of little clothing shops, antique shops, loads of small art galleries as such. Not to mention all the small eateries. There is a little Italian place on the corner just down from Westermarket Church going in the direction of Dam Square. I still make it my business to eat there often when I'm in town. It was the very first restaurant that I dined in while there. It's a very homey type place and the owner and staff know everyone.

On my first stop I learned a bit about dining, as well as everyday life in Europe. My plan had been to eat my meal and split for the nearest gay bar I could find afterward. Well these people were in no great hurry to get to me and help me on my way. Everyone in the place was super nice; they just weren't in a hurry to do very much. I began to realize that the ritual of dinner here - for patrons and staff alike- was something to be savored and enjoyed, not rushed through as if the whole affair was a tremendous nuisance. Slowly I began to loosen up and thaw out a bit. I realized there was no reason under the sun for me to be in such a rush. There was nowhere specific that I needed to be. In fact I could take as much time as I liked and nothing would be ruined, no one would be angry, and best of all I could be that way without sneaking about feeling guilty that I was wasting time. It turned into the most wonderful experience chatting with the proprietor and the waitress who it turned out was his daughter.

There is something about the dark interior of the place. It is very cliché. All the way down to the red checkered tablecloths. The booths and tables are all very old and worn wood. The little tabletop candles in glasses are just as essential to the mood as the fact that you're subject at any moment to look down and see the owner's cat wandering through the room. I don't think I've ever felt as calm, entertained and satisfied in a restaurant in my life.

The food was good. Not pretentious, but very tasty and simple fare. And the fact that the host asked and genuinely seemed to care about my answer made his request for my opinion of the meal the perfect signature. This place was the perfect kick off to my first evening in the city. When I left my stomach was full and I was ready for some fun.

I took to walking in earnest. The little canal bridges trimmed in white lights, the people all zooming past on bicycles and on foot, all the different sights and sounds coming from the various bars and restaurants. All of it was spectacular. There was just enough of a nip in the evening air to make it pleasant.

I found my way over to Kerkstraat and the Spijker Bar. Very much a neighborhood establishment, it was the first bar that I went into. It's not on the beaten path with all the other gay bars and to find it you'd have to look a little. I have since found that a friend of mine that's lived in the next town thirty minutes from Amsterdam all his life had never been to it until I took him there on a subsequent trip! That first night for me was really cool though. There were just enough people for it to feel right. Not a big crowd and not empty. There was even a friendly pool competition going on. Up a narrow spiral staircase at the very back of the club were the restrooms and some of Amsterdam's infamous back rooms. I had heard for years that just about all the bars in Europe had backrooms and back then, for many of them it was so.

Even though the bar was a neighborhood affair I was received well. I could see they were politely curious, and there was a little 'discussion amongst friends' about the stranger; but no rudeness. I immediately did my best to be open and friendly to them. I let them know that I wanted to join in the pool games and they allowed me to. It helped that I played well but lost at the few games that I joined in. It didn't matter. The important thing was that I wanted to show that I was not the aloof American tourist who shows disdain for the natives that many people in foreign countries expect. Before the evening was over I was convinced that I had managed that. They had all loosened up considerably and we laughed at the games whoever won or lost.

Not only in that little bar, but throughout the city for the next few days I had an amazing experience. For the first time in my life I believe I was experiencing how it felt to just be a man.;Perhaps a visitor and a stranger - but a man first, maybe an American second, and THEN a black man. For the first time I was not treated as though my color was the most defining quality about me and that felt really great.

I finally understood the attraction that so many African American artists had for Europe in the early twentieth century as well as now. The cultural overload is staggering and the sense of equality - though maybe not totally without some curiosity - is certainly more welcome than the devaluation that comes all too often here in the United States.

For the next four days I dined well, soaked up museums, and shopped until I thought the soldier on the Amex card would revolt! And I tried quite literally to bathe in the attention of some of the most beautiful and interesting men that I'd ever met. Okay, I mean I just about ran myself ragged!

Moreover I came to realize the image that the media had given me of Amsterdam was nothing like the actual experience. I had been fed images of the freedoms and liberal attitude as something akin to a modern day Sodom and Gomorrah. There was one newscast I'd recently viewed that discussed the handing out of needles to addicts. They had given the impression that people were lounging about in parks and other public venues casually shooting up. I never saw anything like that. In fact the truth as I experienced it is that while there is a much more liberal attitude around sex and the use of 'soft' drugs (marijuana, hashish,etc.) generally people are not just bombed out of their skulls. The usage is moderate. Not only is it not a public nuisance but most will use a type of etiquette around their usage. Meaning if they are in a place where using is not the order of business so to speak, they will refrain from use. Also, it's my understanding from others that often marijuana is cut with tobacco in casual everyday use. I don't smoke myself, so I don't know.

The city itself was, and is, such a menagerie of emotion for me. Down each side street I found myself confronted with a peek into the city's history. I'm sure that to the everyday inhabitant the railing on the apartment building just up from my hotel was just wrought iron railing but I could imagine how many times that railing had been repainted and how many hands had used that very balustrade to descend that flight of stairs over the years. The second morning that I was in town I witnessed a road crew repairing the stone roadway. I was intrigued to find that the method used was just about the same as when the stones were put into place. Years later when I'm sure there are many quicker and perhaps less cumbersome methods of making that repair, the powers that be see the preservation of tradition in their country as that important.

Coming from a culture that's very young in comparison it seems that we're not at all interested in keeping our history evident. I was impressed and deeply touched.

Another big shock to me was that the entire time I'd been there I had yet to hear a sound that's frequently heard here in the States. For three whole days in this supposed 'city of sin' I had yet to hear a siren or see any police presence. In subsequent visits I have encountered the police, so they are there, but my point is for all the talk about this place being dangerous and corrupt, I found that they actually have a pretty low crime rate. One of my theories on this type of situation questions the difference between the two experiences. I have to wonder if having a more open and less conservative environment might not have a more positive psychological impact on a city. Is the idea of taboo always better and/or safer for the populace? This experience had me thinking that sometimes treating the things that we see as questionable as just another factor within our society takes a lot of the mystery out of them. It therefore appears to me that when there's no great mystery people are perhaps not so apt to want to experiment. I walked through this town in the wee hours of the morning and saw singles, couples and even a couple of young Dutch women out on bikes in the city. None of them appeared especially anxious or tense about the hour. Nor did they appear concerned that the streets were not very crowded. Residents there have confided to me that the biggest concern they have is the occasional pick pockets.

Before I knew it and far too soon it was my last day in town. I got an early start because I wanted to drink in as much of the city as I could take away with me. My feelings were very mixed. I was totally taken with the place and hated to leave, but I also knew it would not be realistic to start thinking along those lines. I can say however this was surely the birth of me feeling that at some time I would like to live somewhere other than the States for at least a little while. I was learning there are a lot of different ideas about what makes up daily life; more than just what I've been exposed to.

As much as I'd always loved to travel, going home this time was going to be bittersweet and I knew it. As I was walking around I decided to try and find something that would last as a commemorative treasure to mark this; my first European vacation.

I knew I didn't want or need more clothing as my closets are usually running over at home. No, I wanted my treasure to be something special as well as something that would say Amsterdam without being cheesy about it.

After looking at furniture, light fixtures, sweaters, rugs and just about everything else one could think of I was about to head back to the hotel when I wandered into a small art gallery on Prinsengracht. There was a young woman sitting on a barstool near the back of the shop. As I walked in she looked up from the book she was reading. She greeted me with a warm smile before returning to her reading.

As I browsed the walls I loved the work that I saw there. Many were stunning pieces. The shop was very small and simple. No really elaborate frames hanging anywhere. Several of the canvases were stacked against a wall stretched, but with no frames at all. There was also a small table nearby with pieces that had yet to even be stretched. I went over and started to flip through the ones stacked against the wall. There were many that were quite good.

After a while the young lady came over and asked if I'd found any that I wanted. I pointed out a couple of oils. She told me the artist was local and that his work was beginning to develop a good following there. Both pieces were scenes of canals there in town. I told her I was undecided which I should take, and of course she suggested that I take both! We chuckled and though it would have been nice, I wasn't even sure about making it home with one safely. It would be horrible for them to be damaged during the trip.

After making my final decision I had her wrap it for travel and prepared to pay. I was short about twenty five guilders, which was the Dutch currency at the time. The Euro had not been adopted as of yet. I told her that I had American money with me and asked if she wanted to do a currency exchange there in the shop. She said that she was never very comfortable doing that. She probably would have come out on the winning end of the deal since U.S. currency was much more valuable than Dutch currency at that time. I'd found that most merchants, cab drivers and the like would usually jump at the chance to do this type of exchange if given the opportunity. The fact that she was not willing to spoke volumes about her character.

At any rate, we were encountering a little problem here because I really wanted the piece. It was Sunday evening, she was very near her closing time and there was not a currency exchange shop close by. Though you can find them all over town there, by the time I ventured out to one and returned it would be well past her closing time. I offered to pay with a credit card but the only card that I carried was American Express and she only accepted Visa and MasterCard. The next day was Monday but she would not be open until after lunch. Unfortunately, my flight was leaving that morning.

Then she shocked me completely. She asked me if I intended to go out partying since it was my last night in town. I told her that I did. She then headed back to her desk and took out an envelope. She self-addressed it and then came back over to me. She took me outside and showed me her letter drop. She then asked me how much money I had in Dutch Guilder. When I told her she said, "Ok, you're somewhat short but I trust you. Give me what you have and when you go out this evening you can get some money exchanged. Place the balance in this envelope and just drop it in my mail slot on your way back to your hotel." I was flabbergasted. The fact that this young woman; having treated me with extreme grace, was now willing to allow me to walk out of her shop with her merchandise. Here I was, someone she'd never laid eyes upon, and she was willing to trust that I would leave her the difference on an honor system. That was astounding to me. In the States I would have never even been allowed to browse so freely. I would have been watched and questioned as to "whether I needed help" from the moment I entered. And that close to closing time it would have been made very clear to me that I needed to hurry. And NO WAY would the person here have ever thought that there could be anything like honor about the money!

I thanked her effusively and assured her that I would leave the money for her. I gushed so that I'm sure she must have thought me an idiot, but I couldn't help it. I was just blown away by the incident. I kept my word. I did go out that evening, got the exchange done and left her the balance along with a warm note of thanks.

The next morning I took off from Amsterdam on a flight that had every seat filled. It was so crowded that I had to have the flight attendant put my painting in a closet up front in the plane. Because it was only stretched and not framed I spent the whole eight hour flight worried to death that someone would put something in that closet and slash right through the canvas or something. Happily it made it through the flight ok and hangs in my home to this day.

An interesting little side note about this episode for anyone who doesn't believe in Karma:

It was just over a decade later on a pass through Amsterdam that I ventured over to Prinsengracht in search of that art gallery. On other trips there for one reason or another I had not gone in search of it. But on this trip I decided to. I had lots of time on my hands since the only real reason that I'd come through the town was to visit my friend Joost on my way home. As I remembered, it had been in the 400 block of the street. As I walked down the street looking for it, I almost passed it by when I reached its door. So much had changed in the city I was doubtful that it would even be there. But indeed, there it was! Only now the facade was much different. Though I don't speak Dutch, I do read and speak a little German. The languages are close enough that I could make out some of what was written on the sign. It was informing passersby that entrance was by appointment only.

I could see a very chicly dressed woman at the back of the room at a desk. She was speaking to a gentleman there. I wasn't sure if my intrusion would be welcome, but I decided to ring the bell anyway. She came to the door with a very questioning look on her face. I explained that I had purchased a piece there many years ago and would only be in town for a very short while. I asked if it wouldn't be too much trouble, if I might come in and take a look around. She assured me that it would be fine. She inquired that perhaps I might like to make another purchase while there on this visit as well.

It was quite clear to me that the little shop and its young owner were doing quite well these days! What was on her walls was a bit of a different story from days gone by. From what I could see with just a quick look around, about the smallest and perhaps least expensive piece in sight was a little Rembrandt landscape that was listed at 17,000.500e!

I like to think that her willingness to be kind to who knows how many traveling strangers all those years ago has translated into great success for her and her 'little gallery'.

Returning home when I've been on vacation has always been a challenge for me. I love my home but the re-entry to my world is almost always culture shock. It means facing reality; Bills, work, life, etc. That first time back from Europe was more jarring than most.

I once had a friend that was a German native living here in the U.S. He had done a lot of traveling in his life and in fact owned a travel agency. When I first started to think of traveling outside the country he said, "I think everyone should travel to foreign lands. They may not learn a lot about the countries that they visit but they'll certainly learn a lot about where they come from." That was never more glaringly apparent to me than when I returned home on this particular occasion.

Flying home my seat was near the rear of the plane. I'm usually a person who doesn't really care where he sits as long as there's ample leg room. I'm tall - it matters... I'm not sure if the airlines do this anymore but back then from time to time they would actually de-plane from the rear door of the air-craft. That was the case on this flight, so I was one of the first people to exit.

Whenever you enter the country you have to declare goods and clear customs. My original point of entry on this return trip was Detroit, Michigan. Not having flown inter-nationally before and having been received so graciously when I entered the Netherlands it really didn't occur to me there might be any friction when I returned home. Also there was an Olympic Speed Skating team on the same flight, so with all this going on the last thing I was thinking about was issues with coming home.

I would say I was probably the fourth or fifth person to exit. When I arrived in the customs area I was greeted by an official with a dog. At the time I didn't catch on to what was happening. The man approached me and I said hello. The dog was startling to me and I guess that's why I didn't immediately get it. The officer didn't say a word to me at first, and the dog was sniffing all around me. I was then instructed to proceed to the next available agent. That agent then took my passport and asked me what the reason had been for my visit abroad.

I told him it was for pleasure. He then began asking a whole list of banal questions as they went through my luggage. They scanned my passport, took it and then called it in! I assume that was because it was new and had no other stamps in it. I had packed very tightly and had things in the bag in a certain way so that they would all fit. He found a full size can of shaving cream (there were no restrictions about such things then). Being a person back then with very little need to shave (sometimes I could go three days in between) one can would last me forever. He inspected the can and noticed that it was beginning to rust on the bottom. He immediately asked me what it was. I told him it was rust. He asked why and I said, "Because it's OLD!" This was said in about as sarcastic a voice as I could muster. By this time I was pissed off. I had never felt so violated in my life. I hear people today talk about racial profiling by officials at airports. You don't know how demeaning it is unless you've experienced it. And back then it didn't escape my attention that of all the people on that flight I was the only African American there, though there were other nationalities. One of the first people off the plane, I was dead last to clear customs, and it suddenly dawned on me ; black man, dressed nicely, coming from Amsterdam. It all could only equal drugs to them. One of my sisters had been married and lived in Detroit some years earlier so I was very aware of the divided racial feelings of the city.

Then, to add insult to injury I had to re-pack my bags after their destruction and hurry to catch my connection to Atlanta which, of course, was on the other side of the airport. I was put through the ringer for nothing, and all without an offer of apology or help from them and a snicker at the situation to boot. YES TONY, welcome back to the United States! My German friends' quote echoed in my mind: "you may not learn a lot about where you visit, but you'll certainly learn a lot about where you come from!"

To this day I will not book a return flight to the States from Europe where my original point of entry upon return is anywhere but Atlanta, GA unless there's just no other way. I figure at least I'll maybe get the benefit of the doubt since I live here.

Despite this hiccup my beginning to travel to foreign lands was the opening up of a whole new range of experiences. Not the least was the appreciation for the customs and traditions of other nations and their people. Pretty soon I was seeing other parts of Europe and was becoming very well acquainted with Canada as well. Of the many remarkable things I love about Canada, I found in Toronto a deep diversity of cultures. Here in the States it's still such a big deal to see couples integrated black and white, while there I see Middle Eastern and Black American, Asian and Indian, African and Asian, etc. Any combination that you can imagine was in evidence.

Another breath of societal fresh air was the very first Gay Pride Celebration that I attended there. It was 1995 and it was pure coincidence that I was there at that time at all. I had gone up to visit a friend that I made here in Atlanta while he was here on business. David and I met a couple of years earlier and had stayed in touch over that time. He invited me up to visit with him and his partner Jim. When I arrived they were both extremely gracious and I enjoyed spending time with them. I was a bit surprised to see that David had been as ill as he apparently had been. I could tell he was not doing great, as he was extremely thin. He was thin when I'd met him, but had always been naturally so from what I could see in photos of him that we'd shared over our time of knowing one another. That being the case, I'd let the inquiry drop. After all, it was certainly his right to disclose or not to do so if he were ill. Still, with that being the case, there was no denying that something was up. I was happy that I'd come and that we had many hours to catch up and talk. One of the things that I loved when I met him and that I continue to love about Canadian people is that they are very polite and gracious people usually and will not invade your space. For that reason,to many they appear standoffish. But once you've indicated that you would like interaction with them I've rarely found a group of people more warm, sincere and charming than the Canadians.

David was not only a beautiful man physically, but had a beauty and depth of soul that made him instantly likable.

Because of his failing health he'd stopped working in his primary profession and had begun working with plants ,which he dearly loved. As he went around that week tending to some of the plants of people we talked about many things. He talked of his life that he'd shared with Jim and how much that meant to him. He talked of the success that he'd had in his life. The beautiful home they shared and all the friends they'd known.

I was able to share with him that I was beginning to feel very limited in Atlanta and thought that I would want to leave very soon. He pointed out to me that I was just really beginning to have the time of my life. He said that from what he'd seen when in Atlanta, I was very established there. He thought the wisest course for me would likely be stay in Atlanta and keep it for a home base and then travel.

It was very good advice at the time and it turns out I'm happy that I took it. We decided to go to the Pride parade that week and David was very excited about it. I found out later from Jim that it had always been a favorite time for him. Indeed, he was much like a little kid! We all were once we got caught up in his infectious glee.

My hotel was not far from the route and neither was their condo. We chose to meet and go out on Church St. to watch the parade go by. I was totally astounded by the reception the Pride celebration gets there. I have since found that it boasts of being one of the largest in North America and I can believe it. The entire town gets involved. It helps that the time of year for the celebration is all one long party. It started with Pride on June 24th, and rolled into Canada Day, which is July first, and they just kept on rolling into the fourth of July, since so many Americans come up for the first two celebrations. Then if you're lucky enough to hang about for another week or so they have a Caribbean festival that kicks off later in July.

That particular year their Pride parade was about as big as Atlanta's Fourth of July parade. There, marching right in front of a bus of school kids and the town nudists' group was the Toronto Mayor. The whole thing was wonderful. I had never seen anything like it! It was my first time experiencing such mass acceptance as a gay person and it was downright intoxicating. I decided right then that while it was my first time celebrating Pride in Toronto it definitely would not be my last.

As I finished out the week there I found that I was once again very sad on the ride to the airport. The city had made a tremendous impression on me. Not only with all the great activities surrounding Pride, but also with its love of the arts and culture and with the attention the populace as a whole gives to the upkeep and preservation of their city. To this day I think Toronto is one of the cleanest cities that I've encountered.

Also by this time I had learned to take my recovery with me wherever I go. That was another thing that I found great there. The recovery community is very much alive and fully embraced me. It felt very much like my own home groups just with a few new faces. I made some great contacts on that first trip. Many that I maintain to this day.

As the year rolled on I determined that since I'd never really had a good time at our celebration here in Atlanta I would make it my business to spend the next Pride celebration there in Toronto as well.

All through that next year I would periodically touch base with Jim and David, but didn't tell them of my plans. I intended for it to be a surprise. However, it turned out I was the one that got the surprise. It was a shock really. By the time June rolled around I guess it had been a couple of months or so since I'd spoken with them. I made my reservations and flew up just before the weekend. I just knew that this would be a wonderful surprise, knowing how much David loved Pride. I checked into the hotel and picked up the local community papers on my way to my room as I always try to do when I'm visiting a city. Since my hotel was gay they had a good selection of all. I entered my room, fell across the bed and began to read. I stopped cold.

I got to the memorial page and there was a picture of David. I immediately called Jim. He of course was a wreck. When I told him who I was and that I was in town he immediately said, "Well I'm sorry to tell you this but David is dead." I told him that I knew. I'd flown in with the intention of surprising them. I apologized for not having called in a couple of months. He told me that David had died in April, and that he'd chosen to run that memorial piece that particular week because David had loved Pride so.

We made a few more empty noises and I offered to see him while I was there, which he promptly refused. I totally understood. After all, I was really David's friend, and I was getting the impression by some of the things that were being said that there was a part of Jim that felt that David's outside friends had probably contributed to the situation. Whatever the case, I had no desire to intrude on his misery.

Though it was very hard to hear those tones coming from him, especially since I'd not really known either of them that well, I truly did understand. It was not uncommon during that time for there to exist that feeling of, 'Why'? I didn't know them well enough to know their history; I knew only what they had shared with me. I knew that they had been together for many years; but not the entire story of those years.

What I did know was that if I didn't do something fast I'd run the risk of ruining the entire trip for myself. I hustled up and went over to Church St. I knew there was a community center there and that they usually had a meeting schedule for the entire city. I needed to get this train back on track in a hurry!

I found a meeting that was in session, and then called my sponsor afterward. It helped, and it also helped that I'd met some cool folks there in the meeting too. It allowed me to not be so alone with that pain of loss in a place where that could have easily taken me over without some support to get through it.

I won't go through the entire Toronto saga here. I think I could write a couple of volumes on just that since it actually stretched through a few years. Needless to say I fell in love with the city and its inhabitants. There were a couple of hot, torrid affairs and the place came close to stealing me away from Georgia more times than one. There are still times that I wonder if I made the right choice when I elected not to move there. I actually had the whole thing all worked out and the plan was not half bad. During that time movie and television work was thriving there. Many of the productions from the States were being made there. It's my understanding there was less legal wrangling that had to be done. I know that the schools were really pushing the Theatrical Costuming thing.

That in itself was very intriguing to me. I had the notion that if I registered and went to school there, it would certainly make immigration a lot easier. I thought that maybe I could transfer with the Postal Service to the U.S. side of Niagara, in New York, and commute back and forth. Maybe register in school as a part time continuing education student, yet keep my job.

But then at the eleventh hour fate or cold feet or something intervened and I made the decision to stay where I was.

Was it a good decision, or a bad decision? Thinking about it now I imagine it all depends on how you look at it for I can see it as a little of both. Either way, the next few years would change who I was once again. Even nearing forty years of age I still was not finished growing, learning, maturing...

Chapter 8

Chapter 8

Chapter 8

As I began to travel more my interests in just about all things gay in Atlanta dwindled to near nothing. I'm not sure what all was involved in those feelings but I'm sure part of it was that after being sober for a couple of years I began to see things differently. After twenty years being out in this city I never felt accepted or respected by any of the gay community. I was just very tired and over it all. The treatment I received was so very different in other places. I felt it more in other countries, but in other parts of the United States as well.

This is not to say that everyone in Atlanta is rude and unsociable. However, there was an epidemic of the aforementioned behavior going around. One thing I was sure of; I WAS NOT THE PROBLEM HERE! Earlier on I had wondered just how much of this was the guys in this town and how much of it was me? But then I started to meet men from other places who had either visited or lived in Atlanta. I met all different types of men, and they mentioned the issue as well.

In short order Atlanta holds the reputation for being an attitude filled city with many confused and twisted gay boys in it. It was bad enough seeing it and hearing it here, but then to hear that sentiment on the road as well? It really opened my eyes. The issue even got it's own little nickname; "Atlanta-tude".

I've found that the international gay community is really quite small. We are a very specific sub group of society, and as such tend to localize in niches wherever we are. It has amazed me how I can be in totally different countries and run into people that I know or at least recognize from Atlanta and other places. So perhaps to enter into conversation with different people; tell them that I was from Atlanta, and get a summation on what they thought of the place should have been expected.

All I know is it was becoming very clear to me that the jewel of the southeastern United States had dimmed considerably. Seems that the most popular theory as to why this has happened is simple geography.

For many years there were "Mecca" cities for gay people within the United States and elsewhere. That was an established fact. There was New York City in the northeast, San Francisco out west, P-Town and Fire Island for the 'season',

Atlanta and Ft. Lauderdale for the southeast. These places were what were considered 'the circuit' for the popular gay man. They were the godfathers of what is now the existing party circuit in the United States. All have gone through different phases of popularity. Some have come through very strong, while others - not so strong.

What I think happened in the case of Atlanta is that it had this killer reputation of being the hottest city in the south, which was true at one time. But as times changed and people moved on, the city didn't live up to expectations. Much of its glitter faded.

Even with that happening the reputation didn't immediately go away. Geographically Atlanta was still the largest and closest 'supposedly' hot place for all those up and coming kids from smaller surrounding towns in this state, as well as North and South Carolina, Alabama, Mississippi, Tennessee, and even north Florida. You had some opting for New Orleans and Ft. Lauderdale as well, but I think many found their way to Atlanta.

Pretty soon the small town guys were far outnumbering those that were accustomed to urban life throughout the world. Along with that influx, many of those earlier guys who were just as politically conscious as they were beautiful had decided to move on. They grew tired of trying to force a life in a city where its politicians and leaders were doing everything in their power to make life hell for gay people. During the mid – 1970's and throughout the 1980's, city leaders here were intent on driving off anything that was not thought of as "Family Oriented".

Those gays coming from places where this treatment was the order of the day were nowhere near as eager as the earlier gay people had been to pick up the fight. Many who came here to get away from having that very fight in their hometowns assumed that there would be safety in numbers. I also think that for some, conservatism was a normal part of their background and was all they knew. They clung to the anonymity of the midtown scene and let the ravaging of the community go unchecked in many ways. For all intents and purposes, they traded their closets in their small hometowns, for Midtown Atlanta. Many of them never venturing out of its confines. The result being that Midtown, or the "gay ghetto" if you will, simply became a larger closet.

Then the onset of HIV/AIDS started its sweep and that pretty much sealed the deal on this and many other fights.

Either way, when the dust all cleared it seemed that a great deal of the small-town mentality that Atlanta's gay community had worked so hard in the 70's to shed was more pronounced than ever. Not only was it more racially divided, there was conformity to being closeted or 'discreet' - as many were now calling it. To many, it seemed that the Bible thumpers' claims of "God's Wrath" might just have some merit. In the stronghold of the south, I know that it was much more difficult for many young, gay kids to just shrug those words off.

Though there was definitely an African – American presence in the gay community here by that time, the desire to be 'discreet' amongst black gays was even more pronounced than it was in the white gay community. Many went so far as to distance themselves totally from identifying as gay. They were simply, 'men who enjoyed the company of other men.'

Suddenly there was a huge upswing in hyper-masculinity and people who ordinarily were seen as 'out gay men' were describing themselves as 'straight-acting'. There were confederate flags proudly displayed on pickups in the parking lots of every gay bar in town. And most of the vehicles in those parking lots WERE pickups!

While it seemed we were growing, we were actually falling embarrassingly behind. For all this bluster and bravado and noise making about being 'men', these boys came to the big city and brought right along with them all the hang-ups, bad habits and uncommunicative skills of their heterosexual counterparts back home. The reality was they were the equivalent of Ma and Pa Kettle on the steps of the United Nations trying to fake their way through.

I remember one evening in particular I was in a club called the Armory with a date; A friend of mine from Canada. We were sitting at the bar. It was very crowded and there were limited bar stools. Bob is a very handsome white guy and quite conservative in appearance. He's a university professor, holds a doctorate degree, and is pretty much a walking version of that crush that we've all had on teachers at one time or another. We were sitting there and he was sitting on my lap.

We were kissing from time to time; nothing overt- just light affection. Pretty soon this

blond haired kid walks by, sneers at us and spits on the floor! I saw it clearly though I wasn't sure if Bob noticed at all. He didn't say anything. We kept talking and sitting there. Soon, a couple more guys came by and made rather loud derogatory comments. At that point Bob said, "Wow, they really don't like integrated couples here do they?" This type behavior from guys in the community, along with general fickleness and silliness began to earn Atlanta a rather unsavory reputation.

There was - and still is - a lot of talk about all the games played here. It appeared the gay scene here was more depressing than anything else. I was very disappointed and soon withdrew from socializing here altogether. At that point the only reasons I stayed were my home and a few close lifetime friends.

Between remodeling my home and working on my recovery, whenever I wanted a recreational outlet I traveled. Before I knew what was happening I had gone about five years without so much as setting foot in Midtown Atlanta.

That was a huge development for me. I was building on myself and growing without even knowing it. I believe that wherever you are is just where you're supposed to be at that time. And obviously this was my time to grow my surroundings, my being, and my consciousness of the world around me; the whole world. Not just the space that I'd known for so many years and called home.

By now I had a pretty good handle on my recovery and was quite driven to put together this ideal dream life that I had in mind. Work was about as good as could be expected and I was feeling good about most things.

I was traveling a good bit and though it was fun, it was also tiring. There is a character flaw I have that must be monitored: Once I've decided that things should be a certain way, I can become pretty unmovable. In my mind I had made great strides toward the life that I wanted so now I just needed to seal the deal. It was time to start on the daunting quest to find that perfect relationship; The one that would complete the picture.

I decided that since most of Atlanta was about game playing that I needed to broaden the search within the U.S. but knock off some of the international looking since that would be more difficult and unlikely. I went forward with a 'plan' and was convinced that I would be victorious if I just stuck to the decisions I'd made. Somewhere the man that would complete my life was out there. It was up to me to find him!

Since I was already traveling once or twice each month anyway it was easy for me to decide to just make all upcoming trips domestic. I put out several personal ads on internet sites and checked them daily. I then started communication with those men who seemed most promising to me. Never once did it occur to me that I could not orchestrate a truly loving and committed relationship. I was determined to manufacture the happiness that I so wanted. My interviews took me to Florida twice, almost took me to North Dakota; fresh (1 week) out of surgery. He was a nurse and assured me that he would take care of me. Thank God the doctor told me I couldn't, under any circumstances, board a plane that soon after the procedure. At least somebody in the mix had some sense of reality! When I told the guy that I would not be able to come due to doctor's orders, his response was to completely blow up. He called me a liar and said I was, "like all the other online trash!" I could just imagine going to meet somebody like this being fresh out of surgery. In some place that I had never been and don't know a soul- thousands of miles away from home. Charming! On top of that from what he'd told me, he lived in a totally rural area. Clearly I was not thinking straight to even consider going on that little excursion. A date with the guy voted most likely to become a fatal attraction...

Finally, just a month or so after my surgery, my intense search led me to Baton Rouge, Louisiana. From the moment I descended the escalator into the baggage area and saw him standing there I knew this was as sure a mistake as any that I'd ever made. Though he- like all the other guys I'd met on this country wide tour of dating- had his good points, none were right for me. For one reason or another these were just not love connections. Wonder of wonders. Diana and the girls were right - you can't hurry love! Well the trip to Baton Rouge was such a bust that I just ended up angry and disgusted with myself. We ended up basically sitting in front of the television all weekend. All I really got out of the experience was an introduction to HGTV.

By Sunday I'd decided that the whole thing was just ridiculous. And after seven years of abstinence from compulsive eating of sugar and bingeing on snack food I angrily declared that if I wasn't going to have the man and the life that I wanted then all this was futile. Why was I doing all this work to better myself anyway? My anger and disgust helped me to decide that a little 'treat' would not hurt me. Hell, I deserved it after all I'd been through....

The guy that I was there with had decided to take me out for Sunday Brunch. At that meal I made a conscious decision to go off the plan that I'd been on and have dessert. This was after seven whole years of not eating concentrated sugars. To many people, that may not seem like much. However with my past history of eating disorder and my literal addiction to sugar and carbohydrates themselves this monumentally bad decision was the calling card of complete chaos.

Slipping into relapse with the sugar started off feeling like complete freedom of course. I'd not known total disregard of what I put in my body for a long time now. As is always the case for me, once I take that initial bite, no matter how much I promise that I'm going to 'monitor' my usage, it doesn't take long to become an all-out binge.

This is the way it usually works, and this time, though it had been several years, was no different. It started with that double fudge brownie at the dessert table in Baton Rouge. When I returned to Atlanta and to work the craving that I'd awakened grew considerably. I was working 8:30 a.m. - 5:00 p.m. at the time. When I would take my morning break I would go up to the cafeteria where they had these mega muffins. I started having a bran muffin with a cup of coffee at that break. Before long I was having one then, and also at lunch. What harm could it be doing? After all, they were bran, or so I reasoned.

Then one day they didn't have bran so I chose banana nut- or it may have even been chocolate. No, I'm sure it was the banana nut. Gotta keep it healthy! However the day did come when I had no 'choice' but to try the chocolate. I know that I eventually ended up giving up all pretense and going straight for the chocolate because they were my favorites.

Within a couple of months I was eating those things at every break during the day and hitting the vending machines in between breaks as well. Honey buns and

cinnamon rolls all over the building were not safe from me. Remember, this was a building that you could comfortably land a plane in, and it had vending machines throughout! I was suddenly going through all this hell from re-opening the door to the sugar in the first place. What started out that February Sunday morning in Baton Rouge feeling like 'new found free-dom' quickly degenerated into a misery that was so all con-suming that it was late November that year before I was willing to even consider trying to climb out of it.

By that time I'd abandoned most of the principles that I had based my life on for nearly the last decade. Once again I was always angry, snapping at people, feeling bad about myself and hating my life in general. And of course all this was just in time for the holiday season.

At that time I had a little Toyota truck. I'd started a tradition with a friend of mine where every year she and I would go and pick out our live Christmas trees together right after Thanksgiving. Since it was so easy with the truck we'd hop in and make a day of it. She was pretty much on the same spiritual path as me and we usually had great times together. This time however the conversation turned to food. I was aware on some level that I'd hit a new bottom but was busily trying to convince myself that things were ok. I was spouting off about all the seeming reasons that it now appeared I could partake in the consumption of all this sugar with virtually no consequences.

She immediately called me out on that as being totally ridiculous. It made me blazing mad and we had words a plenty that afternoon. The funny thing about introspection and self-discovery is that once you've learned new things and see their validity, you can't just UN-learn them. My protestation and anger that day was because I knew she was right and I don't think I could have begun the road back from that self-imposed hell without her confrontation.

I knew that it was time to start again though I wasn't sure how. And then- just as before- God stepped in and gave me a little nudge in the direction I needed to go.

I was coming out of a meeting one day at noon and I looked up and saw a familiar face. It was a woman that had been curiously a part of my story from the moment that I'd found myself feeling as though I was coming apart all those years

ago when I first went into treatment. At the time I'd not given much thought to it, but as I looked back, there seemed to be the oddest set of coincidences there.

Back in that week when I first went into the treatment center, as I've mentioned before I almost always went and got the community newspapers. That issue where I found the advertisement for the treatment center also featured a story about a local photographer who was beginning to gain notoriety here in the Atlanta area just as she lost her battle to cancer and died. Her partner was mentioned and interviewed extensively for the story. The reason the article had caught my eye was that I was not very long out of art school, and was always interested in learning how other gay artists were faring and conducting their business.

Though I read the story thoroughly and it stayed with me, I didn't think much more about it. Later on that week in the treatment center I was told that I needed to get a sponsor. This could likely be achieved at some of the twelve step meetings I was required to attend, and I needed to do it as soon as possible. It was a mandatory policy of the treatment program. There was this lesbian woman in treatment with me (the same one I had defended the first week) who assured me that she knew of a gay and lesbian meeting on Sunday and Thursday nights where she had been able to get a sponsor without a problem. She told me where it was and suggested that I meet her there on the upcoming Thursday. As it turned out, I went, but she didn't show. However, the woman that had been featured in the article about the photographer was there. She was one of only a few people at the meeting. I guess since it was just one week before Thanksgiving most people were either away or busy. I don't think there were more than six of us there for the entire hour.

I recognized the woman from her picture in the article and was very surprised to see her there. I didn't know her, but it would turn out to be the first incident of finding out what anonymity really means. I learned that we never know who the person that we see every day on the street may be. Even though they're totally different from us, they may be dealing with the same issues and we do not even know it.

I was introduced to everybody there that night - including the woman from the article. When I returned to treatment on the next day I mentioned to the girl that was supposed to meet me about meeting the people there. I can't remember what reason she gave for not showing up, but it turned out that the woman from the article was the very woman that she'd found to sponsor her!

Well this was the woman that I ran into that day all those years later as I was leaving that noon meeting. It had always been very difficult for me to find sponsors. I didn't like asking people and I hadn't had very good luck with that suggestion. But I'd been praying a lot for some help to get me back off the sugar and onto some semblance of an abstinent program again. I believe that her presence there that day was just one more gift from God to me.   She had been there in the paper, she was suggested to me in the treatment center by a fellow patient, she walked into the first meeting I ever attended and here she was again. We spoke, and on a whim I asked if I could talk to her for a bit. I told her I was having some real trouble and that I needed some guidance. She suggested that I give her a call and we could set up a time to get together. We did that and she became my advisor, my sponsor, and my dear friend.

It was certainly no accident that right at that time- when I had abandoned all the gifts that recovery had given me- here she was again. I was never good at asking for help, but recently had been thinking that was exactly what was missing for me. People say pray for what you need. Well, that's what I was doing! And she turned out to be my angel.

We started to work together and it was the first time that I'd ever taken direction from anyone willingly. I did what she suggested because I respected her and the way she conducted her recovery. I didn't want to disappoint her. I had always been quick to say I didn't do well with authority figures. I was too independent and didn't like people telling me what to do. For me it had always seemed a matter of maturity to be able to follow directions without someone having to guide me. Now I found a certain relief in turning loose the reins for once. There was freedom in admitting that I didn't know everything, and that I needed help.

There were many starts, stops and stumbles. I was not doing this gracefully at all, but I was growing as a person. She was very patient and allowed me to learn

through action. I saw the mistake I'd made before. I'd been attempting to gain positive results in my life without doing any work. I wanted all the good things that I could have in life; friends, a partner ,a good job and home life , but up to now had not been willing to change anything about myself.

Entering my forties brought about all the midlife feelings that others had promised it would. All those questions of whether or not I was doing all that I should have been doing. Whether there was a career choice for me that I was overlooking. What should my professional goals be?

For the first time I looked objectively at my fear of failure as well as my fear of success. I recognized that even if I did have something to offer the world of fashion design it would never be seen unless I could conquer this and move on. I wanted to get honest and as truthful as possible in every aspect of my life. I didn't want to play around the edges any longer. It had become an obsession that I figure out just what I should be doing in my life and get on that path. If I couldn't have the perfect mate be a part of the picture, then I'd damned well better get cracking on the rest of it. Or at least that's the way I started approaching things.

One day as we were meeting my sponsor asked me if I'd ever considered the fact that it may be my destiny to go through my entire life without ever finding a committed romantic relationship. The question stopped me cold. I had never even considered what that might mean for me. While it was a disturbing concept, it was also a whole new direction of thought when looked at it objectively. She told me she could see me becoming a whole individual; One that would be perfectly ok with someone to compliment my life, but that I didn't need anyone to complete me. She said - and I began to believe- that as I came more into myself, I would attract more 'complete' people to me. Not just romantically, but all different types of people.

There appeared to be ample evidence of that to me lately as well. For years I'd looked for that perfect relationship to complete me. This was the first time that it had ever occurred to me that I was perfectly ok just the way that I am, and that I don't need a relationship to have a comfortable and full life.

I sensed a newfound freedom and I was growing more optimistic about my life and the things around me. After several months of working with my sponsor I

could see advances around my fears and my trust of this process. There was no magic bullet. It was however a tutorial on how to manage my life and the everyday challenges that come up.

As I approached the holidays that year I was more centered and comfortable than I'd been for a very long time. There was an absence of the dread that usually accompanied the season.

To grow for me means to change, and it usually takes practice. It's very easy to revert to old behaviors because that's what I know best.

I was talking to my friend Jim and telling him that I found myself completely over the shallow process that we gay men always put ourselves through in looking for love or whatever. He confided that he'd gone through a similar situation and experienced the same feelings while in the dating pool. He had just recently- within the past year - met and become involved with a partner.

He suggested that I try a new site that seemed to be more serious. It was very new and wasn't like many of the web sites that were just about pickups. This was the onset of a new generation of dating. We were just beginning to see that the 'new normal' around dating would largely center around the internet. The name of the site was "My One and Only". He suggested I give it a try. I told him I was sick and tired of all the games and that my last excursion onto the sites had cost me my abstinence. Not to mention a young fortune in airfare on useless weekend excursions. Most of my experience with the sites had added up to a big fat nothing. All the men were really looking for Mr. Right Now, and really just wanted him posing as Mr. Right.

He suggested, and I concurred that if I were to run this ad, I should make it as simple as possible; Direct and to the point. Stating what I was about and no more. I agreed and said that not only would I do that but I would not go on and research or answer any of the ads posted there. If someone were there for me he would have to find me because I certainly wasn't going to look for him.

Fate intervened and though my list was somewhat specific as to what I thought the ideal guy would be for me there was indeed a guy who contacted me who seemed to fit that bill.

Michael first came into my life in November of 2000. He was one of maybe three guys who answered that ad. And he was the only one who actually gave any type of coherent response. In fact, he wrote the equivalent of about a two or three page letter. He was the most expressive and seemingly confident guy I'd ever met. We emailed back and forth quite a bit those first few weeks. I had broken my hand at work and wasn't working, so that gave me quite a bit of free time. I found that he was never at a loss for words.

From the moment we started to chat live on the phone there was always something to talk about. We enjoyed talking about everything and sometimes the conversations would stretch into hours. He was in another state but this was certainly not the first time I'd met someone geographically removed who caught my interest. It worried me a bit but I was determined to monitor my feelings and behavior here. An old habit of mine had been to go after men who were unavailable to me. It could take the form of geographical, emotional or even sometimes situational but that seeming unattainability seemed to fan the flames of my interest into a wildfire. And while this was looking a little that way I really did think that it could turn out differently. There was a quality to the conversation that lent itself to a positive outcome.

As I talked to him there was a nugget of uncertainty because of my recent growing self-awareness. Even if I wanted to entertain the thought of getting with someone, for the first time in my life I was really hesitant about the idea. It looked to me that even a promising man could prove to be more of an inconvenience than anything else. My thoughts these days were more about MY future, not OUR future.

Ironically it seemed that for every negative issue that popped into my head there would be an answer that came up virtually unsolicited where he and said issue were concerned. I was constantly saying to myself, "just let it ride for a bit and see where it goes. You can always get out before it gets too deep if it turns out to not be what you want." It was almost an irritation that I was finally growing and thinking about getting me together, and here he shows up.

As the month wore on he wrote me an email and told me that he needed to go to New York on business and asked if

I would consider meeting him there. He offered to have a car meet me at the airport and promised the weekend would include Dinner at the Russian Tea Room, shows and evenings at the Waldorf Astoria.

While normally I would have jumped at the chance, the fact that I had a broken hand and was not working just then pretty much dictated that I must turn him down. I knew that was the correct course of action, but also knew that it must be done just right. This was obviously a very well-bred and professional man and that told me the invitation was not offered lightly. I certainly didn't want to leave him with the impression that I took the invite for granted. I wanted to convey that I truly regretted not being able to go. So to buffer the refusal I had to come up with a workable alternative. I also knew that I would never put myself in the position of going out of town on limited funds in a situation with someone I didn't know. That scenario offered too much of a chance that I might end up in a compromised position if this didn't go well between us.

I structured my regrets very carefully. I opened the letter by telling him how truly sorry I was that I would not be able to join him, as I was currently injured and it would make travel quite awkward. And besides I said jokingly, where in the world would I find a dinner jacket that would match the cast?

He had also mentioned that later in the month he would be traveling to South Carolina and would be in the area beyond Thanksgiving. I suggested that he contact me when he was in the area. Since he would be close to Atlanta anyway, perhaps we could put together an opportunity to meet then. When we talked again he said that he would see if that would work out.

It was a while before we talked again; after Thanksgiving and on the way to Christmas actually. It was at that time that he told me that things in his life were not going as well as he'd hoped. From the beginning he'd told me that he was married, but was legally separated and attempting to get a divorce. I know this sounds all too much like I should have cut and run then, but there was something about this guy that was captivating. Against my own better judgment, I stayed around. Much of what he had to say had the uncanny ring of truth. He began to tell me that though he was married, he'd known that he was interested in men for some

time. He said that he and his wife had indulged in three ways and that largely the marriage was an arranged situation. She was very much aware of his inclinations and had said that she was willing to divorce now. Well apparently the latest thing was that in the last couple of weeks she had changed her tune and also had gained the support of other family members; HIS family members. She now felt that they should try and work through their problems. He said that he was sure she would relent as soon as she saw he wasn't going to change his position.

I've asked myself a million times why I didn't just get the hell out right then since that seemed like the obvious thing to do. But even now I can't say that I made a mistake by staying there and continuing to communicate with him. There was an awful lot for me to learn and I still think that was the reason I was put there in the first place. As I said earlier my list of demands for the man that I wanted in my life was rather specific to say the least. I was looking for a man close to my age, (around forty at the time), who would be faithful and wanted monogamy, who was not experienced (meaning he'd not slept around). I wanted him to be a bottom who was HIV negative. I also wanted him to be a professional man, though I was not specific as to what profession. I just knew I wanted someone that was making a comparable salary and that I wouldn't have to keep up. Someone who enjoyed the same type of things I did and who knew the world existed outside the bars.

The funny thing is that God sent me exactly what I'd asked for! I found out later that this guy was not experienced as he'd first led me to believe. He was sincere about wanting to finally embrace his homosexuality, but the whole idea scared him somewhat. That fear made the thought of being with more than one person something he wasn't going to consider doing. I found out later the lengths that he'd gone to in making the decision to contact me. All this pretty much squelched the thoughts that he might want to explore the vastness of carnal pleasure the gay community offered. We both enjoyed the same types of recreational things. Both enjoyed theater, dance, classical music, home renovation, antique shopping and a whole host of other things that we seemed to have in common.

At the same time however there were some constant rules that I had in place that I found myself going against. Things like: Never date a guy who makes way less or way more money than I did. I soon found out that Michael was not only in banking, but he came from old money. Not the type of person I had ever sought, or

even considered would likely be in my life. Also there was the idea of going against my newly placed resolve to stay away from unavailable guys. Up to now I'd never considered a married guy as anything serious. So that made this one unavailable in a variety of different ways. But he said he was going to get a divorce, didn't he? <sigh>

Along for the ride just to complicate matters further was the fact that in all the years I'd been out I have never been the pursued party. I've always been the person to initiate contact and pursue the relationship. This was the first time that some-one had ever actively pursued me. It was confusing, a little frightening, but exciting as well. I was thoroughly convinced that this was the difference that would set this apart from all the attempted relationships up to this point.

There actually was some truth to that. To date I think there was probably more genuine affection and sincere desire to build something than I've ever had with any man that I've met previously. I think he was sincere in all he was saying but I was soon to find that his situation was a little more daunting than most. That was the fly in the ointment so to speak.

It turned out that his marriage was indeed arranged and that he comes from a very old and established family. There was to be no easy extrication from this situation at all. I think it took some time for us both to come to that realization. He because he knew it would be a hell of a fight, and me because as yet I had no idea how deep this situation really was. Unfortunately by the time I had the facts and he was willing to face the facts we really had fallen very much in love. We had become friends first, and that made a big difference in how he and I both looked at this. As it turned out, we didn't get together while he and his family were in the South Carolina area. We spoke on the phone and it was then that he told me his wife had changed her position totally. He was totally speechless about what she'd apparently done. She'd enlisted his parents into the fight and they had always been violently opposed to the idea that he may have been anything but heterosexual. Apparently the issue had come up many years prior- back when he was a school boy- and he'd been sent away as a result of it. By the time he was allowed to return to the family

there were strict demands that would be adhered to. One being that a wife had been chosen for him.

All this began to come out in our phone conversations, but I still did not really get the gist of why he didn't just tell them all to shove it and leave. I knew that he had a young child and that she was very important to him, but personally I couldn't see making myself miserable over that. Then again, I'm not a father.

As we continued to talk I could sense that this was really beating him up. It came through very clearly every time we spoke. He sounded as though he was falling apart inside.

By this time Christmas was on the horizon and though we could not be together, it was wonderful to share many hours chatting about things that were important to us. It filled a place in me that usually was left barren during this season. For him, it seemed to give promise that one day things could be different.

I put together a little 'care package' for him and mailed it to him. It was full of little trinkets that said, 'you mean a lot to me' even in their simplicity. There was a stuffed Snoopy doll in a Santa Claus suit, a giant candy cane filled with Hershey's kisses, a heart shaped keepsake box, and I drew a large coupon on a piece of paper with the picture of a troll on it with out-stretched arms. The coupon was good for one hug. It was all very simple but it meant a lot to me to do it. He seemed such a sweet, but unhappy person.

Once it arrived he called me. He was as tickled as a little boy. That made me smile. I was happy I could bring a little joy into what sounded like a hellish existence.

We usually spoke at least once a day by now. I was working a lot as usual during the holiday season. Usually it was a great diversion from the disarray that I found with the Christmas season since the death of my parents. And though I really love the season and always have, it was a big adjustment for quite a while after their deaths.

I received a call from Michael the evening after Christmas. That he was upset was very apparent. It seemed his wife-having agreed to file for the divorce they had talked about- had done an about face and announced in front of his entire family that she was withdrawing the petition and wanted to "work things out" with him. That had been her Christmas present to him. He was fuming. He said that he intended to go and file himself at the first opportunity.

This was turning out to be a monumental mess it seemed. He said that he needed to get away and would go out west to a family owned ranch for the remainder of the holidays so that he could sort himself out. He said that he would try and call,

but that it was very remote, and that I might not hear from him. I offered to come with him, since I hate being alone for the New Year. He said that he didn't want me to. I asked time and time again and the constant answer was no.

Perhaps this should have been another indicator of what was to come but I couldn't see that. The good thing was that in my mind I wasn't really all that involved yet, so as bad as I felt for him I still knew that it was basically his issue and had nothing to do with me.

There was still the issue of what to do about the coming of the New Year for me. I've always had a bit of a problem with it. It drives me straight to a melancholy state. There is a loneliness that has haunted me about it since I was a child. The only thing Auld Lang Syne makes me want to do is cry. So there was no way that I wanted to spend the New Year alone and upset after the year that I'd had. Remember I was just trying to come back from months of all out bingeing on sugar and was still trying to get my eating and the insanity around my life in general under control. As I think of it now, this was another reason that it really was not the time for me to be thinking about falling in love.

As I thought about the approaching holiday, I decided that I needed to get away myself. People always think of the misery that others go through at Christmas as horrible. Screw that! New Year's Eve is a struggle for me. It's international lover's night, and without one I always felt miserable. I started looking around and found a great deal going to Montreal. I'd always wanted to go, and though I knew Canada could be rough this late in the year, I determined that cold had never stopped me from taking an excursion and it wasn't going to stop me now.

I made all the arrangements and prepared to go. A couple of days prior to my departure I heard from Michael and he asked me what I was doing for the holiday. I told him that I'd decided to go to Montreal. I told him that I wasn't going to sit here and if he didn't want me to meet him I'd just as soon take a trip of my own. He asked where I'd be staying and I gave him the information. It was a little guest house that I'd found in the gay guide book. I told him that I hoped he could get things worked out in his head and would talk to him after the holiday.

Unbeknownst to me, this trip would end up being a pivotal point in my decision to get into a relationship with Michael. There were many things that went into that decision but this was probably the first real nudge in that direction.

The decision about Montreal had truly been last minute. I ended up taking a flight that was to leave Atlanta at around 9 p.m. on New Year's Eve. Because I was booking so late that was the best I could do and get there in time to bring in the New Year. It would be cutting it close, but I was determined. As it turned out the flight that I'd chosen was scheduled to be almost empty, but there was another flight that was supposed to go to New York that had been canceled due to bad weather. The airline decided to put those passengers on the Montreal flight and stop at JFK on the way. I and everybody else on the Montreal flight were furious! Not only would this mean that we were delayed about an hour leaving Atlanta, but now the flight was jam packed, and with the stop in New York it meant that it would be well past midnight by the time we got to Montreal.

When we did finally get there it was about one in the morning. The Montreal airport was closed. There were no services open but the ground crew that was to meet the plane and handle the baggage. I didn't know it at the time, but Montreal had just experienced a blizzard a couple of days before so it was like landing in a frozen tundra. There was a queue for taxis and there were maybe five running in the whole area. Of course the people in the line didn't know that yet, but thank God I had sense enough to size up the situation quickly. There was a young businessman at the front of the line and I heard him tell the taxi driver that he was going downtown. I quickly shot forward and said I was going downtown as well. While all the other people were standing there trying to figure out how close that could get them to their destination, I negotiated sharing the cab with the guy. The driver said that he could get me there and I hopped in. It was then that he told us the others would have a long wait because of the conditions and the limited number of drivers out.

By the time I reached the guest house it was about 2 a.m. I'd called the host from the Atlanta airport and explained what was going on and that I would be delayed. I was glad that I had. If you've never stayed in a guest house, it can be quite charming. However there are certain situations that pop up because it actually is someone's home that you're staying in. It's usually a situation where there needs

to be someone there to greet you upon arrival. Once there, you're usually free to come and go at will, but you should always check it out with questions like this because it's not as anonymous as a hotel or lodge or whatever.

The host was glad that I'd finally arrived. Now he could go out or to sleep or whatever. I was thoroughly disgusted with the way the evening had played out and in no way was about to go to sleep. I dropped my bags and headed out into the night to catch the remnants of the revelers. It was well into the next morning before I stumbled back into the guesthouse and went to bed. Though I was no longer drinking, the nightlife could still be a very tiring experience!

When I awakened the next afternoon, the host greeted me and asked if I'd had a good time the night before. I told him that the city was definitely alive despite the piled up snow and

the chill in the air. He remarked that someone had been calling constantly for me. Had called all during the night and had
even called a couple of times that day. While we were talking,
the phone rang and he looked at me. He rolled his eyes as if to
say, "what's up with this?", and handed me the phone.

It was Michael on the other end. Of course I knew it had
to be since he was the only person that I'd told where I was
going. He was being short almost to the point of rudeness demanding to know where I'd been and what had happened. That
pushed me over the edge and I shot back, "hell, I don't even
know you! How dare you question what I do or where I go?" He
immediately apologized and said it was just that he had been
worried. He had heard about the weather issues in the area
and had been concerned. He said he'd also been trying to send
a welcome gift to the place but was having difficulty because
deliveries hadn't been able to get through and there seemed to
be some problem with them locating the hotel. I told him that
was because it wasn't a hotel, but a guest house.

We finished up the conversation and I told him that I
would speak to him when I returned home. It was neither the
time or the place for us to be having this discussion. The
host was looking on with a quizzical look on his face. It was
then that we bonded and he became my first acquaintance in
Montreal. We sat and had a cup of coffee and I told him about
meeting this guy and that he seemed nice. This possessiveness
was something that I'd not seen in him before but then again
I'd never even seen him before! Jon Claude the host shrugged
his shoulders and said,

"Well, either he's a nut job or he really cares about you." He
then said that he had to get busy on his daily chores. I said
I thought I'd get dressed and take a stroll around the area. It
had been so late when I arrived that I never got a chance to see
much of the place in the dark.

I dressed and headed out for the afternoon. Since it was New Year's Day there wasn't much open. But there was a little diner up the street on the opposite side. I walked up there and went in to grab a bite to eat and think a bit. I was still fuming over Michael's behavior. It was very puzzling to me. I really didn't even know this man. If this was any indication of how he would act, I wasn't sure I wanted to know him. On the other hand I reasoned, when was the last time somebody cared enough to care what I did or where I went? The latter thought apparently won out because by the time I'd finished lunch I'd determined once again to let this play out and see where it went. I'd talk to him when I returned to Atlanta and follow it up then. I think that was the real beginning of me thinking 'relationship' in earnest with this man.

To try and describe Michael's family situation I would say you should think "Brideshead Revisited".(If you've never read the story or seen the movie it's about a relationship between two men of European descent; One of Aristocracy, and the other a commoner)

From the moment I first met him I was caught. He came across to me as very intense and just a little bit overwhelmed with life. I had no idea how much truth there would be in that first impression. Though we'd talked on the phone and in email a good bit, it was actually four months into our correspondence before we physically met. It came about because I was frankly getting very suspicious that perhaps he didn't want to meet me at all and was just fascinated by the phone communication.

There have been many guys that I've come across that are insincere. I don't give them much of a chance to play games with me anymore. So in that spirit when plans for an upcoming trip to visit a family member would put me in close proximity to Michael's home, I suggested that we should meet at that time. I would only be a few hours from him and didn't think that I would be willing to continue

with the current state of affairs if we didn't meet soon. We were on the phone for hours each evening and it all seemed pretty futile to me if it were going no further.

I was planning on taking the trip in mid-February and Michael explained that he would be having a rather serious surgery on his head the first couple of days in that month. He said that due to that he wasn't sure if he'd be up for travels anywhere, but would try. I immediately thought it was awfully convenient, this serious surgery that he'd not mentioned before now. I didn't believe a word of it. I told him that I hoped it would work out, and with that, I left off talking about it for the time being.

As the week for his supposed surgery came about he mentioned that he was really worried about it since they would be cutting into his cranial area. He didn't talk much about it, but I didn't accuse him of any falsehoods. I just went along with all he was saying. He told me that he would be hiring a private nurse to take care of him at home once the surgery was done, and that he would have that person give me a call as soon as he was out of the operation.

On the day that his surgery was to take place someone that I'd never spoken to did contact me to tell me that his operation had gone well and that he was resting. I thanked the man for calling and asked that he tell Michael that I wished him a speedy recovery.

I'm sure it will make me look cynical to some but my thoughts at the time were that the person who called me could have been anyone. There was no way for me to know if it were an actual nurse as he'd said it would be or some friend of his that he'd put up to do this. It was a few days before we spoke again. When we did he sounded just fine. He told me a little of what all had been done. He said that his head had been shaved and that he'd had several melanomas which had to be removed. His description of the ordeal sounded dreadful but I still wasn't ready to just accept. I didn't say anything right away, but I soon would make it known that I still expected to meet with him in a couple of weeks and if we couldn't arrange that I couldn't really see the sense in us continuing to communicate.

When I expressed that sentiment to my surprise he didn't complain. He said simply, "ok then, I'll make it happen."

Michael lives very close to the D.C. area and I arrived there to visit my nephew on the third weekend of that February in 2001. Somehow it turned out that my eldest sister and I had both chosen to go and visit at the same time. I was actually glad this was the case. Sometimes, even though my family could get on my nerves, it was nice to spend time with them. By now I was very comfortable with who I was and any issues anyone had with it was their issue not mine.

Michael and I had agreed to meet at the Hyatt Capitol Hill that Sunday afternoon. He had warned me that he still had stitches from his surgery and also reminded me his head had been shaved. He said he would have to have his housekeeper prepare some type of headdress so he could appear in public and not look like a freak. When I walked into the hotel I went directly to the front desk to check in. When I turned around there was a man standing there behind me in a distressed leather bomber jacket with a mink collar and an Arabian type headdress(Keffiyeh) on. With his dark coloring (a product of his Italian heritage) it actually looked quite authentic! He had a full beard and prescription sunglasses on. He broke into a smile which lit up his whole face.

He introduced himself and told me that our room was ready. He showed me to the elevator and up we went. He had taken a two-room suite and it was a very nice setup. Before long there was a knock on the door. It was a delivery of fresh flowers and a fruit and cheese tray. We settled down and talked and really got to know one another. It felt as though we already did, we'd been talking for so long.

When he took his glasses off I could see there was a bright spot of blood in one of his eyes. It was a ruptured blood vessel. Also when he turned to the side I could just make out the gauze and even the stitches into his scalp. You could have knocked me over with a feather! Suddenly it dawned on me that I had caused this guy to get up from his sick bed and take a car trip only two weeks after this type major surgery with that stupid and selfish ultimatum. I felt like a complete heel. He noticed me studying his injuries intently from the corner of his eye and yelled for me to stop looking at him! I've never been so ashamed. And yet my heart has never swelled so large so quickly. I think I started to fall in love with him right at that moment. We cuddled a bit and I apologized for staring at him. I knew that I needed to put him at ease about his injuries.

The housekeeper had done such a wonderful job with the headdresses that you really couldn't see any of the taping or gauze covering his injuries unless the thing shifted. She had made several to go with his outfits and they were really sharp!

We dressed for dinner; he was in one room of the suite and I, in the other. When he came out dressed I was speechless. This man was positively made to wear fine clothing. I don't think I'd ever seen anyone so stunningly well-tailored and well fit before. Everything he wore was top shelf and looked like it had been made just for his body. I've worked with clothing for over thirty years and I've never seen a man that looked as good in a blazer, shirt and tie and slacks as he did that evening. I knew right away that if I were going to date this man the first thing I'd need to do when I returned home was shop! I knew that I was dressed ok and that I usually look pretty good in dress clothing but that night there was to be no contest on who would be winning the glances here.

We headed out to a restaurant in Georgetown and I was so captivated by the setting and conversation that I couldn't tell you if the place was half crowded or near empty. This was straight out of some movie. I NEVER had dates like this. Though I had known guys with style, and this is what we'd strived for, it just never seemed to happen like this. Michael had my attention completely. He was very vibrant and alive. His conversation was quite interesting and his extensive knowledge in subjects ranging from art to world affairs - and practically everything in between - was impressive to say the least. During the meal he asked me about preferred cuisine. I told him that I was very open - minded about food. (Ha! that's a laugh!) I told him that I would generally try all types though my favorites were country French and just about any type Asian cuisine.

When the meal was completed we went out into the night and spent wonderful time walking the streets of Georgetown. There was a slight chill in the air, so we chose to go back to the hotel before long. After all, we had the whole of the next day to explore the city together.

After breakfast the next morning we went out to several of the art galleries and shops in the area. Most of the time was spent just getting to know one another and chatting. He was still wearing the headdresses and we had great fun with the reception that received from people. Even many of the Middle Eastern people that

we passed attempted to speak to him in ways that had to be custom, though they were unfamiliar to us. There were even a couple of instances where a couple of gentlemen spoke to him in some language that I assume was Farsi. I didn't understand and neither did he! Michael just mumbled and grunted a bit and we sped past. Once we were in the clear we cracked up about it!

On one of those stops in an Art Gallery there in the city he'd asked me to give him some privacy while he spoke to the gallery owner. I was a bit put out. So far this had been a great day but now I felt as though I'd been dismissed or something. When we left I was angry and I let him know it. He was mortified that I felt that way and went on to explain that it was never his intention to make me feel bad. I could tell that this really upset him. His reaction was so swift and complete that I ended up feeling like a real asshole for even taking such a strong stance over such a minor issue. Because it seemed to be bothering him so I told him it was ok and really wasn't that big a deal.

I asked him why he was so upset and to just let it go. He explained that the reason he'd wanted to talk privately to the woman was because she was a friend of his mother. I said, "oh great! I'm with a guy that's not only closeted but ashamed to be with me!" He said that wasn't it at all. It was more like he was ashamed of his people. From this point it all began to sound just a little fantastic, but as time went on I came to understand.

This was when he told me that his family is one of the oldest and well-known names in America, and most of his concern was that all his life whenever people found that out suddenly the good times and comfortable feelings with them were usually over.

Most people would not understand that or even believe it for that matter. However, the family name is one of those straight out of the Guilded Age. In the next few years I witnessed personally the exact reason he felt that way and can attest to the fact that there's definitely merit to the sentiment. All too often the minute people hear their family name it conjures up many preconceived notions, prejudices, jealousies, and general imagery that's somewhat akin to royalty. I was totally surprised by his lineage and certainly had not even had a moment to think about the ramifications of what that might mean. I was more stunned than

anything. I can't truly say that I viewed it as positive or negative yet. I've never been particularly star struck. Having worked in the hospitality industry for all those years I'd met some very prominent people. Some who were quite famous and many who were very, very wealthy. Those experiences had allowed me to see them in a wide range of situations; usually what you'd expect, but all too often at their worst or near it. The good thing was that it helped me to keep firmly on the ground as far as viewing the extremely wealthy as just people with flaws like everyone else.

In addition I'd learned that the upper classes usually shake out into two types: Those who are comfortable with who they are and what they have, and those to whom it's a big deal, so they think everyone else should think it's a big deal also. I didn't know yet which type he would turn out to be, but I did know that one thing all notable and wealthy people seem to have in common is that along with the wealth and notoriety comes the burden of rarely being able to relax and be comfortable completely; Especially with people whom they've only just met, or don't really know. That gave credence to his claim on the day that he disclosed his heritage to me. I'm fairly certain that his comment about being more ashamed of them than of me simply meant that in meeting them I would likely be treated as insignificant at best.

I think that the true test for this elite group is how they learn to handle it all. Part of that education for this man is that he's well aware that there are people in the world who think they know him and have formed opinions about him simply because they may be familiar with his family name, and the history as it's been reported. And incidentally, since our getting to know one another he has shown me much evidence that shows the reporting to be at best flawed, and at worst totally erroneous.

Either way, I wasn't sure just what to make of all this on that day in D.C. The afternoon was wonderful and as it neared the end we were less than ready to say goodbye.

When he dropped me off at the airport we agreed that I would come to Virginia to visit him in another two weeks. To say the least things were moving along. I was pleased but a little on edge. Things like this never happened to me.

Chapter 9

Chapter 9

Chapter 9

Upon my arrival back in Atlanta my sister was already in town having left D.C. a day before I did. I'd promised her I'd accompany her to the doctor upon our return since she'd been ill throughout most of the trip.

Two days later it was time for her appointment. She came over to my house and asked me how the remainder of the weekend with my friend had gone. I told her that things had gone very well but there was an issue that I wasn't at all certain about. She asked me what the problem was and I disclosed to her what he'd shared with me about his family. Her response was to look at me and say, "Well, I don't mean any harm, but if that were true what in the world would he want with you?"

I looked at her, shocked that she would voice this even though I could understand her thinking it. I was sure that anybody who became aware would certainly be thinking the same exact thing. I began cracking up with laughter. She had this puzzled look on her face. I asked her, "Have you ever thought that perhaps because I'm NOT from that background, and in fact, the farthest thing from it- may be the very reason he chose me?" I could see her giving this some thought...

Although I didn't know it when I voiced the sentiment that idea turned out to be very prophetic. In time, I could see that to some degree being with me was an escape from the strict, conservative structure of his day to day life within his family.

The next few weeks were a whirlwind. There was a lot going on around me. As it turned out, I went to the doctor with my sister and what we thought was just food poisoning or an extreme elevation of her blood pressure turned out to be a series of small strokes. After performing the necessary tests the doctors told us it was likely she had been having them all through that previous weekend. He told her what she'd need to do in the near future to guard against a major stroke. He said that often people will have several minis for years and not even know it. That there would be definite safeguards that she would need to take and several changes to her routine that it would be best if she made.

While it was very upsetting to me that all this was going on with her, I knew that I could not force her to take his advice and that preaching to her would be largely useless. It had been just a few years earlier that we'd lost our other sister to a stroke at the brainstem. All I could do was impress on her that I loved her and that I would do anything I could to help her. Her stress level at that time was very high and that was certainly no good for her. Over the years we'd had our differences but that in no way changed the fact that she was my sister and I didn't want to see anything happen to her.

In the following week I was to go to Virginia to see Michael. We'd talked a good bit since I left D.C. and I was content to just follow this and let it 'play out'. I had no idea at this time just what I felt or didn't feel. I knew that he was a very nice guy, and that there was a sensitivity about him that was adorable to me. My experience has been that the image that successful white men like presenting to the world is all about controlled and controlling strength. Rarely do they allow themselves to be seen by the world as people with feelings and sensitivity. I think that's a major mistake. While it may serve them well in business, those that I've gotten close to who adopt this warrior trait have almost no defense against the backlash that it brings when they need compassion from people as we all do from time to time. Often, the world regards them as cold and unfeeling, so in times of compromise, that much needed consideration is often withheld. They sometimes can't even get it from their own families.

That single solitary trait made Michael human for me. He allowed me to see that tender side of himself. He talked to me about the personal things that really bothered him. In time I would be treated to that 'boardroom persona' as well, but by that time I knew of the other so it was somewhat balanced.

I arrived in Virginia that Sunday evening. He met me at the airport and told me that we'd have to hurry. I had no idea what he had in mind. He just said that we'd need to hurry and get changed because we had dinner reservations very shortly.

When we walked into the restaurant it was quite beautiful. It had a wonderful lush atmosphere complete with roaring fireplaces and draperied private dining alcoves. There were a couple of people sitting at the bar who spoke to Michael as we entered. I didn't think much of it since he was from the area. We were shown to a private alcove and the waiter was instantly there. All the regular amenities were in place; Water, wine selection, appetizer menu, etc. We chatted quietly and in no time at all our selections began to arrive.

As the evening went on I couldn't help noticing that the place was very slow. It was the end of winter/early spring, and I would have expected that they would be doing a very nice business on a Sunday evening such as this. Yet, other than the couple at the bar we seemed to be the only patrons in the restaurant. The other odd thing to me was that though I'd dined in restaurants often where servers worked in teams that usually consisted of two people and it was largely done when a place was busy to keep the guests from having to wait. We seemed to have about three or four servers and there was no one else here. I'd mentioned to Michael when we were in Georgetown that I liked country French cuisine and this place was just that. I looked at him sharply. "Wait a minute, I said. Are we the only people here?" He looked at me and smiled. It turned out the couple at the bar were the owners. He'd had them open on this - a night when they were usually closed - and paid for the privilege so that we could have this experience in private. That really blew me away. I'd be lying if I said that I wasn't impressed and just a bit overwhelmed as well. What I learned from him early on was that it is a privilege to have money. One that he didn't take for granted. But managing money also was a big responsibility, and should be treated with care.

We were together for a good while and during that time displays like that evening were a rarity. I think had that not been the case those times would not have been so special. We began a system of him coming to Atlanta to spend time with me and then two weeks later I'd go to Virginia to spend time with him. Sometimes we would meet in the middle and go somewhere completely different for the both of us. The Michael that was most impressive to me was the person who would meet me in the kitchen of my little house with an apron on when I came in from work. This was the man who could find beauty and enjoyment in simple comfortable times at out of the way places. In the early days of our relationship he would fly in during the day while I was working and I'd come home to find he'd cooked dinner and cleaned up the place too! I'm no slob, but I'm no white glove housekeeper either. Although he'd been raised in an environment where there was always live-in staff, he was never above picking up a broom or a sponge and rolling up his sleeves. He enjoys cooking and will spend great amounts of time preparing recipes and meals that are very tasty. Whenever we traveled we always preferred country inns and smaller private guest houses over the four and five star establishments.

One of his earliest trips to Atlanta happened to be around the Memorial Day weekend. I was having some of my family in for the holiday and he jumped right in and ran me out of the kitchen. They took to him right off and I think he was surprised how easy they were to be around. For all our issues with each other, none of us were raised to treat others badly or behave badly in front of other people. Our spats were our own, and not situations for others to be drawn in.

We were getting very comfortable with our alternating weekends routine. Between my work scheduling and Michael's very capable assistant, we were able to maintain this arrangement for quite a while. People would ask how I could see this as acceptable, since it was a long distance relationship. But the truth was that with our scheduling it was rather like being in a relationship with someone who traveled for work. The times that we were apart weren't that long, so it wasn't too bad. We managed to do this for a few years. It was something of a challenge for sure, but do it; we did.

No matter what type of Nirvana we created for ourselves though, the big issues weren't just going to go away. Michael still had responsibilities to his parents and to his wife and child. They apparently were making it abundantly clear that they were not happy with his choices of late. They had reportedly all joined forces to stand against his decision to leave the marriage. According to him, his parents - who had not agreed upon anything for about as long as he could remember - were in complete agreement over disputing his decision to come out and leave this marriage.

My heart went out to him as I saw him struggling against the tide of all that opposition. In time, it began taking a real emotional toll on the both of us. Stress of the family issues, the geographical distance between us and the continual separation/re-entry were all destructive factors.

After about four years of battling opposition I think we both realized the situation was getting the better of us. We still talked everyday- sometimes multiple times throughout- and still loved each other very much, but despite our best efforts we knew that things couldn't continue as they were. It was just too difficult and painful. We began to drift further and further apart with our physical connection. Up to now, twice a month almost religiously he'd either come to Atlanta or I'd gone to Virginia or we'd met somewhere in the middle. His business was suffering from his absences and my home was totally neglected since every time I had off time that consisted of more than a few hours I was jumping on a plane. The end of the romantic relationship was staring us in the face, but neither of us was strong enough to admit it. The fact that we really did love each other very much made the situation nearly unbearable. It's the first time I've ever had a relationship tank and the reason really had nothing to do with either of us having a problem with the other. It was predominantly outside issues that would ultimately force us apart. I think any other issues could have been worked on but his family ties are just too demanding. It's more of an institution than just a family. People say, "Well, if he really loved you, he would have left." I have to challenge that statement though. He's one of those people who really feels strongly about heritage and – to him – going against his family; all that history was just too much.

Everything was so tied together. Even his business was basically overseeing family interests. So my understanding is that for him to extricate himself would be akin to just ripping the fifth floor out of a seventy story building without using any type of plan. Just going in with a bulldozer and tearing the thing out. Not going to happen with major upset all around. It was one of the most painful and difficult times that you could possibly imagine.

Like most people when I'm faced with what seems to be an insurmountable issue I will often start to think of what I may be able to do to change things. By now I was really becoming restless with the fact that the relationship seemed doomed. That made me sad and angry. What happened? I was not supposed to be here again! How in the world had I let myself spend so much time away from my goals and how had I lost myself so completely in this affair? Suddenly I wanted nothing as badly as I wanted to continue my growth in my own life. It was like there were two people living inside me. One minute I was raring to go and making plans for all I needed to do to get my life back on track and in the next instant I'd be so mad at Michael and that whole situation that I'd want to murder somebody.

It didn't take long for me to see the pain of thoughts like, "here we go again", meaning another failed attempt at a relationship after all that time of thinking that I'd been super careful not to get involved with another dud. The only consolation when I start to think about situations in that way is to focus on the lessons that they bring. Sometimes it takes making mistakes to grow.

Thoughts of travel and faraway places were still running about in my head. I've always had that wanderlust even as a child. Since I'd started traveling I'd often thought about how it would be to live in another country. The difference this time was that the thoughts really had some fertilization. There was really nothing holding me here now. This time, even most of my family had died, so for the exception of the job and the house I really had no great need to think of Atlanta as 'home forever' anymore.

As a few of those seeds started to germinate I started to wonder what my next step should be. I really had not challenged myself with anything in a very long time. I'd been fascinated with language for a very long time and thought that it would be nice to learn other tongues. Along with the thoughts of seeing just how far I could go in fashion was also the knowledge that if I ever were to make good on the thoughts of living abroad it would be useful to speak another language anyway. It had been brought to my attention while traveling that the most widely spoken languages in European business are English, German, and French.

I've always been intrigued by the German language and how orderly it is. And I think French is one of the most beautiful languages around when spoken. So I decided to start with German and go from there.

I enrolled in classes and despite feeling like I was at the bottom of the roster as far as catching on, I stuck with it. I got pretty good and can form simple sentences ok, but then my work schedule changed and I had to drop classes. I did however make it through the first year and have every intention of going back and finishing.

The immediate plan when I started was to try and become at least conversational and then seek opportunities to go over and live. It didn't really matter to me how I got there. If fashion could be the ticket, then so it is. I did think that would probably be my best bet, but at that point my mind was open to whatever presented itself.

By now I was moving along in my forties at a good clip. It was 2004 and though I was still focused on growth, I no longer felt the rush of mid-life crisis. I wasn't obsessed with thoughts of having to make a change in my life and doing it NOW. Rather I was feeling more comfortable in my own skin than I had in a while. Though Michael was still on the radar, we both talked around romantic issues, and never really discussed it. We had our heads in the sand and seemed content to just let the whole affair decompose around us rather than deal with it in any way. He was consumed with business affairs there and I was caught up in my personal affairs here, and when we talked, it was about ANYTHING but 'us' as a unit.

I had started going to the urologist about a year earlier because of frequent urination. And though I had not thought much about it, he informed me it was time that I start to have an annual prostate exam as all men should at my age. No man looks forward to that. However since an earlier intestinal surgery back in 1997 I had matured a great deal around the issue of healthcare and taking care of myself in general. I now looked at any trip to the doctor as just one of those worrisome things in life that everybody has to do. And as much as I may not like it, to put it off would be totally irresponsible.

Though I didn't know the cause, the frequency of the urination was certainly a concern. I was going as much as eight to ten times a night. It made for an awkward situation because I didn't know whether this was about something being wrong or if it was just about aging.

I don't know if it's this way for everybody but for me reaching forty seemed to be bringing about a lot of changes; in mind, in body- everything. And with all the changes going on, who could be sure what was happening here? It seemed I was seeing the doctor more than I ever had. It appeared I was having trouble with just about every part of me. I was having trouble with my knees, the aforementioned intestinal surgery, there were questions suddenly about blood pressure; you name it....

On top of it all there was still this business with Michael. The whole thing felt very estranged. Like we were role playing. We'd never felt that way with each other before, but things had definitely changed. We were both staying at our respective homes more and visiting each other way less. As this happened we were less tolerant of one another's fundamental differences. He was a diehard Republican. And as a result of family connection, deeply entrenched in politics.

All this was going on during the first and second 'reign' of Baby Bush. In fact, one of the worst arguments we ever had was the day that Bush was elected to the second term.

He had decided to come and spend the weekend with me. I'd warned him that it was not wise as our politics don't mesh very well. Long story short, he ended up packing up and storming out on election day. We argued badly and that trip ended just as I'd thought it would.

There were plenty of things that made our situation difficult, but this one really put a lot of fuel on the fire. So I really wasn't surprised at all that the distance was growing ever wider. What did sadden me was that it was happening over what should have been very trivial things and that was what made it so hard for us to say goodbye. It seems like such a contradiction, but we were still very close in many ways. We each gained an understanding of the other's world that would not have been possible unless we experienced it just as we did- through each other's eyes.

Even though it was largely unspoken we spent the next year trying to transition from lovers back to good friends. It's still very painful to me if I dwell upon it. There are still volumes here that could be written about the feelings we both went through, but it would serve no purpose but to create a sort of emotional wake.

There have been a couple of times when we could see opportunities to get together. Frankly I think the idea frightens us both. Time softens blows and I think for now that's the best that both of us can hope for.

By the end of 2005 I decided that I needed to regain some independence and spread my wings a bit. I had always wanted to attend the Winter Olympic Games and decided this would be my year. I had wanted to go when they were held in Salt Lake City in 2002, but that was still so close to the 9/11 incidents that I was not sure that I wanted to take the chance and go to such a large public event.

Torino, Italy four years later however would offer an opportunity to kill two birds with one stone. I had always wanted to see Italy so this would be as good a time as any to do that as well. I had thought about it but really had not made any plans in that direction and when I did start to get serious it was already fall of 2005. That meant I had to acquire tickets to the events, map out places to stay, arrange travel itinerary, and make sure the funds were as they should be.

It was surprising to me how easy I was able to pull it all together. As I'd experienced in the past, buying for one in situations like this is often much easier than buying in any multiple quantities.

The deal with the tickets was that they were all being handled by brokers. In some ways that was probably best but it was a bit of a hassle trying to navigate through it all online. First, you had to input information into the system that only gave you a limited time to do so. If you didn't get it all in within the allotted time, it would cancel the transaction altogether. Then, to add insult to injury the way the thing was set up you could not purchase tickets to the most popular events unless you also purchased tickets to the unpopular events. For instance, I wanted tickets to both men's and women's short and free figure skating programs. I also wanted tickets for the men's downhill skiing competition; all very popular events. So for each ticket that I purchased for an event like that, I also had to buy one ticket for something like curling, for which it was likely there wouldn't be much attendance. It felt a little like blackmail, but I have to admit I found it an amusing way to guarantee ticket sales. I think my curling tickets were something like twenty bucks whereas the men's figure skating tickets were more like three hundred. And the women's events that year were even more expensive. I thought, "what the hell, I might as well watch curling too". I didn't know anything about it, but since I'd bought the damned things I may as well go.

I had set up the trip to get me into Rome the weekend before I was to attend any of the events at the Games. I landed there with no problem and found the shuttle to my hotel. Anyone that's planning a visit there who hasn't gone before, make sure you ask about shuttles to your hotel. They have different ones from the airport that will list your hotel by name if they go there. It's worth a check. I think it works out to where the shuttle is about fifteen dollars (U.S.) whereas a cab ride- of which there is abundance - will run you about sixty dollars (U.S.). Be careful of the cabbies! They will practically attack you as you exit baggage claim trying to get to you before you can find out about the shuttles.

My hotel there in Rome turned out to be a delightful little place. It was very clean and neat with a very small restaurant downstairs. When I first entered my room I was very impressed. There was a bottle of red wine and a cheese and fruit tray awaiting my arrival. Even though I no longer drink I thought this to be a very nice touch.

Since I knew that I would only be in town a couple of days I immediately scheduled a bus tour for the next day. This is something that I ordinarily would not do; preferring generally to explore a city at my own pace. But I wanted to see as much of it as possible and quickly since I knew I'd be out of there and on to Florence on Monday.

The tour was great though the clientele was much what I'd expected: Old people- and all in couples! Fortunately there was one young lady who was there alone. Since she was by herself as well the tour guide paired us up. Turned out she was there for work. She was with Microsoft and had a couple of days to kill there in Rome. She was fun and talkative and we had some really good conversations. I usually am not one to come out of my shell easily, but I enjoyed her company. We ended up spending the day together-even enjoying each other's company through lunch. At the end I was glad I'd gone through with it. I know me well enough to know that without her company I'd probably have gotten off the bus given half the chance.

That evening I chose to go out to the baths. I couldn't imagine spending time in Rome and not doing so! I knew that I wouldn't be spending any time in the bars there. Besides, who goes to Rome and leaves without having at least one sexual/romantic interlude?

I checked my guide books and to my surprise there was a bath house very close to where I was staying. So I got cleaned up and headed out that way.

Though I probably shouldn't have been, I was surprised to find the place small and rather dingy. As great a city as Rome is, I fear she's a grand old lady whose age shows in most of her establishments; no matter the type. In this particular ensemble let's just say that her frock was rather worn and tattered.

There was a good crowd there but most were just looking around. Not a lot of action. It was very apparent to me however that the age old myth about black men was alive and well. At first, I was a little put out by the behavior of the guys there. They were all trying to catch a peek and see if the myth was true. It was obvious by their behavior they were wondering did I have this gargantuan penis, or was all 'normal' down there? Now mind you, nobody was stepping forward to attempt to find this out first hand, but they were all acting like school boys; huddling in clusters, looking at the crotch area of my towel and whispering amongst themselves. It actually was rather funny.

There was this one guy that was like the ringleader. He spoke the most English and as a result I guess he became a designated speaker. He came up to me and wanted to know how big it was. I grinned slyly at him and asked if he wanted to come along with me and check it out. "NO WAY!" he exclaimed. But he wanted to know if I would allow him to touch it. Like I said it was all funny and just a little bit childish.

Though I didn't meet anyone of interest I did get to experience what I found out later was the most popular bath house in the city.

The next couple of days I got out and did some more sightseeing on my own. Rome is so chock full of things to see and places to go that it's a little overwhelming. There's no way to do it all in just a couple of days. I have every intention of returning so that I may see it properly. The little shops around the Trevi fountain alone will take days to explore.

One thing that I found very interesting there is that people believe in dressing. That was very refreshing to me. It was interesting to watch people going about their business in the evenings just out of work or whatever. I found that no matter what the employment or apparent economic level, Italians all like to wear quality clothing. It was an education to see people even in clothes that were obviously older and somewhat worn, but kept at a level that showed concern for one's appearance. ALL women that I encountered past, say, twenty years old; wore hose and heels in public. The heels may not have been high- though believe me there was plenty of that - but they all wore decent and well-made footwear. I saw only seasonal dress. It was February and I cannot remember seeing one person in anything that would have been associated with another season. Not even a pair of white sneakers. I even saw a girl on a motorbike with stilettos on! There is such a rich appreciation for good food, good clothing and art there.

And yes, the men are all that they've been promoted to be. Such gorgeous guys! Straight, gay, all of 'em! And quite the peacocks I might add. It's very apparent that Italian men appreciate that they are a sexy breed. They all have this air about them that lets you know they are certain about their position in the world. Heads held high, confident smiles, and flirtatious eyes. I've never been anywhere that men who were obviously straight relished being looked at so much. And I was pleased to see that they knew how to acknowledge your appreciation and at the same time make sure you knew they didn't want things to go any further. They graciously accepted the compliment, yet didn't scorn your glances. Tastefully they would let you know they were not of that inclination. But trust me, as far as eye candy goes, it's overload!

That Monday I was to move on to Florence and had to be at the rail station by 10:00 a.m. I arrived about forty-five minutes early because I didn't want to miss my train. To my surprise there were not a lot of places to sit and what few benches existed there were occupied. It was Monday morning and there was plenty of activity there. Lots of places to eat and get coffee but I wasn't interested, having eaten a full breakfast before checking out of the hotel.

My experience in train travel was very limited until I started to go to Europe. There, the rail systems are so well maintained and well run that it's often the more preferred method of travel over air. There in the main station in Rome they still had one of the old style arrival and departure boards where all the numbers and letters flip as they change. It fascinates me to watch those. The clatter sounds like a million tiny wings flapping simultaneously to me.

I was just standing there watching the board when I realized that I'd stumbled into perhaps one of the top cruising locations in the city. It didn't take long for me to notice that men were going out of their way to walk past and catch my eye. Many were making no attempt to be clandestine about it, and several were quite tempting, however I was not about to chance doing anything in a public place; especially in a foreign country. On top of that I was leaving the city and on a tight schedule.

Then along came Gianni. As he came toward me I could tell the sight of me had shocked him. I think it was the fact that I'm so large and was wearing an oversized jacket which made my shoulders and all look even larger. That will shock some people speechless. And in a place like Italy- where most men tend to be rather small in stature anyway- I look like a giant.

As he came up to me I remember that he had on a bright yellow parka. He spoke and his eyes said volumes! I give the little guy credit because his English was no better than my Italian, but he didn't let a little issue like that deter him. He was adorable! In our broken language efforts we managed to have the following conversation: He asked me where I was going and I responded that I was off to Florence. He then asked if I would come back into the city with him for a while. Apparently he'd come into Rome to party over the weekend. I told him that I could not, as my train was about to depart shortly. He told me that he was headed home- I can't remember where home was, but then his eyes lit up. He motioned for me to stay there and he would be right back. He ran down the corridor to the lower level. When he returned he was smiling broadly. He informed me that he had changed his ticket and was now on the same train as me. He said he had an aunt in Florence and would visit her while I was sightseeing there. All he wanted was to spend the night with me!

I was totally undone. I had no idea if I wanted to get with this guy, and certainly didn't know if I wanted to spend the night with him. The thought was intriguing though. He was such a little character! Anyway he'd already bought his ticket and was ready to go.

In a couple of minutes they were calling the train number and it was time for us to board. As I took my seat I thought to myself that I must be out of my mind. Here's this guy that's gone and decided he'd like to spend the day with me and we didn't even speak enough of the same language to be certain of what the other was saying half the time! Kind of reminded me of a weekend in Dublin years before with a beautiful German boy named Chris..... Ah well, but that's another story.

It had been a long time since I'd traveled and -even without my knowing it - I'd changed a lot. The time that I'd spent with Michael had 'domesticated' me somewhat. I found that I'd taken on many of his fears about the world and life in general. Because of his sheltered upbringing, Michael was often wary of everything and everyone. I think that the close proximity to his fear during our time together had me a little frightened to experience life. I'd never been flighty and had always kept my wits about me. At the same time since I'd first started traveling I'd never allowed my fears to keep me from experiencing whatever life and fate sent my way. So as we pulled out of the station I began to review the rules of the game about pickups in my mind. I know how to take care of myself and generally I'm very good about being attentive to situations around me.

When we arrived in Florence I was not prepared for the city. It's quite small and- like lots of cities in Italy- they've managed to cram a lot into such a very small space. Right off the bat I knew that I'd have trouble finding the hotel I had booked. Since I didn't have a map, I had no idea how close it was to the train station. Gianni knew of a place where he usually stayed when visiting so we decided to go there instead. It was not bad, but I admit it probably wouldn't have been my choice. However it was considerably less than the place I'd booked and who was I to complain about saving money?

After we checked in we both felt the need to freshen up a bit. I let him take the first shower and while he was in I secured my things. I was willing to spend the day and the evening with him, but I certainly wasn't about to let him anywhere near important items like my passport, tickets, money, etc. I needn't have worried. He was turning out to be a really sweet little guy and I felt very glad that I'd gone through with the idea of us spending time together. We had a few intimate moments together and then agreed that we should both get moving. He had called his aunt when we arrived and she was expecting him. The day was moving quite fast so if I wanted to see any of the city I'd better get moving as well.

Florence in one word is BEAUTIFUL. It is such a small place that walking the streets seems to be the best way to get around. They all are pretty narrow and it's quite congested. Then add to that the fact that all the streets look the same.

Most of the time I will learn my way around using landmarks rather than street names in a new place but in Rome and Florence this system was not working. Both are so overcrowded and close that it meant paying close attention at all times.

I had decided to do some picture taking while there because from the moment I stepped off the train I could see the architecture was phenomenal. Once again here, as in Rome, statuary was everywhere and it was breathtaking.

One of the places that I most wanted to see before it closed was the National Museum. It's located in a city square not too far from the hotel where we registered. It's actually a castle that was once home to the De Medici family. It's the home of many of Michelangelo's great works.

I managed to get there before it closed and was speechless. There's an outside gallery in the square that holds many, many copies that are just exquisite and this is before you even enter the building. Once inside, there's a huge gallery with statues lining the walls all the way around the room. Paintings cover each wall as well as the ceiling panels done in frescos. This room has to be around one hundred feet wide and probably just as long, with ceilings maybe thirty feet high. It's an auditorium and each and every piece of art is more beautiful than the one that precedes it.

There was no way I would get to check out the entire place before it closed that day since I'd arrived so late, but I did get to see the statue depicting the wrestling match of Hercules and Diomedes. Here also is a place that I know I must return one day to experience it all. Sadly, I learned that the statue of David – which I certainly didn't want to leave without seeing – is located in a different museum, so I didn't get to visit on that trip.

I was very good as far as shopping was concerned while there. I found a great little leather shop and very much wanted to pick up a couple of bags, but knowing that I still had Milan, Torino, Munich and Amsterdam in which to make stops, I thought it better to forego the purchase. For me to travel and not shop is almost unheard of. It's one of the few times that I allow myself to splurge. I did manage to pick up some souvenirs for the guys on my pool team back home though. I decided that would have to be the extent of my shopping this time.

With one last wistful look at the courtyard out front of the castle I started my trek back to the hotel. Once in Florence I was sorry that I'd not planned to stay another night. That's the only thing about pre-planning (and pre-paying) an itinerary in an unknown place. You don't know how you'll feel about it until you get there. I couldn't afford to go off my schedule, as many of the hotel rooms had already been paid for. I'd already ditched the one here in Florence. I vowed to myself right then and there that I would return to this city and soon. It's a promise that I intend to keep here in the very near future.

By now it was perhaps 8:30 p.m. and I decided that I should make my way back to the hotel. It was not all that late, but there was no sign of Gianni yet, so I decided to go back out and grab a quick bite to eat. When I returned an hour later he was there. He asked about my sightseeing and I told him that I'd had a great time. As I'd suspected he had eaten with his aunt and was not hungry.

We spent a while trying to chat and make a little small talk. It was rather comical and we both laughed at our attempts. Rather than going out to the clubs we decided to make an early night of it. I'd done more than my share of walking around the town and was tired. He too agreed that he was ready to call it a night.

He turned out to be very warm and loving in bed. He was all too ready to be wrapped up in my arms and like most of the Italian men that I've known, took intimacy very seriously. He was simultaneously very much an equal man, yet appeared docile and innocent. I had the feeling that if things got really intense he might get overwhelmed and a little teary-eyed on me- but not this little guy. He was a fantastic kisser and really knew how to touch another man. I cannot stand guys that touch like girls. If you want to touch me, then TOUCH ME! Don't run your fingers lightly over my skin. That's more irritating and annoying to me than exciting.

We soon had exhausted ourselves and were more than ready for sleep. I suffer from Sleep Apnea, and have often had people say that it's rather disturbing to sleep with me for that reason. They say it bothers them that I stop breathing from time to time and that I snore loudly. So on top of being worried about the stopping breathing, they can't get to sleep because of the racket. Although I'd heard about it I had never experienced it until Gianni. He suffers from the same condition. I now knew exactly what people had been talking about where my condition was concerned. There were two beds in the room and I finally had to move to the other one because he was keeping up such a ruckus. Who knew such a great deal of noise could come out of such a small person? For those of you who've had to put up with me over the years, you now have my sincerest apologies!

The next morning broke beautifully and after our hurried goodbyes we were both off to our respective destinations. He, to his home and I, to Milan where I would be staying for the days that I would be attending the Games.

The train ride into Milan was rather uneventful and truthfully I remember little of it. What I do remember is that it was a rather gray and rainy day, and that the station was very confusing due to construction. downstairs in the station was where the taxis should have been, but were not. I finally found my way into a waiting cab and got him to take me to my hotel. While it was the nicest hotel that I'd stayed in so far, it was quite a ways from the train station and that was of concern to me. No time to really peruse the area or get much of my bearings. I would have to return to the station by 4 p.m. that day in order to make it over to Torino in time for the men's short program in figure skating that evening and it was already after noon.

That was the other issue that I'd faced with the pre-planning. Torino is not a very big town and the closest I could get a hotel room was in Milan, which is between one and two hours away by train. I was never able to get a clear answer from the EuroRail customer service while I was in the States about when the last train would be leaving Torino in the evenings. The overall schedule said that the last train would leave at 10 p.m. but the people were telling me that they would run a later train. I asked again once I got to the station that afternoon, because I was sure the event would last later than ten. Once again I was getting mixed responses. However, after having paid what I had for the tickets, I certainly didn't want to come all this way and miss part of the event. So I just decided to go with it and play it by ear...

When I arrived in Torino on the train, I didn't realize that there were actually two or three stations in town, and got off at the first one that we came to. I should have waited for one of the later ones to be closer to the arena. By and large however, despite the language barrier I did ok as far as getting around.

This was the first real mistake that I'd made on transportation. It wasn't the end of the world. I just decided to hop a cab and go on from there.

That was certainly the solution to the issue but my God, traffic was a nightmare. My taxi driver was a delight though. He spoke almost no English, but was such a happy and up-beat guy that he made the journey a delight. He was by far one of the most jovial people that I'd met since coming this far north in the country. My experience on this trip was that the further north I traveled in Italy the less hospitable and more ill-tempered the people seemed to be. So far, I'd had a run in with a rail station attendant, the porter on the train and also a young 'lady' who was a passenger on the train. God knows I try and honestly admit when something is my fault but these folks were just rude assholes. From the attendant who pre-tended to not speak English while I was merely attempting to ask a question about the ticket, to the porter who then went off on me because same attendant had not properly notated the ticket, to the bitch who then got an attitude because I wouldn't give up my seat to her just so she could sit by her school friend. The train was crowded but she had a seat. It was just not where she wanted to sit. Her seat was a window seat, which is inside and uncomfortable for someone my height. It also was about three rows up and from her girlfriend, whose seat was just in front of mine. Jeez! I wasn't even in Torino yet and already there were issues.

By the time I got to the cab driver it was a welcome reve-lation to find that not all northern Italians were crazy people. He told me that he had family in Boston, so he did have some connection to the States though he'd never been. He said that someday he would like to visit. I said that I was sure he would enjoy it. Somehow we got on the subject of politics and he wasted no time telling me he didn't like Bush and wondered why the American people would pick such a leader. I told him that not all Americans embraced Mr. Bush's ideals. He then - even in broken English - immediately came back with the eternal question we were all asking at that time: "If you didn't all like him, how did he get a second term in office?" That floored me. For the entire remainder of the cab ride I attempted to explain to him that even though there were many people in the United States who were unsatisfied with the administration, the general consensus seemed to be that we had to allow him to continue his path because no one really dared trying to make a change in the middle of the mess he'd made. I told him the belief in the country was largely that he had basically started all that was going on so now we had no choice but let him try and finish it.

I think he understood what I was trying to say. Interestingly for the remainder of that trip to Europe I began to watch people's reactions to me. I began to deliberately inject politics into conversations with them just so I could observe their responses. There was a tremendous amount of negative sentiment. Even once I reached Amsterdam and was among people that I knew and who were familiar with me.

I had often encountered a sort of impatient tolerance of American ideals amongst Europeans, but that trip was the first time that I'd encountered what I would call blatant hostility from many. It was at that point that I understood just how deeply America's relationships abroad had been damaged. It had been nearly a decade since I'd traveled abroad, and I got to see first what had transpired in that time.

When we finally made our way through all the traffic and got to the arena I was as excited as any kid. The arena, called 'The Palavela' was enormous. Out front they had constructed a giant topiary that had to be about twenty feet high in the shape of a pair of ice skates. It was a masterpiece in itself. I got there just in time to make it to my seat before the first skaters took the ice.

It turned out that I was sitting in a group of fellow Americans. We all had a great time watching the skating and chatting in between about our various vacations here in Italy. It was ultimately this group of people who told me that the train schedules had not been adjusted as promised. Many had tales of how they had coped with the misinformation as they'd been caught in the same fix the night before. It appeared they had all been told the same thing as me from the rail company while still home in the States. Some said that the city there had tried to make the schedule change happen, but it was a no go. Regardless of what was going on, the last train to Milan would be leaving around ten p.m. each night.

Well, as caught up as I was, I was not about to leave the short program that early. Only about half the competitors had skated, and the field of competition was looking far too good just to get up and go in the middle of it all. So that evening I just decided, "The hell with it - What's the worst that can happen?" HINT: Never ask that question in a crowded European city- that's a small city at that- when half the world is there.... I waited and watched the last skater that evening and at the conclusion of the competition I made my way out to the taxis. I beat it over to the train station. The effort was to absolutely no avail. Not only was the last train long gone, but there would not be another until around six a.m. It was cold and rainy and I was stumped as to what to do. At first I thought I'd just wait in the main terminal area until morning, but the Police put an end to that thought rather quickly. As I was standing out there two officers came out and told me that the area was closed and I would not be allowed to wait there. The station had a waiting area, and I was welcome to go there and wait. The only problem was the place was full of drunken street people trying to get out of the cold and it smelled like piss. There was no way I was going to stay in there with thirty or so drunks and druggies and a stray dog all night.

There was a hotel just across from the rail station and I went there. Of course every room was full but the bellman was very nice and pulled out the local phone directory and started calling around to see if he could find a place for me. Not one decent place had a vacancy it seemed. I had suspected as much since I had tried from home. Also, even though Torino has a gay bath house, the place closed down at midnight, so I couldn't even go and hang out there.

In a last ditch effort the bellman suggested a small hotel up the street from where we were. I had noticed the place earlier and it looked anything but inviting. However, by this time I was getting desperate. It was around two in the morning and it was still raining and cold. So I walked a few doors up to see if they had a vacancy. I swear the place was straight out of a horror movie. Complete with a neon sign sporting a couple of burned out letters.

When I rang the bell I was admitted to the lower foyer, which was very dark. I went up to the top of the stairs and was buzzed into a very warm, but cluttered room. The woman who let me in was old with leathery skin. She appeared to be Middle Eastern, and had a way of looking up at you even though her head was lowered and her back stooped.

I inquired about a room and she said that she had one at a cost of about 80 Euros! At that time that was about $130, U.S., but I was over a barrel here. That was a lot to spend for about six hours sleep and when she showed me the room I was really disgusted. It looked like she'd taken an old sofa style bed; the type where the back used to lift up and off, and thrown some quilts on it to make it up. I lay down but refused to take my clothes off. It felt filthy but by that time I was cold, angry and tired. All I wanted was to get some sleep.

At the first light of day I was up and out of there. It was still raining but the trains had started to run. I went directly to the station and caught the first thing going to Milan. When

I arrived at the Milan rail station it was still so early that the subway was not running yet. No matter. I hopped into a taxi and was off to my hotel room. I was never so happy to see a luxury hotel in my life! Usually I'm fine with a bit of roughing it while traveling , but the previous night had taken all that out of me for the moment.

The original plan had been for me to go back over to Turin that day and try to find a room. I still had tickets for the men's long program a couple of days later and didn't want to go through the same thing all over again. But once I got into my room, had a shower and lay down on that wonderful bed all thoughts of going back to Turin that day completely left my mind. All I wanted to do was close the drapes and sleep all day.

Once I was up later and moving about I found out that day was the beginning of Milan Fashion Week for that year. Ah, to be so close and yet so far away! Had I known earlier it surely would have been worth a couple hours sleep to catch a couple of Europe's up and coming designers. Not to mention the top names that I'm sure were there also.

As it turned out I did go to the Men's long program a couple of nights later but had to leave early. Though I'd always wanted to attend the Winter Games, I've now been fortunate enough to attend sessions of both the winter and summer games at least once. And while both are moments that I'll always cherish, I also now know that attendance at the games is mostly about the party. Both times I've actually been able to see more of the sports by watching on television than I've been able to see at either of the Games I've attended.

By the time I left Italy I was thinking that I'd have done better to just forget about the games altogether and spend that additional time in Rome and Florence. I'll certainly keep that in mind should the opportunity present itself to go to a third Olympics.

I planned to leave Italy and stopover in Munich for a couple of days. From there I would go on to Amsterdam to see my friend Joost (pronounced like "Host", but with a "Y") just before flying home. Much of the train ride through Bavaria was gorgeous that winter. Snow and ice were covering the mountain sides as the train wound its way through the tunnels there.

The dry heat in the train cars was aggravating my sinuses so it was a little annoying while trying to enjoy the scenery but I was determined to make the best of it. You live and learn. Once I arrived in Munich the air was crisp and fresh and I was happy to make my exit. It would be good to see my friend Walter here and spend a couple of days allowing him to show me his city and all it had to offer.

In all honesty by the time I reached Amsterdam I was exhausted and more than ready to go home. But since I rarely get to see my European friends I try to fit in as many stops as possible when I go over. By this time it had been years since I was last in Amsterdam.

Joost was doing well and looked wonderful. While I was thrilled to see this, the city itself was not as I remembered it. Lots had happened since my last visit. Things had been 'modernized' in some ways that I felt didn't enhance its appeal. Where there were once smart little shops and galleries now stood shopping centers in the very buildings that gave the city its charm. The Mall culture had certainly come calling.

I had to hang out for a couple of days because Joost was working and couldn't see me before then. The rest was exactly what I needed. It was so nice to just lay about there and do some reading and journaling. The rest was good and the reunion with my friend was superb.

Joost and I had a great time that evening. He knows that I love Asian cuisine and that my absolute favorites are Thai and Chinese. We found a great little place and had lots of fun catching up and talking. When we get together we can talk for hours. He's such a sweet and gentle person. After dinner we went out for a little while. Since we had been doing a lot of 'remembering when' that evening I decided that I wanted to revisit the very first bar that I'd ever gone to there. We were very close to the Spijker Bar so I suggested that we go there. It was a week night and still not too late so we were about the only patrons when we went in. It turned out that Joost had never been there.

While it's not that gritty a place, it isn't Mrs. Astor's tea room either. Watching him I realized for the first time just how gentle and somewhat protected a person my friend was. Even having grown up no more than a half hour from this part of Amsterdam and its nightlife he wasn't really aware of what was here in this world. It's funny to me how I see that as I've grown I end up coming in contact with people on different levels all along the journey. These days my life is much less about the gritty underbelly of gay life and I seem to have moved away from that part of the gay world. Not just in my social life but in all the connections that I seem to make. It seems that my sponsor was right when she said that I would become a whole person and in doing so I would begin to attract different types of people; People who would gravitate to that positive energy. Joost is a shining example of that. I'm not saying that any one set of people is better than any other - just that the interests are different and seem to seek each other out. I guess the old saying that water seeks its own level is true.

This growth has been very enriching in so many ways. I have the opportunity to see life in many different ways. To experience things through my own outlook and then to be understanding of others without judgment has turned out to be the most wonderful gift that introspection has given me. I am really beginning to see the changes clearly now.

My evening with my old friend was coming to an end. It had been great to see him and was painful to say goodbye knowing that it might be years before we would see each other again. We've been great friends for more than a decade now, but still the time in between visits makes it hard to say goodbye. Especially when the visit is as short as this one has been.

I knew that life would not stay on hold at home forever though. My flight was leaving the following day and I had to return to work.

Getting back to my routine was hard. I found that the longer I stayed in the job I was in, the harder it was to return after a break. The mind numbing boredom of it all would drive me up the wall. It took a minute for me to slow life down to that pace once more.

For all that however there is a certain comfort that comes from the safety of routine. I think we often mistake that safety for satisfaction. But is it true satisfaction, or is it just settling for what's there? As usual, within the Post Office it didn't take long for the madness to begin again.

I'd experienced a lot of treachery in the Postal Service before but I had never experienced it as blatantly as I was about to.

Somehow the word got out amongst my co-workers that I'd gone to the Olympic Games during my vacation. By the time I returned to work it was all over the place that I'd gone. It seemed to many that this had been a big deal. I've always believed in doing what I want to do and having a good time. The fact that I'm single and have no kids has made it possible for me to do a lot of things that I otherwise would not have been able to afford. For this reason I was well past thinking that this- or any other trip that I'd taken - should have been necessarily big news to anyone else. I do what I like and you do what you like, etc.... But their reaction reminded me that for many this was really something that was outside the scope of what 'normal everyday people' were doing.

Many wanted to know of the experience and I was happy

to share with them some of the experiences that I'd had while abroad. I brought the pictures to work and shared them with all that wanted to see.

At the time we had an administrative supervisor that everyone had labeled a troublemaker. To me she had been ok. We seemed to get along and I didn't really have any problems with her. Others said that she had done really deceitful things to people ; really mean things, and later would laugh about it at their expense. I guess now it was my turn.

We also had a new relief supervisor working in our section. The relief had never been in the area before and really had no knowledge of how things worked. As was customary, the administrative supervisor had worked on the time records for the upcoming pay period. I was gone for about three weeks all total and had surely done my share of spending while away, so upon return I really needed my paycheck to be there. The time had been covered by vacation so there should not have been any discrepancy in my pay. As it turned out, no time had been put into the system for me even though it should have reflected that I was on paid vacation.

When I got my pay stub it had a zero balance. I was livid. I asked the administrative supervisor and she replied in all innocence that she had no idea what happened. She said that apparently the relief had failed to run my time in. It was a problem that was easily remedied but I learned then - and also through watching other things she did later on - that it was all great fun for her watching me panic at the possibility of having no money on the heels of taking such a great vacation. It was a malicious and vindictive trick to play on someone who did nothing to deserve that treatment, and this was exactly the type behavior people had accused her of in the past. It seemed that now I had made some imaginary list of hers and from that time forward there would never be another period where I would be free of her insanity. When people ask me why working for the Postal Service was so nerve wracking, I can point to situations like this as a prime example. While this seems like a harmless prank, by her not knowing what my situation was, it could have turned into a calamity.

At this point in my career within the Postal Service all I really wanted to do was finish out my time in relative peace and quiet. I didn't want any friction, and expected nothing more from the place than the bare minimum I was receiving as far as reward or job satisfaction. But it seemed that even sitting here in this one place, not moving or trying to climb professionally, was too much to ask for in this hell hole. Too many people found comfort in others' misery.

For the most part, I had allowed things to settle into a steady routine. I had been a clerk for far too long. I didn't really know what I wanted to do, but I knew that I had to do something else. The job was getting the best of me in more ways than one. I was eternally grateful for the opportunity, and never forgot where I was before I got on here, but I could no longer just continue doing the same thing day in and day out and hope that I would feel better. The mind numbing boredom and the viciousness of the immature people were no longer just passing me by.

The problem is that when you're dealing with small minded people the last thing that you can afford to do is allow them to see that you can think for yourself. I'd made this crucial mistake within the ranks of the Postal Service. I'd allowed people to see that I was not dumb, could think for myself, had goals and was not afraid to go after them. All that seemed to label me as a threat and from the time that I'd shown some potential as a relief supervisor until the present there were those who had thwarted my every attempt to make any moves beyond my present position. That one vicious supervisor was only the tip of the iceberg of hatred and maliciousness in the place. For these reasons any thoughts of motion in position were pretty much stifled. Favoritism and Nepotism ran rampant in the entire organization.

Always before when I was stumped by my work situation I would refocus my attention on outside projects. That usually helped. These days I was trying to think of what I could do to increase my desire to resume working on my housing remodel. Quite frankly that was beginning to bore me as well. I had not been active in seeking contract costuming work in quite a while now, and as a result my regulars - as they were- had all gone away.

There is nothing like feeling as though you're in a box with no way out. When that is the case physically maybe it's different, but my box seemed to be in my mind. If you asked me what was wrong in my day to day I could not put my finger on a specific thing. It was a collection of things. Everything felt 'incomplete' is the best way that I could describe it. I was still struggling somewhat with the food. Not as I had been in the past, but not a really clean abstinence either. I would get a few days free of the sugar and then I'd slip right back to the old behavior. It seemed I couldn't live without sugar. I knew this was not true, but that knowledge wasn't worth much when I was acting like any heroin addict when it came to letting it go.

Though I had stepped away from Michael, there were still lingering feelings there that had not been resolved so they were yet to be dealt with. And that of course created another problem. I've always been the type of person that has a real problem getting involved with someone else where situations overlap. So not having totally concluded the situation with Michael was blocking any chance of me meeting someone else and moving on, and this was very frustrating.

Then there was the whole thing about living where I was. While I loved my little house and all that I'd done to make it my own, there was still the problem of the neighborhood. It was a really bad area when I moved in. There were hopes in the city that it would turn around. It was happening, but very slowly. Meanwhile I was having issues with break- ins and less than desirable neighbors. I would best describe it as loving my house, but hating my neighborhood. That's what I think was most affecting me with continuing to work on it. I had put it up for sale once so far but hadn't had much luck in trying to sell it. Seems people wanted the remodel vision complete for total value to be paid or totally not started and at a rock bottom price. I guess I was somewhere in the middle there.

I didn't quite know what to do with the feelings around all these issues. Combined they were beginning to make me feel really crazy, but I didn't know just what to do about them. Slowly the frustration was beginning to move closer to depression. Talking at meetings was not really much help, since the issues weren't really about acting out in addictive behavior anymore. Sure, I was still using the food to battle feelings but at this point I knew the problem was the feelings underneath, not the acting out behavior. That was only a symptom. I was beginning to accept that once again I needed to talk to someone outside the fellowships that I attended. Recovery programs have taught me that not all the answers will always come from there. Sometimes I may need outside help. That was clear to me now. Although I didn't know it yet, before I could even seek that help something was coming along that would make all those issues seem pale by comparison.

Chapter 10

Chapter 10

Chapter 10

While continuing to deal with the craziness at my job and the other issues that were present in my life, I found a growing sense of unrest about it all. I wanted very much to just get away from it all but not even the traveling was working for me anymore. You can't run away from yourself.

The time came for my regular annual trip to the urologist for my prostate exam. I had been generally taking care of myself, and it seemed that the earlier problem with frequent urination was under control with the aid of medication. So this was really viewed as one more bothersome thing that I just had to deal with in my daily life. I don't know any man that finds the exam particularly pleasant but it's a necessary evil. In my case it felt even more invasive because my doctor will at times take on new physician's assistants in his office for teaching purposes. Sometimes the students will be guys and often they're women who are training as well. To me, as a gay man there's nothing more dehumanizing than having some twenty something girl stick her finger up my bum. But endure it I will, to find that all is ok up there.

My usual routine is once the exam is done and my blood is drawn they tell me I should come back in a couple of weeks for the result. My doctor has a reputation as being one of the finest urologists in the business. I understand that this is because of his total dedication to prostate health in men.

As a result the walls in his office are littered with pictures of celebrities, star athletes, and even a couple of dignitaries that come from all over to see him. I'm very accustomed to him going that extra mile that not all doctors will see as necessary. I'm told that because of his attention to detail he has one of the highest percentages of successfully recovered patients from prostate related issues in his field.

When I returned for my results from the examination he told me that he'd like to do a biopsy just to be on the safe side because my PSA (prostate specific antigen) reading is slightly elevated. We had done this before so I really wasn't all that concerned. He is known to sometimes order biopsies with numbers that other doctors would not consider elevated enough. Knowing all this I went on and scheduled the test. I think it's pretty hard to do these things and not think about them at all but since I'd had one a couple of years earlier and nothing was found I thought of it all as pretty routine.

Two weeks later - on the morning of 06/06/06 to be exact - I went in at nine a.m. for the results. From the moment I walked into the examining area I began to get hot all over. The nurse that I usually shoot the breeze with was all business that morning. When I asked her why she was so serious she dismissed it as nothing. She got me settled in the exam room and told me the doctor would be in shortly.

Not five minutes later the man himself walked in and with little more than a 'good morning', he looked at me and said, "Well, we found something". I don't know what I expected, but only about .01% of me thought that there might be a chance I'd walk in and get a prostate cancer diagnosis.

He told me how far along it appeared to be. We then discussed options available to me. He told me to take a couple of weeks to make up my mind what I wanted to do. I thought about it for a few days, but for me it was a no brainer. I know myself and the only viable option seemed to be surgery based on the facts I had been given.

The irony of that day would not end with just the date and that diagnosis. I remember walking from his office feeling as though I were wading through Jell-O. I was in shock and thinking how I would make it through the rest of the day. On top of the calendar date, I had to return home right then to dress for an aunt's funeral that I was attending in a couple of hours. Throughout the service I was continually chanting to myself, "this is not your story, it belongs to your aunt". I wanted to make sure that I didn't alert my family members as to what was going on with me yet. The pressure of their fears along with my own would be just a little too much for me to bear. In fact, for the exception of Greg, the only person that I told about my diagnosis was my supervisor at work. The reason for this was that once I made the decision to have the surgery, I would have to schedule the time off for it as well as the recovery. Beyond that it was about two weeks before I told anyone else about my diagnosis.

Eventually it was my cousin who remembered that I'd mentioned having to go to the doctor for test results when we were all together the night prior to her mom's funeral. Within the next week she'd thought about it and remembered to ask me. Prior to her asking, I'd been content for the time being to just leave the whole family in the dark about the entire matter until I was just about ready to go into surgery.

When I told them, it turned out much as I'd suspected. They were all a little misguided about the whole thing. Their reaction was much the same as everybody's the minute you mention cancer. They immediately thought the worst. It was actually very helpful to me that I had to educate them about where I was and what the prognosis was. I found in that experience the power that I needed to keep myself from becoming worried. I was able to draw strength from the telling. My brother was the one person that I'd wanted to talk to in person, and was glad that I did. Since we are the only two survivors of our nuclear family I had a pretty good idea that he would indulge in a bit of catastrophic thinking. He did not disappoint. The first thing out of his mouth was, "oh great, and you can't live without it can you?"

I knew just how he must feel. Though I never want to think about it, the fact that we are the only two naturally makes you think that one of us has to go sometime. So it was nice to be able to share with him in person exactly what was going on and how I planned to deal with it.

I had definitely moved into kick-ass mode. My attitude was, "ok, I've got this thing. Now what the hell are we going to do about getting it out of me?" Not for one minute did I think I would not be going ahead with the surgery for removal. I felt very blessed that the cells were still 'encapsulated'. That is, they were still concentrated in the prostate. There were thoughts that went into my final decision for surgery, but this main fact was the cornerstone of my thinking that removal was the best solution for me.

There are several options available to men these days. I was told about the watch and wait method, which is exactly what it says: Because the disease is often slow moving some people feel that if you get a diagnosis early in your life you could wait and possibly nothing will ever come of it. The belief is that you'll be very old before it poses any serious threat- if it ever does. To me that would have been totally nerve wracking. Then there are the radioactive pellets. This is where they insert the pellets and they supposedly attack the disease from the inside- hopefully eradicating it and yet preserving your prostate. That too seemed a stretch to me since it's my understanding that the PSA exam will often still show an elevation during the period and if the pellets don't work you're still faced with removal. Not to mention the fact that in the time you've waited the cancer could have then spread.

The other option that was presented to me was Cryosurgery. It was my understanding that at the time of my diagnosis it was a somewhat new procedure which I'm still not so sure I understand. I do know that it involves freezing the prostate, but I wasn't really able to get a lot of information on it and didn't find anyone in the patient advocates that I talked to who had made the choice to go that route.

I was surprised at how smoothly the whole thing went. I went into surgery a couple of weeks after I informed my doctor of my decision and was back home a couple of days after I checked into the hospital. The recovery was also rather simple, though lengthy. I was off work for eleven weeks. There was very little pain, however the first two weeks were challenging due to catheterization. However once the catheter was removed I was up and about with very little hindrance. My stamina was somewhat unpredictable but tended to be good most of the time. It was pointed out to me this was the reason for the long recuperation. Sometimes I would get up in the morning and feel great. I'd stay up for hours and run errands or whatever. Then there were mornings I would get up only to find that I'd need to return to bed within the hour.

The first day I came home from the hospital Greg, his partner Peter, and our friend Terry all came over to the house to see me. They really helped cheer me up and raise my spirits. We sat there all afternoon and laughed and talked. It was truly the medicine I needed at the moment. It was invaluable.

One thing I discovered rather quickly was that when something like this happens there's tons of information about what one should do in relation to their marriage. There are pamphlets on how to talk to your spouse, what to do if you want to have children, etc. But there's not one word of information about what to do emotionally if you're a single gay man. How do you deal with the feelings that not only are you alone now, but possibly because of this latest occurrence you could very well be alone from now on....

Areas like this are the times that I've found my gay and recovering family - my family of choice- to be my rock. It was these guys (and women) even though they had no firsthand experience with the issue- who were there for me and propped me up emotionally. As gay people I think that most of us who are from an earlier generation realize that when hard times visit us, all too often birth family is not there for us, so we know that we must go to bat for one another.

On my first follow up I had the chance to talk to the doctor and he informed me that from what he could see inside all looked good and that he believed that I would recover well. Of course I would have to undergo the customary scale of examinations and visits to be certain. That means a thirty day follow up and then progressive time period checkups that would be graduated in lengthier periods over the next five years.

I love it when life shows me my decisions have been correct. By the time I went for my second checkup I was already wondering whether another of the choices would have been better for me. I was ninety percent sure that my decision was right, but once out from underneath the immediate threat there was that secondary thought. Now that I felt my life was no longer in danger, my manhood was the primary issue.

Part of the preparation for having removal surgery was for my doctor to tell me that while I would be able to perform sexually afterward, the chances were better than not that I would require chemical assistance. And what's more it would be about six months to a year before I'd know the true extent to which my sexual function would be affected. Quite naturally absent the threat of mortality from the condition I then saw my sexual performance as the next biggest priority. The fact that the operation and solution seemed to come so easy was a catalyst to me wondering; 'what if?

I was only forty-seven years old when I received my diagnosis. My question was answered as I sat there in my doctor's waiting room on that day.

There was a young man who came back into the waiting area from the examination rooms with a woman who appeared to be his mother. Though I was not intentionally listening to their conversation it was very clear to me what they were discussing. From the look on his face it was clear that he was anything but relaxed, appeased or comforted.

Apparently he had chosen to have the radioactive pellets implanted, and since that time his PSA readings were still coming in quite elevated. The first shock to me was that this guy had to be in his late twenties or at the very most his early thirties! Though I'd heard there were cases of men being diagnosed with this condition early in life, I never expected to see one right here in my doctor's office. Most of the men that I'd seen there were at least my age; usually older.

His mother or whoever the woman was reminded him that the doctor had told him this could possibly be the result. Even though he had the implants he might still show a high reading. She assured him that if he wanted they would seek a second opinion.

My overhearing that conversation immediately put to rest for me any doubts about the decision I'd made. I had begun to think perhaps I'd moved too soon but hearing them talk and seeing the look on the young man's face reminded me that the mental hell I would probably go through of not knowing what was going on with this thing inside me was the very reason I'd rejected the implants in the first place. It also helped me to realize that I certainly had no business feeling like the universe had dumped on me because this was happening to me so young. My heart truly went out to that young man. He was even younger than I. Whatever his life path I knew that the knowledge that his future might likely include sexual dysfunction or worse could not be an easy thing to handle emotionally. Especially at such a young age.

In the upcoming months there would be much to learn about coping with the changes my experience with prostate cancer would bring. Throughout it all I've managed to maintain an open mind and have- for the most part- been gentle with myself. I've tried to treat this as a learning experience and keep in mind that though I will have to learn to do some things differently it doesn't mean that a good sex life is not possible or that I should feel compromised in any way.

So far thinking in that way has served me well. I've been able to take the struggles right along with the triumphs and explore making them work for me. Today I know that I'm blessed to be here - cancer free- and looking toward a beautiful future.

About a month after my surgery the thoughts of my own recovery were thrust to the background. On the way home from an appointment with my doctor I received a phone call from Greg. From the moment I answered I could tell there was something up with him. I asked him where he was and what was happening. He said, "Tony I'm in Piedmont Hospital. I was feeling bad and the other night I got really sick. My stomach was hurting really bad, so Peter brought me to the hospital."

He said they checked him in and started running tests. "The news is not good", he said. I asked him what he meant and he told me they had diagnosed him with liver cancer and said after reviewing his case they thought he might have six months to a year to live.

I went hot all over. I told Greg that I was on my way. I was just about to turn into my neighborhood. I didn't even stop. I made a U-turn and headed directly to the hospital.

I don't know if I can adequately describe how things were that first afternoon at the hospital with Greg. I think what we both needed was just the comfort of being together. I know that we both talked from our hearts. There was very little that we couldn't say to one another, and in this case there was no need for descriptive expression between us. We had been friends and had loved each other far too long for that. We spoke when and of what we needed to, but there was a great deal of pensive silence in that room as well. I knew he was shocked, scared and mad. The whole gamut of emotion was evident. I could also see that he was determined to put up the best fight possible. I had watched him fight tooth and nail just as I had, to build a life in a world that all too often did every-thing it could to thwart the efforts of people of color. He had not only survived, but thrived as a black man. Having gone from being a kid who left school very early before graduating, to getting his G.E.D., and then becoming one of the most cele-brated and highly regarded chefs in the city of Atlanta. He had done well, and I know that he felt that there was still much to do in this life.

I too had those feelings, though I know my torrent was nothing compared to his. We talked for a while then both slept for a bit. Watched a little television and all the time wondered what was happening to us? For years now it seemed that we'd covered just about every possible life occurrence either to-gether or in support of one another. Lately however the chal-lenges were becoming more demanding and more frequent. It's very hard to see the reasoning when you think of yourself as eternally young. The whole concept of difficulty as a result of aging just doesn't compute.

I think that was probably the hardest realization for both of us just then. Up to that time I think that on some level we both were still those two little teenage guys who had become friends in Piedmont Park so many years before.

As the days wore on, Greg withdrew more and more into himself. It was the first time since I had known him that I didn't think I could reach him. I certainly thought that I understood where he was and that he needed to go there mentally for himself- but it didn't make it any easier to watch or to handle. Near the end I don't think he was communicating much with anyone, save Peter his partner. As his condition worsened, it became a situation where communication was difficult for him. He could not speak during one period after a procedure when they had him in the intensive care unit. I went in and took his hand. When he looked up at me I knew that he was very much aware that I was there and that I was with him. I would be there when he needed me no matter what.

That was the last time that I would see him alive. It was a few days later that his sister called me to tell me that he had passed in the hours just before. I don't know if I can describe the feeling that I had at that moment. It was unlike any other grief that I've ever experienced. I've buried just about my entire nuclear family; not to mention a staggering number of friends. Yet the feeling that I had during those first days after Greg's passing was like none of the others. It was similar to the feelings around the family members that I'd lost, all of whom I certainly loved and missed, but they were all family as a result of birth. Consequently there was a built-in support group and somewhere to take my grief where the people expected and understood it. Greg was my chosen family and in many ways was much closer to me than many of my blood relatives.

As a result the grief that I felt at times was all consuming but I didn't know where to carry it. It was much more than the feeling of loss that I'd had in the past with other friends, yet I knew that I could not go to his family with these feelings. I knew that as close as Greg and I had been, we'd never particularly spent a lot of time with each other's families. Oh sure our families knew each of us respectively, but it wasn't the type of closeness with them where we could be in their midst without ritual formality. Their grieving would be personal to them and I felt that I would be an interloper. And my own family would probably react just as I would expect. Though they knew he was my very best friend, I just didn't think they would grasp the depth of feelings that I was having.

About the only person who seemed to get it was my sister-in-law and friend, Diane. She and I were always very close and she knew how close Greg and I had been. I think also what helped was that she had suddenly lost a best friend and confidante to a terminal illness in much the same way; suddenly and with very little prep time. I clung to the conversations that she and I had during that period. They were one of the things that truly sustained me.

The next few days were a surreal blur for me. It was Tuesday when Gloria called me and told me of Greg's passing and the funeral was scheduled for the following Saturday. In the midst of all this I had two projects that I was working on and both had definite timelines. My niece's first prom was set for that very same Saturday and I was making her dress for that. I had always promised that since she was my only niece I would make her first formal and her wedding gown as gifts to her.

My other project was for a friend of mine who was to attend her first Kentucky Derby Weekend. That too, for those that are unaware is a really big deal. It's a rather substantial spring social event here in the country.

Grateful as I was for the distractions, it was torture trying to be creative when I was in such a dark hole emotionally. I'm happy that I was able to function at all and thankful that the two ladies were somewhat understanding about what I was going through. In fact, the Friday night before I was totally happy to sit up and do late night finishing work on the prom dress. Anything was better than having to go to sleep because I knew what the following morning would bring.

That Saturday dawned bright and sunny. It was a beautiful day though I felt anything but joyous. I had always made it a point not to go to funerals of people who were my age or younger. Here I was doing just that and it was for the person that I'd been closest to for the past thirty-two years.

Fortunately the night before Diane had given me two little tablets that she assured me would help me to calm down and make it through the funeral that day. Thank God she did. I don't know that I would have made it otherwise.

I arrived at Greg's house just before eleven that morning as requested. I was to be a pallbearer along with Terry and Howard; his other closest two friends. The family had requested that we ride in a family car rather than drive ourselves.

When I got there it was just about time to go in, but not quite. I sat in the car for a while and watched some of the family members arriving. I did not want to go into that house. However I knew that it must be done so I screwed up my courage and got out of the car. The scene inside was just what I'd imagined and more. There were family members all gathered and in the den there was a DVD of photos of Greg's life continually running on the television. It had been prepared by the mortuary.

Though I understood the desire to do things this way it didn't make it any less painful. If anything I felt it made this situation nearly unbearable. I spoke to Peter and he introduced me to a couple of his friends that were there. I also had a chance to talk with Terry for a brief bit. Otherwise I felt very alone. Howard was there but we were not close. He had been Greg's friend and that was our only connection. To tell the truth even if I'd had an army of best buds around me I don't know if I would have felt any less alone.

Just as with my own parents' funeral services I was happy when they started to load up the cars. The quicker we could go and get this over with, the better. I had not gone to the wake the evening before so walking into that church would be my first encountering Greg in that casket.

Much in the style he'd lived, the selections they had made were very nice. He was laid out in a beautiful beige suit and a burled walnut casket. There was an actual calm that came over me when I saw him. It was something of a relief to know that my friend was no longer suffering as he had.

The service was very orderly and I could see at once Gloria's steady hand at work there. It was put together precisely even down to the number of guests who would be allowed to come up and remark about their lives with Greg.

Though I caught this immediately in the program Terry, who was sitting beside me, had not. When the second speaker had finished he jumped up and told me to let him out. He headed directly for the pulpit and microphone.

I had expected to speak if there had been an open call. After all, I don't think there was another person there who wasn't family that had known Greg longer than I had, so many would have expected it. However I was somewhat relieved when the minister quickly took charge after Terry spoke and indicated that the program would return to its outlined order. I understood that Gloria's intent here was to make this as short and sweet as possible for the sake of her mother and all of us.

When Terry returned he urged me to get up. I leaned over and explained to him what was going on. He then got it. Later he told me that Gloria had apologized to him. She said-just as I'd expected - that it didn't occur to her that we might want to say anything. She was trying to keep the service brief.

Soon the minister was giving the benediction and we were exiting the sanctuary. Pallbearers in front to line up and receive the casket at the door of the hearse.

Casket loaded, I then turned to notice a couple of people from earlier days in my life that I had not seen in years. One was Carl, who had spoken. We had known each other from school. Although he had known Greg from when they were kids his connection to me was different. We had gone to high school together but had not seen each other since. I knew that he'd known Greg. We had talked about it. However I don't think they had kept in touch.

The other person I recognized was Skip, Greg's cousin. We had gone to school together from kindergarten to sixth grade, and had been good childhood friends. We had not seen each other since that time and frankly I was in no mood for these types of reunions just now. While I think he recognized me, he didn't approach and I didn't acknowledge.

Soon we were once again loaded into the limousines. This time headed to the cemetery. As we made that journey my mind was moving at an impossible rate of speed. There was so much going on in my head that it was a jumble. I hadn't known before now just how close Terry had become with Greg's family. It felt a little funny sitting there with people that I know of through Greg's talking of them and that know of me, but we've never been close. All the same I'm glad that I was able to be there on that day. I don't know that much of anything would have made sense had I not chosen to go through with attending. This was a heart wrenching but necessary closure.

When we exited the cars my sedative had all but worn off. I was here now more fully than I'd been all day. As we carried Greg's casket up the hill to the gravesite a degree of calm had come over me. As with every member of my family that has passed I seemed to get to that point when I accept all that has happened. The knowledge that it can't be changed puts me into a place of resignation.

Once the minister had done the committal, the graveside ceremony was over in the blink of an eye. I saw PJ, a friend of ours, and asked him if I could grab a ride back to the house to pick up my car. In no way did I want to ride back in the limo. I had moved into escape mode. He said that he wanted to go back to the church for the repast and talk to some of the people there, but wasn't sure that he knew how to get back there. I quickly struck up a deal with him and told him that if he would take me by the house so that I could collect my car, I would lead him back to the church. I was really in no mood to go back there, but figured that I should at least show my face.

The fellowship hall of the church was of course filled to capacity when we arrived. Bones Restaurant- which is one of the finest steakhouses in the city and had been Greg's employer for years up to the time of his death - provided the refreshments. I managed to wander through and offer more condolences to Greg's brothers. After that I made a beeline for the door. I thought I'd just made it out scot free when I looked up and saw Gloria out in the parking lot. I think she was taking this the hardest of all. She had been Greg's closest sibling and they had been extremely close. She was just wandering around out there looking lost when I saw her. My heart went out to her and I went over and gave her a hug. Times like this are the most draining when someone has passed. There's always the desire to do something to solve things, yet there's nothing that can be said or done to make one shred of difference. It was those times that the hugs of others usually meant a lot to me.

My plan for the day was to leave the church and head over to my brother and sister-in-law's. They were throwing a little party to give my niece and her friends a little send off for their first formal dance. I also wanted to be there in case there was anything last minute that was needed on her dress.

My car was already loaded up. Not only was I going to attend that party, but afterward I was heading straight out of town to Ft. Lauderdale for a week of getaway. I needed to unwind badly.

I had no idea just how much the day had taken out of me until I reached their home. I had a splitting headache. I walked in, headed straight for a bedroom and fell across the bed; asleep in minutes.

When I awakened people had begun to gather. The festive atmosphere did me some good. I needed an uplift and this group of kids was providing it. As in most situations, time that day proved to be the great healer.

There were many days after Greg's passing that I wondered what life would be like without him there to discuss and work through things with me. Just as with most losses I eventually found a way to move on. These days it often feels like a challenge to make new friends and to start a social life all over again. There was a time when I thought the friends I had would be my friends for life. I truly thought that I would be settled into a relationship and totally out of that market. Having to shift gears after Michael; as with so many other changes that have happened in my life, has been rather difficult to say the least. However the positive is that as I've grown. My outlook and expectations in life have changed.

There will always be challenges and new goals to set in life. Those are the things that keep it exciting for me. My desire to work more with the creative side of myself is coming more to the forefront than ever before, and given the opportunity I'd love the chance to develop that consciousness.

As I look back on the years that have passed there's no way that I could have scripted things as they've happened. It's been a tremendous journey for me and I don't know that I would change it even if I could. As a friend of mine pointed out to me a short time ago, there should never be any regret about the periods and occurrences in our lives. It took each and every situation to bring us to where we are. That could not have happened without the good and the bad.

All the things that I went through in the school years I can now see are the very things that fed my desire for a better self-image. Just as all the things that I went through with my family around my sexuality are the very things that made me an independent and strong person.

I also know today that it took the myriad of deaths that I and so many others went through since the 1980's to make me appreciate life and all the gifts it has to offer. Today I'm very appreciative of those in my life that I'm honored to call friends, having lost so many. The loss of my parents and later the loss of both my sisters have helped me to cherish the family that I have remaining. I find today that my brother and I go that extra mile to be there for one another. I think we've both learned that in the grand scheme of things just how little the differences and small issues matter. It's not easy to lose two families - the chosen and the natural ones- at much the same time.

I thank God every day for my sobriety and my abstinence. Had I not developed dependency issues and gone through treatment it's possible I could have gone through my entire life thinking I was the only person who had the feelings and thoughts that plague us when we're caught in the addiction web. As a result of honestly looking at these issues I've met an entire worldwide community of people who realize that life is not always easy and that it's ok to admit that. They've taught me to surrender to that knowledge and learn a healthy way to deal with life when it does get difficult. I've learned to appreciate my body as the precious gift from God that it is.

Even those early years out there in the bars where things seemed so unbalanced has helped me with the acceptance of others. I don't think I would have ever learned to take people on a case by case basis had I not gone through some of the pain and heartache that I felt in those days of the biased gay community. In the world that we live in it has been imperative for me to learn that. This world is populated with all types of people. I must have some type of system for managing to live in it. There will always be people with whom I have no desire to associate. However unless I can utilize a method of discerning them from the masses I - like many others in our world- will begin to stereotype. I believe that's the culprit that has gotten us in so much trouble all along in this world.

Epilogue

Epilogue

In the late fall of 2009 I was granted disability retirement from the Postal Service. As a result of sustained injury, I was required to have a four level fusion of the cervical vertebrae; C3 – C7. Even though the ordeal was quite painful and the recovery was long and slow, I can see grace and the hand of a Higher Power even here. First, I've been blessed that my treatment seems to be going well. I've not had many of the difficulties that others I've known with this or similar conditions have gone through. I do know that things could have been much worse than they've turned out to be.

Once again, out of a seemingly hard time comes growth and advancement. Though I cannot continue doing the work that was my career for the last 22 years, the surgery has restored the feeling in my right hand; which was totally compromised as a result of the herniated discs pinching the nerves.

After having almost no use of my right hand for nearly a year, I can now once again enjoy working with fabrics and designing clothing. I'm making a move toward building this into a profession. I have been given the gift of imagination! I cannot just sit here and think of myself as 'retired', or whatever. There is FAR too much life left to live for that!

After the first few months of recuperation, I started to get moving on getting my strength back. The physical therapist has told me that even when I'm done with the surgical follow-up therapy with him, I must still concentrate on exercising correctly to keep my body in shape. I'm done with lifting any substantial weight from now on; either recreationally, in exercise or professionally. However, I can do cardio, yoga, and other things to keep myself in shape and viable. He has also not spared any words in telling me that it's IMPERATIVE that I watch my weight. It will be very damaging to my neck and back should I gain or hold onto a lot of bulk.

No matter, I'm anxious to get up and get moving about! Already, I'm rolling around my cutting table sketching, planning and making clothes. It's been so long since I've been able to sew. Now I can do it with abandon. My mind is free to create without the complications that have bogged it down in the past.

At this point I don't know what my life or Higher Power have in store for me. But then again, have I ever known? Whatever comes, I will embrace it and run with it with the knowledge that I'm free and open to make my life whatever GOD directs me to. The possibilities have never been so endless!

Peace...

Author Bio

About the Author - Tony Holland is a native of Atlanta, Georgia. the youngest of four children, he spent much of his childhood dreaming of far off places and beautiful landscapes. The remainder of the time was spent learning to craft beautiful clothing, which is still his vocation today. This is his inaugural effort at the art of writing.

Acknowledgments

Special Thanks to Maxx Yin Photography ; Atlanta, Georgia - For the cover photo.